AF566740

# HUMAN RIGHTS
## Third Millennium Vision

# HUMAN RIGHTS
## Third Millennium Vision

V. T. Patil

First Published 2001
by Authorspress

E-35/103, Jawahar Park (Shree Ganesh Complex),
Laxmi Nagar, Delhi-110 092
e-mail: authorspress@yahoo.com
quantum_soul@mantramail.com

Copyright © 2001 Authorspress

Typeset in NewCenturySchlbk by Chitra Computers

*Human Rights: Third Millennium Vision*
ISBN 81-7273-073-X

Printed in India at Mehra Offset Press, Delhi.

# Preface

The problem of human rights has been receiving the attention and concern of all the wise men and nations since long but the society is still deprived of concrete and lasting outcome. Since World War II we have seen an unimaginable progress in human rights activities. We witnessed its institutionalisation and normalisation. The human rights law has manifestly expanded, merging with other areas of law and extending its normative reach. For even as contemporary developments in human rights law reflect a millennial urge, there is also a sense in which the current moral climate and even the build-up of international criminal law is also anti-millennial, for it evidences both persistent human rights abuses and the general impotence of the international community.

Violations of human rights is one of the most worrying problems of our times for the entire world civilisation. The responses to the worst human rights violations of the twentieth century, to totalitarian oppression—to apartheid, to the political executions and disappearances of the national security state in Latin America, ethnic cleansing in the Balkans and Africa—have created a veritable human rights culture. This culture focuses less on the punishment of transgressive behaviour than on establishing a broader discourse of rights.

Human rights are largely procedural. Whereas human rights are often conceived of as coming after the fact, as trumps that check the outcomes of political processes, contemporary practices suggest that human rights come into the picture much earlier, as a form of discursive engagement within the broader public domain. International human rights has come to offer nothing short of a global language by which to represent violations of human dignity. The discourse of international human rights has become a medium for the condemnation of local abuses, regardless of how these abuses may otherwise be characterised or rationalised within domestic political schemes. Rights talk can affect local dialogue and in this way structure domestic political developments. This role of rights talk is most evident in the recent wave of liberalising transformations, where the language of international human rights has served to inspire and galvanise a liberal opposition and an imagination of hope.

Today's international institutions of human rights exemplify the impetus toward the normalisation of international criminal human rights law. They gesture toward a millennial view of international justice and of the rule of law, but themselves proffer only a thin and symbolic image of that fulfilment, one which lacks historical context and political authority. Such gestures reduce justice to a principle applied *ex post facto* and without necessary ancillary humanitarian intervention. Normalisation of a permanent human rights culture ought not to be predicated on a utopian legalism that outstrips the international community's capacity to respond effectively to extreme dehumanisation. Instead, international human rights processes and institutions constantly remind us that the notion of radical transformation through law remains a messianic vision, still at the dawn of this new millennium, beyond our reach.

This book has tried to explore the varied dimensions and new visions on human rights with the changing world scenario, in a lucid and readable style. It will help administrators politicians, researchers, students and the lay alike, to understand the millennial vision of human rights in its proper perspectives.

1.8.2001 ***V.T. Patil***
Pondicherry

# Contents

# Contents

# 1

# Human Rights: Millennium Concepts

Human rights are not derived from some understanding of human nature, instead they are the articulation of aspirations immanent in a culture. As ideals, human rights define the community within which people want to live, but have their roots in the community in which they in fact live. Based on our common humanity, human rights differ from rights grounded in domestic law, but in other respects they operate much like rights grounded in domestic law: violation of one of the enumerated human rights would serve as a predicate or justification within the legal system for exercises of the state's coercive power.

Human rights might be better viewed more as social ideals than as legal claims. In the domestic sphere, some rights operate in both these ways, that is, as legal claims and as social ideals. For example, the right against racial discrimination—one of the architectonic rights of United States legal system today—has such a dual character. As legal claim, the right against discrimination stems from the Fourteenth Amendments promise of the equal protection of the laws and is also instantiated in myriad federal, state, and municipal civil rights codes. It entities all American citizens to be treated without harmful prejudice and to call on state agencies, including the courts, to use their power to honour.

The right against discrimination defines the conception of the good and the just; it projects an understanding of the ideal community. To demand recognition of the right against discrimination is to demand that a community be brought into being in which all persons enjoy equal respect and concern, regardless of the colour of their skins. Viewed from this perspective, the right against discrimination should be understood as referring not just to a claim that will be enforced by the state, but also to an ideal that expresses our hopes and that might structure all our social interactions.

Ideals of a right may of course have its historical origins in the actual willingness of the state to honour certain claims. Indeed, the right may be nourished and strengthened by frequent and forceful exercises of state power on its behalf. But even in such cases the ideal is not reducible to the legal claim.

Even if every single law protecting the right against discrimination were repealed, Americans might still invoke that right, though they would now understand it purely as a social ideal rather than as a legal claim. Admittedly, the adoption of a constitution, the enactment of a statute, or a series of judicial decisions may well give life to ideals, but the causal dynamic often works in the other direction as well.

Social ideals have given rise to legal claims and often endow those claims with special force and potency. While some domestic rights are solely legal claims, and others, such as the right against discrimination, have a dual nature, human rights should be seen primarily as social ideals. They have a universalistic quality, and thus are of equal force in the United States or Argentina, or for that matter, the world over, but they always operate as ideals do as aspirations. They identify the features or qualities every society should embody. They are not a projection of an idle utopia, but inform and infuse the expectations and demands of the here and now.

Human rights, now understood as social ideals, may give rise to legal claims in either the domestic system or in the international sphere through international agreements, but even when that occurs they should not be reduced to or confused with their legal embodiments. In these situations, human rights retain their separate existence—they persist as social ideals—and provide the moral energy needed to enforce or otherwise to actualise the claims to which they have given rise. All too often, of course, this culture of human rights is ignored, and the good they promote is flouted.

Confronting this fact, many human rights activists acknowledge the role of human rights as social ideals, but deeply regret that these rights are not fully treated as legal claims. They bemoan the gap between human rights as ideals and human rights as legal claims and see this gap as an unfortunate consequence of the absence of an agency say a world government. Viewing human rights as social ideals, transcending any existing legal order, enables us to use those rights as an independent standard by which to judge all social practices, including the law. As social ideals, human rights can move the law toward the creation or recognition of certain claims as a matter of positive law, both international and domestic, yet they will always stand apart from the world as it is presently constituted.

## HUMAN RIGHTS IN TRANSITION

The history has witnessed a revolution in the modern moral imagination over the last few decades. The important features of this revolution include the emergence of human rights as the prominent language of the good in international politics and the growth of non-governmental human rights organisations around the world. Until 1945, international protection of individual human rights was confined to the treaties abolishing the slave trade, the laws of war, and the minority rights treaties concluded after Versailles. It is only since 1945, in effect, that the rights of all human beings as individuals have come under the protection of international law. While religions and doctrines have preached equality for millennia, it has only been within the last fifty years of our species that equality has received international and national legal protection.

Today's human rights culture has been accompanied by the global diffusion of psychoanalytic ideas about the healing properties of truth. Since the 1980s, with the truth commissions in Latin America and now in South Africa and the de-satisfaction processes in Germany, it has become axiomatic that truth about human rights abuses is a precondition for national healing and reconciliation. We are all so much in the midst of this revolution that we barely see it for what it is.

Most histories of international law regard the dense new fabric of international human rights law and the number of states who ratify these covenants as self-evident signs of progress. But there are historical traditions that vigorously dissent: post-modernists who insist that progress and especially moral progress is incoherent; those Marxists who represent human rights as bourgeois ideology; those within the Islamic world who dispute the universality of human rights standards; those who interpret the proliferation of international human rights as a continuation of European imperialism by cultural means. Besides all these problems there are also practical issues about the nature of the gulf between intention and result, between statute and enforcement, between what we proclaim and what we do. Every human rights activist has to work in this gap. It is the essential metaphysical difficulty of doing human rights work on the ground. The statutes exist; the rhetoric is noble, but implementation, enforcement, and follow-through are often lamentably deficient.

Immediately after World War II, the moral rules of state behaviour and the entitlements of individuals within states, together with the language of human difference itself were all rewritten in authoritative international documents. A bare list of these indicates the scope of change: the UN Charter of 1945, the Nuremberg case law in regards to war crimes; the

Universal Declaration of Human Rights of 1948, the Genocide Convention of 1948; the revision of the Geneva Conventions in 1949, redefining the laws of war and the international legal protection due to civilians in conflict; the European Convention on Human Rights of 1950; and the United Nations Educational, Scientific and Cultural Organisations' (UNESCO) statement on the race of 1950, in which prominent anthropologists sought to ban the scientific use of the word race.

All these documents spoke the same language and arose from the same moral impulse: to rebuild public morality after the abominations of a world war. While these documents all sprang from the same impulses of repentance and renewal, they were not consistent with each other. Many of our contemporary difficulties stem from these original contradictions. The UN Charter is addressed to states as moral actors, while the Universal Declaration addresses the human individual. A conflict between the rights of states and the rights of individuals was built into the very foundations of the post-war world, though the signatories probably did not see this conflict as we do. Initially, the charter was intended primarily to rewrite the rules of intrastate conduct. Hence the primary emphasis on state sovereignty and non-interference.

The human rights of individuals were seen as contributing to the internal legitimacy and hence of the stability of the international system. But there was less recognition than now of the intrinsic conflict between the rights of states and the rights of individuals and still less perception that the chief threat to the human rights of individuals was going to come from states themselves.

In the past fifty years, all regimes practising human rights abuses have taken refuge behind the UN Charter's guarantees of state sovereignty and non-interference. In response, international law has gradually shifted the balance in favour of human rights claims over the rights of state sovereignty, so much so that after the operation to protect the Kurds from the

Iraqi regime in 1991, French authorities began speaking in terms of a right of humanitarian intervention. This was clearly premature, but there seems little doubt that there now exists a presumption in favour of human rights over state sovereignty in humanitarian emergencies where the violations are gross.

The Geneva Conventions define human rights norms in battlefield conditions; but there remains a tension between the Geneva Conventions, which tacitly accept war as a normal, even lawful means of resolving human disputes, and the Universal Declaration, which tacitly treats war as an intrinsic infringement of moral norms. These tensions and contradictions were not always apparent at the time. What was problematic then was whose norms they were. They were written while the Cold War was locking itself into place with the division of Berlin, the establishment of Communist governments in Eastern Europe, and the formation of North Atlantic Treaty Organisation (NATO).

In this context, language crafted as a statement of shared universals was quickly turned into a weapon in the ideological battle between the superpowers. Many Communists of the period saw the new human rights norms as bourgeois humanism, promulgated as a universal ethic by imperialist powers bent on ideological expansion. The Communist bloc succeeded in excluding the right to property from UN human rights covenants. In turn, Western governments used human rights language to attack the denial of political rights in the nations of the Soviet bloc.

Below the surface of these exchanges lay a philosophical disagreement between the legal and political rights tradition of Western liberalism and the predominantly social and economic rights tradition of the Marxist world. Both traditions flowed from the Enlightenment conception of the rights of man and both laid claim to its emancipatory heritage, though with differing degrees of plausibility.

For twenty years after 1945, each side used the Universal Declaration to denounce each other, while protecting their own rights regimes behind the UN Charter's guarantee of state sovereignty. They also competed within UN bodies and international conferences for the allegiance of the emerging nations of Africa, Asia and Latin America.

With the Helsinki Final Act of 1976, the Cold War conflict between the two rights traditions began to evolve toward new forms of cooperation. At Helsinki, the West, in effect, acquiesced in a Soviet sphere of influence in Eastern Europe in return for guarantees of human rights protection. This *quid pro quo* had unexpected results: first in Poland, then in Czechoslovakia, human rights groups sprang up to defend the norms agreed at Helsinki, while Eastern European regimes continued, *de facto*, to persecute human rights activists and to denounce outside interference in their domestic affairs.

Against Communist oppression, human rights proved to be a powerful language of mobilisation. Dissidents exploited their own government's ratification of human rights covenants to defuse the charge that they were in league with foreign espionage or were bent on the restoration of capitalism. They sought, in effect to hoist their rulers on their own petards. This internal human rights resistance was doubly important because, externally, detente policies were reducing human rights pressure from the West.

Over fifty years, the Cold War evolved from outright ideological competition into a system of complicity, in which the West agreed to keep silent about human rights abuses in return for Soviet cooperation in the maintenance of geopolitical order. In effect, detente traded rights for order. Such mutual collusion created the conditions in which civil society actors—the non-governmental rights activists—came into play. Since government-to-government contact on human rights issues seemed to be bogged down in the collusive polemics of the Cold War, a people-to-people strategy seemed to offer the best chance to break the deadlock.

Amnesty International, Index on Censorship, and Human Rights Watch were only the best known of the international human rights organisations that came into being to combat this conspiracy of silence by states and to create indigenous constituencies for human rights reform. A new style of human rights activism came into being—ordinary people signing petitions and writing letters on behalf of specific prisoners to the rulers of foreign states.

Organisations like Amnesty and Human Rights Watch monitored human rights conditions in more than eighty countries around the world on a continual basis. Through their fund-raising and information campaigns, these organisations have created vocal, well-informed domestic constituencies who have forced human rights issues onto the political agendas of most Western societies.

Human rights questions are now obligatory in bilateral meetings between democratic and despotic regimes. A generation ago, Cold War *real politik* and cultural relativism combined to keep human rights off the agenda: liberal capitalist and communist societies agreed not to challenge the values of the other. The existence of a single normative rights standard leaves no room for such moral and political evasions, though the actual realities of international human rights politics are necessarily impure.

Nation states with indigenous human rights traditions like, France, Britain, and the United States are often guilty of what might be called rights narcissism. They find it disagreeable to have their own human rights record brought before the scrutiny of international bodies. Rights narcissism makes the British resistant to appeals against British court decisions to the European Court of Human Rights.

The developed nations are often willing to soften human rights criticisms of other powerful nations, like China or Iran, for the sake of trade or other economic benefits. The frequency with which human rights standards are compromised for the sake of economic benefit or geopolitical deal making makes it easy to forget that, until a generation ago, human rights criteria did not figure at all in these exchanges between states.

The case of South Africa—an exceedingly powerful and strategically important country engaged in abhorrent human rights behaviour—is illustrative of the increasing effectiveness of human rights norms in international politics, while internal domestic struggle by South Africans themselves was the decisive factor in overthrowing apartheid.

Since Marxism's ideological eclipse, the chief critique of international human rights has passed to those working within the cultures and traditions of colonial nations. But it was not always so. In the 1950s and 1960s, these new nations who signed up to a rights tradition derived from European Enlightenment sources did not mount an ideological or intellectual challenge to the American, French, and English rights traditions from which it was derived.

While there were obvious contradictions between the values of traditionalist societies and the individualist bias of Western rights language, most emerging nations were so anxious to sign up to the modernising project in general that they made little initial objection. They ratified international human rights treaties in somewhat the same way that they sought to have their own airlines: as part of a general wager on modernisation. But when modernisation and state building ran into difficulties, a cultural backlash against the individualist bias of human rights language began.

The Iranian Revolution of the late 1970s provided the focus and the leadership for this revolt. It is not surprising that Islam should have been the source of the central intellectual challenge to secular human rights. *Shariat* law is an ancient legal tradition and its re-imposition in the daily life of the Islamic world became the central element of the Islamic revolt against Western modernisation.

Islamic law and human rights discourse have encountered each other in the 1980s and 1990s and a curious process of hybridisation has taken place. In Afghanistan, for example, women use Western human rights talk to defend their right to education and health care, while insisting that they wish to be faithful to Muslim traditions in respect of female decency, marriage, and participation in public life.

Attachment to human rights no longer needs to imply purchasing the whole package of modernity: secularism, Western dress and sexual mores, and advanced technology. These hybrid mixtures of human rights language and local tradition and custom permit complex forms of accommodation between the unquestionably individualising bias of Western moral discourse and the communal and familist impulses of traditional society. Whether these accommodations are stable over the long term remains to be seen.

Muslim fathers have understandable reasons for being alarmed at their daughters wishing to have the right to a scientific education, for with educational qualification comes the means to a career, independent marriage choice, and possible departure from the patriarchal order of the family. It remains to be seen just how far Western liberal rights language can be accommodated with traditional religious and patriarchal identities.

But there is no doubt that human rights language is something more than a Western imposition or form of cultural imperialism. It has become something quite different: a hybridised vernacular in which the victims of traditional society mount their claims against the ethical claim of community. In every context this demand for freedom will mean something different, and it will not necessarily mean what is meant in the West.

The legitimacy of human rights is not so much its authoritative universalism, so much as its capacity to become a moral vernacular for the demand for freedom within local cultures. Nor is the meaning of human rights fixed or stable in the West. The dissolution of the Cold War stand-off between the Soviet and capitalist rights traditions has brought to the forefront the significant differences within the Western tradition.

Human rights are involved as trump cards on either side of debates about abortion, cloning, assisted suicide, and medical experimentation. Human rights is misconceived if it is understood as a breviary of values: rights talk can do no more than formalise the terms in which conflicts of values are made precise and therefore rendered amenable to compromise and solution.

In 1945, women, blacks, and homosexuals in Western societies were denied many of the basic protections of the Universal Declaration. The domestic history of most Western societies since 1945 could be written as a struggle for enfranchisement by these groups. The international human rights revolution abroad would have been inconceivable without the rights revolution at home. This illustrates a central point about rights language itself and its dynamic, destabilising character in any society that ratifies or adopts its provisions. Once rights language exists in public consciousness it sets up a dynamic directed at the inevitable gap between what a society practises and what it preaches. This dynamic of enfranchisement has powered liberal society for centuries.

The genocide convention has certainly not prevented genocide. The convention may even have been counter-productive, causing nations to avoid formal use of the word lest its use entain treaty obligations to intervene which come into play once a situation is defined as genocidal. This is only one example of a bigger problem: the gulf between word and deed, formal commitment and actual performance, in the human rights behaviour of governments. On such a reading of the history of the past fifty years, the so-called set-backs that human rights activists lament are not set-backs at all, but the norm of human rights behaviour around the world.

Proliferation of international statutes and human rights organisations to lobby for their enforcement might only prove that the human rights practices of dozens of states remains abominable and therefore requires the constant Sisyphean labour of human rights monitoring to keep it from getting worse. The human rights activity is driven by the logic of insatiability: the more that is accomplished, the more remains to be done.

The existence of an international human rights law amounts to progress, even if the gap between statute and practice remains discouragingly large. Indeed, the key function of human rights language is to keep us aware of the gap between what we say and do. It is there to make trouble, and it will most certainly continue to do so. It has legitimised individual self-hood and authenticated every form of discontent with injustice, ascribed and inherited status. Rights language has been central not simply to the protection, but also to the production of modern individuals.

## MODERN CONCEPTS OF HUMAN RIGHTS

Human rights were not invented overnight out of nowhere. They are a product of history. They have their roots in the practice of states and societies the world over. Many people erroneously contend that the concept of human rights is basically a Western concept. This misunderstanding is partly the reason why the concept of the universality of human rights has been questioned by different groups of states and individuals at different phases of their history. That human rights is a Western concept is to ignore the practices of other great ancient civilisations of the world. They are equally universal because every human being living in every corner of the world needs them and every civilised society in every orderly and civilised country has recognised them as such since time immemorial.

The claim of the universality of human rights can be sustained if we look at it from the angle of universal values, found in all major civilisations. International law reveals examples of individuals being afforded rights by treaty, including asylum and religious liberty during early historical periods and in all regions of the world. Similarly, international law imposed duties directly on individuals, reflected in prohibitions on privacy and war crimes, and later, on the slave trade. Both have their origins in the relations and conflicts which developed between the first human societies.

The modern concept of human rights is a contribution of the UN since there exists no general history of the law of human rights as such prior to the establishment of the UN. Certain people of Western origin were instrumental in developing the modern concept of human rights through the mechanism of the UN in the early years of the UN which resulted in the adoption of the Universal Declaration on the 10th December 1948 by the UN General Assembly. But these people were not the only persons who did the job nor did they ever intimate that they were advancing the values of Western civilisation through the Universal Declaration.

At the time of the adoption of the Declaration, the UN and the General Assembly was dominated by Western States who had won the Second World War and the General Assembly passed many resolutions during that time to suit their interests. But when the decolonisation process accelerated, the Western States were no longer in the majority in the General Assembly. As such, most of International Human Rights Law in existence today was developed after the developing countries gained majority in the General Assembly of the UN.

Many of the declarations and the resolutions of the UN adopted since the late 1960s express the aspirations of these developing countries. That is one reason why it is inaccurate to say that the International Human Rights Law is basically an imposition of Western values on other states. Human rights are therefore universal, international and represent the aspirations of humanity as a whole. As former UN Secretary General, Perez de Cuellar said in 1988, The gradual and growing acceptance of the Universal Declaration and the evidence of general practice by the international community have led to the conclusion that, the Declaration constitutes binding law as international custom, in accordance with Article 38 of the Statute of the International Court of Justice.

Through a widespread acceptance by states of the 1966 Covenants on Civil and Political Rights, and on Economic, Social and Cultural Rights, most of their provisions and subsequent conventions protecting children and women, could now be considered part of customary international law. The provisions of these international instruments represent the opinion of the international community from which no state should derogate.

In early September 2000, United Nations' 'Millennium Summit' was held in New York City. In the meetings, the leaders of 150 countries tried to address the most pressing problems of the new century. At the end of the 20th century the summit was remarkable in that conflict and war did not dominate centre-stage. Instead, the heads of state focused their rhetoric on the problems of widespread poverty, the AIDS epidemic, environmental destruction, and the lack of education for millions of the world's children. Talk of globalisation dominated the discussion throughout the summit. The heads of state were nearly unanimous in challenging the shape and direction globalisation has taken until now.

The most pointed attacks came from leaders of the Global South. But even representatives from the world's wealthier countries sharply questioned the global economy's benefits. Prime Minister Bertie Ahern of Ireland said: "The statistics of poverty and inequality in our world are shocking and shameful. Half the world's population is struggling on less than $2 a day, over half a billion on less than $1. A quarter of a billion children of 14 and under-working, sometimes in terrible conditions".

All speakers, came before the General Assembly noted that the increasing interconnectedness of the world means that—questions of morality aside—the wealthy nations cannot afford to ignore the world's deepening social injustice. The Nigerian President, Olusegun Obasanjo, chairman of the Group of 77, a forum for developing nations, said.

> The wishes of the developing world are simple. We are all living in the same house, whether you are developed or not developed. What we are saying is that some of us in this house are living in superluxurious rooms; others are living in something not better than an unkempt kitchen where pipes are leaking and there is no toilet. We are saying, look, in the interest of all of us, let us live in the superluxurious rooms, pay a bit of attention to those who are living where the pipes are leaking, or we'll all be badly affected.

During the post Cold War period, the emphasis on social and wealth divisions instead of geopolitical ones makes perfect sense. War and conflict perhaps no longer pose the greatest threat to human rights. Rather, increasing wealth inequalities within and among nations now represent the most immediate attack on human dignity. In a world where malnutrition and preventable disease kill more people than wars and state-sponsored repression, it is clear that the concept of human rights is long overdue for a redefinition.

Since the end of World War II, the concept of human rights has gained near universal acceptance. Advocacy and research by organisations such as Amnesty International and Human Rights Watch have been invaluable for popularising the idea that each individual has certain inalienable rights. But these organisations, along with multilateral institutions like the UN and the Organisation of American States, have for the most part limited their focus to certain kinds of abuse, those involving civil and political rights. And these same groups have looked mostly at repression directed by nation-states, leaving aside the sorts of abuses committed by multinational corporations.

Division of political rights and economic rights arose partially from the political manoeuvrings of the Cold War. During that ideological conflict, the capitalist democracies, always looking to delegitimise the communist nations, frequently charged those regimes with human rights violations, while at the same time ignoring the social and economic rights abuses occurring within their own borders. The communist countries would respond that political freedoms are meaningless without social equality.

Today, a new space exists for fundamental redefinition of the term human rights. Adopted by the UN General Assembly in 1948, the Universal Declaration of Human Rights is considered the foundation of modern international human rights defence and promotion. The declaration is built on the common sense idea that human rights are based on the inherent dignity of every person. This dignity, and the rights to freedom and equality that derive from it, are undeniable.

The declaration explicitly establishes economic security as central to human dignity on equal footing with freedom of conscience essential to human rights. The declaration says, "the right to work, to free choice of employment, to just and favourable conditions of work and to protection against unemployment" are basic human rights. The "right to equal pay for equal work" as well as a worker's "right to form and to join trade unions for the protection of his interests" are considered essential liberties.

The declaration asserts:

> Everyone has the right to a standard of living adequate for the health and well-being of himself and of his family, including food, clothing, housing, medical care, and necessary social services, and the right to security in the event of unemployment, sickness, disability, widowhood, old age or other lack of livelihood in circumstances beyond his control.

Political rights can be enjoyed only when basic human needs have been satisfied. Without economic security, freedom of conscience—the liberty to grow as an individual—is impossible. According to Article 22 everyone has the right to social security and the economic, social and cultural rights indispensable for his dignity and the free development of his personality.

Today, multinational corporations are increasingly more powerful than the governments that are supposed to represent their citizens, the argument that economic rights are also human rights must be made as urgently as ever. When 51 of the 100 largest economies in the world are corporations, not countries, company managers are just as likely as any callous dictatorship to brutalise people. The abuses taking place in low-wage factories around the world mirror the sort of repression often directed by military governments.

In the Mexican city of Tehuacan, for example, jeans factories employ armed guards to keep workers in line. Local human rights groups there report that the pistoleros are paid up to 10 times as much as the employees they guard. Then there is a worker's right to form independent unions and bargain collectively. Essentially, this right is the same as the freedom of association. Just as individuals must be allowed to gather together to create political parties or civic groups, so too should individual workers be able to come together to bargain collectively.

In countries such as China and Vietnam, where US companies do business, authoritarian regimes prohibit the formation of independent unions. But even in the growing democracies of Latin America and Indonesia independent unions are uncommon. In these places it is not state-sponsored repression that restricts freedom of association. Rather, it is intimidation by factory managers that crushes democratic efforts to establish collective bargaining.

In the political realm it is agreed that governments should not use force against peaceful demonstrators, but in the economic realm it happens all the time, as when companies' private security guards attack striking workers. Multinational corporations also routinely violate communities' basic economic rights, as when they press for lower wages or avoid paying their share of social costs in the countries where they operate. Certainly governments, not private companies, have the final responsibility for ensuring basic social security. But when corporations constantly seek, through tax breaks and special subsidies, to widen their profit margins at the expense of spending on health and education, they undermine any chance for economic justice.

In the coming decades, human rights campaigns will increasingly have to be directed against companies, not countries. The demand is simple: Basic liberties must not stop at the workplace door. Article 21 of the Universal Declaration of Human Rights states that "the will of the people shall be the basis of the authority of government".

Abuses against people's political rights are less common in liberal democracies than in autocratic states. No society freely chooses to limit speech or the right of association. Equally, it is the authoritarianism of economic decision-making that allows for violations against individuals' social rights.

In the 21st century, democracy must become the central value of the refashioned human rights movement, for only the vigilance of self-governance can ensure against abuse. Until we bring genuine democracy to economic decision-making, we will be unable to end violations against basic economic and social rights. Unless we establish popular governance of the global economy, there is no chance of creating the sort of social justice that guarantees individuals' basic dignity.

## HUMAN RIGHTS EDUCATION: AN INVESTMENT FOR THE FUTURE

Notions of individual freedom and liberty and of dignity of person which are the most cherished values of the free society governed by the rule of law, would sound as empty words for those who are illiterate and ignorant about them. Education means knowledge which leads to liberation from ignorance. The fundamental purpose of education is to transfigure the human personality into a pattern of perfection through a systematic process of the development of the body, the enrichment of the mind, the sublimation of the emotions and the illumination of the spirit.

Today, it is principal instrument in awakening the child to cultural values, in preparing him for later professional training and in helping him to adjust normally to his environment. In the context of a democratic form of government, education is at once a social and political necessity. The foremost need to be satisfied by education is the eradication of illiteracy which persists in a depressing measure. A true democracy is one where education is universal and where people understand what is good for them and the nation and know-how to govern themselves.

Awareness of human rights is equally important in times of peace and war. Human rights education, which is essential for the formation of public opinion and the generation of public pressure for compliance with human rights, is thus a *sine qua non* for the observance and advancement of human rights. Only those people who are educated about and aware of their human rights can demand that their governments observe those rights.

Knowledge of human rights is essential as a tool for the observance and the promotion of human rights and for the creation of a climate of public opinion in which gross violations of human rights are unacceptable. Human rights education is a priority in that it contributes to a concept of development consistent with the dignity of the human person.

In its 26(l)st Article the Universal Declaration of Human Rights proclaims:

> Everyone has right to education. Education shall be free, at least in the elementary and fundamental stages. Elementary education shall be compulsory. Technical and professional education shall be made generally available and higher education shall be equally accessible to all on the basis of merit.

Clause (2) of Article 26 of the declaration further provides:

> Education shall be directed to the full development of the human personality and to the strengthening of respect for human rights and fundamental freedoms.

Right to education has also been recognised by the International Covenant on Economic, Social and Cultural Rights. Article 13(l) of the Covenant states:

> The State Parties to the present Covenant recognise the right of everyone to education. They agreed that education shall be directed to the full development of the human personality and the sense of its dignity, and shall strengthen the respect for human rights and fundamental freedoms....

Clause (2) of Article 13 of the Covenant further provides:

> The state Parties to the present Covenant recognise that, with a view to achieving the full realisation of this right:
>
> a) Primary education shall be compulsory and available free to all,
>
> b) Secondary education in its different forms, including technical and vocational secondary education, shall be made generally available and accessible to all by every appropriate means, and in particular by the progressive introduction of free education;
>
> c) Higher education shall be made equally accessible to all, on the basis of capacity, by every appropriate means, and in particular by the progressive introduction of free education;
>
> d) Fundamental education shall be encouraged or intensified as far as possible for those persons who have not received or completed the whole period of their primary education; and
>
> e) The development of a system of schools at all levels shall be actively pursued, an adequate fellowship system shall be established, and the material

conditions or teaching staff shall be continuously improved.

Right to free and compulsory primary education has been universally recognised. Further, the basic object of the elementary education at the fundamental stages is to develop human personality and the sense of its dignity and to strengthen the respect for human rights and fundamental freedoms.

## Human Rights in Primary and Secondary Education

Today, peoples around the world live together as a global community and we are each day more conscious of responsibility for anyone beyond all frontiers. The present condition of global interdependence obliges us to reflect about our past and common future—to strive towards the practical implementation worldwide of our rights as enshrined in the Universal Declaration of Human Rights, for as the Declaration states, human rights are international and universal.

Some aspects of development education in schools in fact relate to human rights, but development education is not normally taught within the context of human rights. Courses are taught in some schools, colleges and universities which include human rights as part of other courses. Several universities, centres and institutes offer teaching and undertake research in human rights, mostly in law. Work on issues of gender and racial equality in the school curriculum and in the organisation within schools depends on the initiative of teachers.

The concept of human rights are based on the equality and freedom of all humans. The notion of educating children on these rights seems to be radical, if we can judge from the lack of interest in the subject, or indeed the political resistance to its incorporation in primary and secondary school curricula.

One of the main concerns of integrating human rights in children's curricula is that human rights are normative, and so should not be imposed on children. This objection rests upon the illusion that it is possible to teach other curricular subjects objectively. The case in Japan in August 1997, where the Japanese Supreme Court held that the state has the right to censor education material, highlights the fact that all teaching is subjective.

The curricula already contains the teaching of values in the form of religious concepts and national legal principles. Even if we leave aside the inflammatory question of whether religious concepts should be taught at school and concern ourselves with the teaching of legal principles, we find that the case for including human rights in primary and secondary school curricula is very strong. Hardly anyone would contest the fact that children must know the law, or at least its main principles of justice, equality before the law, and proportional retribution.

Human rights, as embedded in two global and one regional convention to which the UK is a party, are very much a part of the legal framework for this country. When we say that children must know the law, there is no argument for limiting this law to national legislation. Indeed, how can we possibly justify not teaching children about their rights and obligations from a global perspective when the accelerating globalisation process makes it quite clear that what they have to learn to make sense of most probably will not be confined to their own country.

Another objection is that the concept not only is normative but also political, the argument being that children should be left to develop a political opinion by themselves in due course. Political opinions, however, do not develop in a vacuum. A quick overview of the flux and prominence of ideologies in modern history shows that political opinions are very much relative to the historic, social, and economic context from which they grow: national socialism as a response to the economic hardship in post war Germany, socialism as a response to industrialisation and the creation of a working class, and neo-liberalism as a response to the apparent inefficiency of the welfare state in the 80s, and to the debt crisis in developing countries.

There are, needless to say, commodities between human rights and political ideologies in general. Human rights, like political ideologies, are based on moral assumptions, and they are very much the basis for advocacy work. However, unlike political ideologies, human rights do not represent an entirely subjective perspective on the political, social, and economic reality of society. The Universal Declaration of Human Rights was unanimously adopted by the United Nations General Assembly in 1948 in a vote that included countries of very different and even contrasting ideologies, implying that the vision of human rights is common to most political systems and so trans-political rather than political.

In a society that is increasingly distrustful and cynical with regard to politicians and politics in general, it is perhaps not surprising that the teaching of a subject that seems to be political is regarded as undesirable, especially in primary and secondary schools. Considering the impressionability of young minds, it is healthy to have an open debate on what values should prevail in the education system. Blocking such a debate by insisting that the current education system is value-free is not only unhealthy but wrong, and the most interesting thing in this context is that if such an open debate existed, the discussion of whether human rights should be part of children's curricula or not would be dismissed as superfluous.

## Human Rights in Adult and Continuing Education

Adult education is essential part in assisting the right of each individual to social and cultural development. Adult education is also essential for assisting those whose schooling did not enable them to achieve their full potential to catch up and regain their access to educational opportunities. This possibility is especially important for women, those from lower social strata and ethnic minorities. Adult education has suffered over 20 years from major policy shifts, cuts in public funding, administrative re-organisations and financial changes.

The United Nations recently placed a heightened emphasis on education by proclaiming the Decade of Human Rights Education (HRE), which will promote awareness and understanding of global and individual human rights issues. This change to promote human rights education creates additional responsibilities for both world governments and various non-governmental organisations.

## REFERENCES

Avishai, Margalit, *et. al.*, "The Uniqueness of the Holocaust', *Philosophy and Public Affairs*, 1996.

Berman, Marshall, 'Modernism and Human Rights Near New Millennium', *Dissent*, 1995.

Cranston, *What are Human Rights*?, The Bodely Head, 1973.

Kalaiah, A.B., *Human Rights in International Law*, 1986.

Patil V.T. and Trivedi, P.R., *Human Rights and Refugees*, Authorspress, New Delhi, 2000.

__________, Migration, Refugees and Security in the 21st Century, Authorspress, New Delhi, 2000

Rai, Rahul, *Human Rights: UN Initiatives*, Authorspress, New Delhi, 2000.

Robertson, A.H., *Human Rights in the World*, 1972.

Thakur, L.K., *Comparative and International Human Rights*, Authorspress, New Delhi, 2000.

Torres, Rosa Maria, "Repetition: A Major obstacle to Education for All", *Education News*, No.12, UNICEF, April, 1995.

# 2
# Challenges to Universality of Human Rights

Many people have been unsatisfied with the notion that what is right or good is simply what a particular society or ruling elite feels is right or good at any given time. This unease has led to a quest for enduring moral imperatives that bind societies and their rulers over time and from place to place. Fierce debates raged among political philosophers as these issues were argued through. While a path was paved by successive thinkers that lead to contemporary human rights, a second lane was laid down at the same time by those who resisted this direction. The emergence of human rights from the natural rights tradition did not come without opposition, as some argued that rights could come only form the law of a particular society and could not come from any natural or inherent source.

One of the earliest precursors to human rights might be found in the notions of 'natural right' developed by classical Greek philosophers, such as Aristotle, but this concept was more fully developed by Thomas Aquinas in his *Summa Theologica*. For several centuries Aquinas' conception held sway: there were goods or behaviours that were naturally right or wrong because God ordained it so. What was naturally right could be ascertained by humans by 'right reason'— thinking properly. The moral authority of natural right was assured because it had divine authorship. Further reinforcement of natural rights came with Immanuel Kant's writings later in the 17th century that reacted to Hobbes' work. In his view, the congregation of humans into a state-structured society resulted from a rational need for protection from each other's violence that would be found in a state of nature. However, the fundamental requirements of morality required that each treat another according to universal principles. Kant's political doctrine was derived from his moral philosophy, and as such he argued that a state had to be organised through the imposition of, and obedience to, laws that applied universally; nevertheless, these laws should respect the equality and freedom of the citizens.

The divine basis of natural rights was still pursued for more than a century after Hobbes published his *Leviathan*. John Locke wrote a strong defence of natural rights in the late 17th century with the publication of his *Two Treatises on Government*, but his arguments were filled with references to what God had ordained or given to mankind. Locke had a lasting influence on political discourse that was reflected in both the American Declaration of Independence and France's Declaration of the Rights of Man and the Citizen, passed by the Republican Assembly after the revolution in 1789. The French declaration proclaimed "rights as the natural, inalienable and sacred rights of man".

Jeremy Bentham's critique of the Declaration, in a publication entitled *Anarchical Fallacies*, argued vehemently that there can be no natural rights, since rights are created by the law of a society:

> Right, the substantive right, is the child of law: from real laws come real rights; but from laws of nature, fancied and invented by poets, rhetoriticians, and dealers in moral and intellectual poisons come imaginary rights, a bastard brood of monsters, *gorgons and chimeras dire*.
>
> Natural rights is simple nonsense: natural and imprescriptible rights, rhetorical nonsense, —nonsense upon stilts.

After *the French Declaration*, Thomas Paine wrote a defence of the conception of natural rights and their connection to the rights of a particular society. In The *Rights of Man*, published in two parts in 1791 and 1792, Paine made a distinction between natural rights and civil rights, but he continued to see a necessary connection:

> Natural rights are those which appertain to man in the right of his existence. Of this kind are all the intellectual rights, or rights of the mind, and also all those rights of acting as an individual for his own comfort and happiness, which are not injurious to the natural rights of others. Civil rights are those which appertain to man in the right of being a member of society. Every civil right has for its foundation, some natural right preexisting in the individual, but to the enjoyment of which his individual power is not, in all cases, sufficiently competent. Of this kind are all those which relate to security and protection.

Contemporary theorists have developed a notion of natural rights that does not draw its source or inspiration from a divine ordering. The ground work for this secular natural rights trend was laid by Paine and even Rousseau. In its place has arisen a variety of theories that are humanist and rationalist; the 'natural' element is determined from the prerequisites of human society which are said to be rationally ascertainable. Thus there are constant criteria which can be identified for peaceful governance and the development of human society. Contemporary notions of human rights draw very deeply from this natural rights tradition. In a further extension of the natural rights tradition, human rights are now often viewed as arising essentially from the nature of humankind itself.

There are strong objections to the manner in which human rights have been conceptualised. Many lists of human rights read like specifications for liberal democracy. A variety of traditional societies can be found in the world that operate harmoniously, but are not based on equality let alone universal suffrage. A question that will recur in later discussions is whether the human rights advocated today are really civil rights that pertain to a particular—liberal—conception of society. To a large extent, the resolution of this issue depends upon the ultimate goal of human rights. If human rights are really surrogate liberalism, then it will be next to impossible to argue their inherent authority over competing political values. In order for human rights to enjoy universal legitimacy they must have a basis that survives charges of ideological imperialism.

## THEORETICAL BASIS OF HUMAN RIGHTS

Human rights exist in order to protect the basic dignity of human life. Indeed, the United Nations Declaration on Human Rights embodies this goal by declaring that human rights flow from the inherent dignity of the human person. Strong arguments have been made, especially by Western liberals, that human rights must be directed to protecting and promoting human dignity.

As Jack Donnelly has written, "We have human rights not to the requisites for health but to those things needed for a life of dignity, for a life worthy of a human being, a life that cannot be enjoyed without these rights. This view is perhaps the most pervasively held, especially among human rights activists; the rhetoric of human rights disputes most frequently invokes this notion of striving for the dignity that makes human life worth living.

The idea of promoting human dignity has considerable appeal, since human life is given a distinctive weight over other animals in most societies precisely because we are capable of cultivating the quality of our lives. Unfortunately, the promotion of dignity may well provide an unstable foundation for the construction of universal moral standards. The inherent weakness of this approach lies in trying to identify the nature of this dignity. Donnelly unwittingly reveals this shortcoming in expanding upon the deliberate human action that creates human rights. "Human rights represent a social choice of a particular moral vision of human potentiality, which rests on a particular substantive account of the minimum requirements of a life of dignity.

While one of the most basic liberal beliefs about human dignity is that all humans are equal, social division and hierarchy play important roles in aspects of Hindu, Confucian, Muslim, and Roman Catholic views of human life. Indeed, dignity is often achieved in these views by striving to fulfil one's particular vocation within an ordered set of roles. But, if human rights are meant to be universal standards, the inherent dignity that is supposed to be protected should be a common vision.

Human rights are not just a product of morality but are meant to protect the basic freedom and well-being necessary for human agency. Gewirth distinguished between three types of rights that address different levels of well-being. Basic rights safeguard one's subsistence or basic well-being. Non-subtractive rights maintain the capacity for fulfilling purposive agency, while additive rights provide the requisites for developing one's capabilities. Gewirth differentiates between these rights because he accepts that humans vary tremendously in their capacity for purposive agency. Through what he calls the principle of proportionality, humans are entitled to those rights that are proportionate to their capacity for agency. Gewirth's approach, however, has been strongly criticised by those who argue that human rights cannot be universal if they are derived from one's capacity for agency.

Douglas Husak has used Gewirth's theories to argue that there can be no rights that extend to all human beings. He makes the crucial distinction between humans and persons, and he points out that some humans may be considered non-persons because they are incapable of ever performing any purposive agency. Even if one accepts Gewirth's rebuttal that all humans are entitled to at least basic rights because they are either prospective or former purposive agents, there still remains in his theory the notion some will find unsettling: not all humans possess all human rights to the same degree.

John O'Manique put forward another basis for human rights based on evolution and human development. He was motivated by the desire to find a truly universal basis for human rights theories that are not as susceptible, as is dignity, to controversial interpretations or denial by others. Thus, human rights should be founded upon something inherent to humans rather than some moral vision that is created by human action.

O'Manique argues that a satisfactory basis may lie in the following set of propositions:

— P1: I ought to survive
— P2: X is necessary for my survival
— P3: Therefore, I ought to do/have X.

The finding agreement in P1 is the real hurdle in this set of propositions. The requisites for survival are fairly easily ascertained by scientific inquiry. Thus if there is concordance on the notion I ought to survive, then the logical construction of this model produces the conclusion that one ought to have X if it is necessary for survival.

O'Manique is on fairly firm ground when he asserts, "The belief that survival is good is virtually universal". He does concede that there are religious beliefs which hold that a person's life can be sacrificed, but usually this sacrifice is done to further the survival of others. So he determines, "The exceptions do not prove the rule, but they do point to the strong probability that the belief that survival is good is found, explicitly or implicitly, in almost all human beings. One might add that some value in human survival may be found in any society, since no culture comes to mind that has tolerated unrestricted, recreational homicide. He also draws from theories of evolution to establish that the goal of humans has to be the survival of the species. So, there would be universal agreement with the statement, "Humans ought to survive."

O'Manique explicitly dismisses the idea that the source of human rights lies in the needs for human subsistence. He wishes to propel human rights into a further plane, by basing human survival upon the full development of human potential. The initial proposition P1 in the model above really becomes "I ought to develop". As he says, "Human aspirations are not to the maintenance of existence but to the fulfilment of life. If we believe that one ought to survive, it is because we believe that one ought to develop".

In O'Manique's vision, human rights would include rights to things needed for subsistence but also go on to cover all aspects of intellectual and emotional development. He tries to limit in some way the range by insisting that the needs for development can be ascertained through research. However, he also reveals the broad sweep of matters that could be included when he addresses this issue: "The existence of such needs for human development—the need for association with other human beings, for self-expression, for some control over one's destiny, and even the need for love and for beauty—can be observed and even empirically confirmed within the social sciences and psychology".

O'Manique may well lose some support with this incredibly vast range of issues that he would include within the human rights rubric. A fundamental difficulty with using the fulfilment of human development as a basis for human rights is that it can have a meaning that is relative to each culture and individual. This relativism even creeps into his discussion when he concludes, "A community and its members will develop to the extent that the members of the community support the development needs of others in the community, in ways that are appropriate to that community". Just what is needed for fulfilment in expression, love, or autonomy will be given profoundly different interpretations in Bedouin, German, or Japanese societies.

Human rights may be limited to providing all humans with the needs for their physical subsistence. But, this subsistence would involve a certain degree of minimal comfort beyond merely keeping one's organs working, because human subsistence also consists of being able to function. Advocates of the other approaches to human rights have dismissed needs to subsistence as too narrow a foundation, but this criticism may not account for the ramifications that flow from the range of human needs.

Human rights would guarantee the provision of the food, clothing, and shelter without which anyone would perish. Since most households are not simply provided with the requisites to life but buy them with the wages of their labour, one can easily extend the range of human rights into other benefits relating to the work force. This extension is particularly true if the satisfaction of needs is accomplished not by directly supplying the specific goods needed, but in providing the capacity for individuals to provide for themselves.

Theories of human rights based on dignity, well-being, or development all are motivated by a desire to protect and cultivate some quality of life; because one is alive, one should lead a life filled with dignity, well-being, or continuing development. A view of human rights based on subsistence is ultimately concerned with simply preserving life itself. But this distinction should not ignore an overlap, as a common ground among all theories of human rights is the assumption that human rights include subsistence rights.

## MOTIVATION FOR HUMAN RIGHTS

Human are often thought to exist beyond the determination of specific societies. They set a universal standard that can be used to judge any society. They provide an acceptable benchmark with which individuals or governments from one part of the world may criticise the norms followed by other governments or cultures. With an acceptance of human rights, Muslims, Hindus, Christians, capitalists, socialists, democracies, or tribal oligarchies may all legitimately censure each other. This criticism across religious, political, and economic divides gains its legitimacy because human rights are said to enshrine universal moral standards. The prime rhetorical benefit of human rights is that they are viewed as being so basic and so fundamental to human existence that they should trump any other consideration. Any conception of rights trumps other claims within a society, human rights may be of a higher order that supersedes even other rights claims within a society.

Due to the currency given to human rights in contemporary political debate, there is a danger that such a denial will provide support for brutal regimes who defend their repression on the grounds that international human rights norms are simply a fanciful creation that has no universal authority. The United Nations conference on human rights held in Vienna in 1993 saw some of the world's most repressive governments making precisely this argument, and few people would wish to provide further justification for this position. Without the appeal to human rights, democratic champions would have to argue the desirability of values such as equality and freedom of speech across the often incomparable circumstances of the world's societies, rather than asserting that such benefits just inherently flow from human existence.

## HUMAN RIGHTS HOLDERS

All humans hold all human rights; after all, human rights are said to be those benefits to which we are entitled simply by being human. But what is meant by being 'human' is vague since the life-cycle of homosapiens ranges from conception to death and decay. There is profound controversy over how and when a human acquires and then loses human rights between those two periods. Even before conception, sperm and eggs exist that contain human genetic material.

One may decide easily that these are human cells but not 'human beings', because they contain incomplete sets of human genes. After conception, however, controversies arise about the status of the developing foetus. From a mass of undifferentiated cells, the embryo quickly grows into a recognisably human entity. Many distinguish foetuses from babies that have emerged from their mothers and say that separate human life only begins with 'birth'. This can be an arbitrary distinction since a very premature baby is at much the same stage of development whether inside or outside the womb; the differences centre on how a baby receives nutrition and oxygen. One can specify an arbitrary point for the acquisition of rights, such as conception, neural development, viability, or emergence from the womb. But this approach is bound to erupt in controversy, because not everyone will agree on a given point. Abortion is such a divisive issue precisely because various groups hold different beliefs about when human life starts.

There is some special quality of human life that provides a basis for possessing rights; when that quality is acquired, so are rights. This approach is favoured by many, since it allows for the distinction between humans and other animals. Human rights are rights particular to human beings, thus the basis of the claim to rights should be something that differentiates humans from other animals. With a sharing of an enormous proportion of genetic material between humans and primates, the distinction is usually drawn on the basis of some quality of human life not shared by other animals rather than physiological characteristics.

Douglas Husak has written a poignant critique of the notion of human rights based on his objection that some human beings merely exist. Some mentally-ill patients lack any basis for purposive agency; they are seemingly unaware of their surroundings, incapable of rationale thought, or unable to distinguish right from wrong. Husak distinguishes between humans and persons, and he points out that some humans, such as the comatose, are non-persons. Persons are human beings with capacities beyond mere existence that produce a quality of life. Non-persons simply lack the qualities of life that one wishes either to protect or use as the key to acquiring rights. Distinction between humans and persons is often used to justify aborting foetuses, because the human foetus is not considered by many to be a person. In the end, Husak argues that the phenomena called human rights are really rights of persons.

The rights of children and the mentally ill may depend greatly upon what foundation one adopts for the possession of rights. Similarly, the existence of rights to life in abortion, infanticide, and euthanasia are directly related to what status one accords to undeveloped foetuses, mutant newborns, or terminally comatose adults. According to Donnelly, human rights are properly held by only individuals. Others contend that human lives are lived within group settings and the full enjoyment of human life can only be realised when those groups are able to flourish. Whether human rights can include collective rights is a particularly crucial issue in analysing whether the human rights regime protects a group's culture, language and the right to self-determination.

## THE RIGHTS IN HUMAN RIGHTS

The universality and inalienability of a human right depends to a large extent on the character of the 'rights' involved. It is necessary first of all to distinguish between the adjectival use of the word 'right', which means good or proper, from the substantive 'a right', which is a special, possessable benefit. Not everything which is right (good) is a right, although many people mistakenly inflate the concept of a right by asserting benefits they believe are 'right' to be 'rights'. This confusion has become evident in the assertion of what are known as 'second-generation human rights'—such as the right to economic development and prosperity —and 'third generation human rights'—which cover the rights to world peace and a clean environment.

While some human rights advocates accept the inclusion of these benefits as rights, others argue that prosperity and peace are 'right' but not substantive rights. Even with the substantive term 'a right', however, there are several different meanings. In 1919, Wesley Hohfeld laid down a useful set of four distinctive connotations that can be given to the phrase "A has a right to X". Perhaps the most common meaning given to this phrase conveys the notion of a claim—right. It is a claim that A has against a correlative duty of another, B; A has a right to X, and B has a duty to let A have or do X. The duty B has may be positive, in the sense that action is required on B's part to allow A to enjoy X; if A has a right to health care, B has a duty to provide it. There may also be a negative duty, in the sense of B having to refrain from interfering in A's possession of benefit X; if A has a right to privacy, B must refrain from prying in A's affairs. It is important to note that the duty may be owed by a particular person or official, or the duty may generally lie in the whole community. The essential characteristic of a claim right is the inherent connection between A's claim to a benefit and B's duty—A can make a claim that B must perform the duty.

There are other connotations of the phrase 'A has a right to X' that do not involve a corresponding duty on another's part. The term may mean that A has a liberty with respect to X. In this view, A has no obligation not to do or have X, which may be different from the status of other people. Also, A can make no claim against another, because no-one else has a duty with respect to A's enjoyment of X. A liberty may be enjoyed by all, such as the right to wear what one pleases while doing household chores. A subset of liberty is privilege, because A may have no duty not to do X but others do. For instance, in some English colleges the dons have a right to walk across the grass in the quadrangle, although others must use the pathways instead. In any liberty there is no duty on anyone to provide the X involved; i.e., no one has a duty to provide the lawns simply for the dons to walk upon.

To connotation 'A has a right to X' may also indicate that A has a power to effect changes in X. Thus an owner of a bicycle has the right to sell it, and a customs officer has the right to confiscate property or detain people at the border.

Another interpretation of 'A has a right to X' conveys the notion that A has an immunity that B is unable to change. Thus, MP's have a right to free speech that protects them from prosecution for speeches given in the House of Commons, and it is a right which cannot be changed by the executive, police, or courts. There are other uses of 'having a right' that should be added to those identified by Hohfeld, because these other uses refer to ideals, needs, or wants that are simply expressed as rights. The confusion between adjectival and substantive right has led to the frequent use of rights to describe ideals.

Thus, the rights to prosperity and peace are ideals or goals to strive for, that some express as rights. Another confusion arises when people assert a right to a benefit because it fills a need. But, not all needs are rights; I may need a car to drive to work in, but few would agree that I have a right to a car. Many confuse benefits they want with benefits they have a right to; free, post-secondary education and complete bursaries may be desirable, but are not viewed as rights by many. These uses of rights also involve a confusion between making a claim and having a right. One does not hold a right simply because one claims so, neither is it necessary to make claims in order to possess rights. It is not the act of claiming that creates rights. Thus, the claim to a right to prosperity or world peace does not establish that those benefits exist as rights.

The most common interpretation given to the 'right' in human rights is that of claim-rights. There is a defined benefit to which individuals are entitled, and there is a correlative duty on others in relation to that benefit. This tendency may be partly due to the increasing codification of human rights into legal documents. It is far more efficacious if human rights are conceived of as claim rights, because those who are deprived of their rights may argue that others must be compelled to fulfil a duty to provide the benefit.

Since much human rights activism centres on the respect for rights contained in international agreements, it is natural for attention to centre on governments as duty-holders since they are the entities directly bound by the human rights documents. If human rights are claim-rights with a correlative duty on somebody to provide or safeguard the benefit, however, a major problem arises in identifying that duty-holder. Most often it is assumed that if an individual is being denied some human right, the duty falls on their government to rectify the situation.

If the correlative duty lies only with an individual's government, a serious difficulty emerges because the abuse of human rights may occur by private individuals or corporations. For example, tremendous injustices result from the caste system in India because of the way people treat others who belong to a lower caste. In this instance, the actual infringement of human rights is largely perpetrated by individuals rather than the government. While the government has accepted a responsibility to try and end the practise, caste is so deeply entrenched in Indian society that it has so far proved impossible to stamp out. A further complication arises when a government either is incapable of providing a benefit protected by human rights or when a government simply fails to respect human rights.

If human rights set moral standards for the treatment of all humans, those standards should bind anyone who is capable of infringing those rights—be they corporations, governments, or other human beings. Thus, the correlative duties involved in human rights as claim-rights are duties that do not necessarily reside solely with an individual's government. The violation of some human right may be perpetrated by one individual against others, such as an employer who discriminates against a racial group in hiring.

A duty to respect human rights may be held by a group within a society, such as a religious majority's obligation to tolerate other religious practices. There may be a general duty on the community to act collectively, as with the example of community efforts to run food banks. An individual's own government often has a direct duty, for example, to refrain from arbitrary detention and torture. On some occasions, many will argue that foreign governments have a duty to intervene; for instance, the Front Line States in southern Africa believed they had some duty to help liberate the black majority from apartheid in South Africa.

There may be a duty that lies with all humanity; such an obligation is often expressed in private, international relief movements to alleviate suffering among famine victims. Governments may only be intermediary duty-holders who should try and intervene to safeguard human rights from actions by their citizens, but those citizens bear the direct duty to respect the human rights of others. With any form of rights, but particularly with claim-rights, there are problems that arise with their definition, exercise, and enforcement. There may be conflicting views even on the existence of a particular right.

There can also be profound debate when two or more rights conflict in a given situation. A continuing problem is posed for women's rights by several religions that stipulate particular roles for women that are subservient to men; in these instances the right to equality conflicts with the freedom of religion. Another difficulty may arise over whether a benefit is really a claim-right, with correlative duties, or some other type of right or claim without corresponding obligations. For instance, academic freedom may be viewed as either a privilege or a claim-right. If a claim-right is involved, there may still be many questions about who in particular holds a correlative duty, and what type of action is required to satisfy that duty.

If human rights operate uniquely in a moral plane, then the definition, acceptance, and respect for rights can involve a controversial, tortuous route. In the end, fulfilment of human rights will depend upon a spirit of consensus and the effect of community opprobrium. Disputes that involve profoundly different value systems, however, may go unresolved. With the codification of human rights into legal documents, one may limit some of the range of debate, but only with institutional structures for adjudicating can there be authoritative resolutions.

The record of national courts reveal that judges within the same society can be deeply divided over the definition and enforcement of human rights; for example, almost 31 per cent of the Supreme Court of Canada's Charter of Rights decisions between 1983 and 1989 involved dissenting opinions, where one or more judges disagreed completely with their colleagues on the resolution of the rights issues at stake. Within many societies there are patterns of deference to the judiciary that allows their court's majority view to settle authoritatively most disputes over human rights.

However, some societies are so divided that deference is not voluntarily given, such as enforced black acquiescence to the white judiciary in South Africa during the apartheid regime, and the discretionary choices made by judges will not be accepted as final resolutions of rights disputes. There is an even deeper problem if international institutions are to adjudicate rights disputes that involve societies with very different cultural norms; losing parties may simply not recognise the adjudicators' authority to impose what are seen as alien values.

## CHALLENGES TO UNIVERSALITY

Human rights are universal since they are said to belong to all humans in every society. Human rights are also supposed to be inalienable; because they flow from and protect human existence, they cannot be taken away without endangering the value of that existence. However, these universal and inalienable qualities of human rights are disputable in both their conception and operation. To some extent, the universality of human rights depends upon their genesis.

Moral standards, such as human rights, can come into being in two manners. They may simply be invented by people, or they may only need to be revealed to, or discovered by, humans.

If human rights are simply an invention, then it is rather difficult to argue that every society and government should be bound by something they disagree with. If human rights have some existence independent of human creation, however, then it is easier to assert their universality. But such independent moral standards may arise in only two ways: if they are created by God, or if they are inherent in the nature of humankind or human society. Unfortunately, both these routes pose substantive pitfalls.

No divine origin for universal human rights would be acceptable, nor is it often advanced, since there is no one God that is recognised universally; just because Christians or Muslims claim that their divinity has ordained and proscribed certain treatment of humans does not provide the legitimacy needed for that moral code to bind devotees of another religion. The alternative origin that could justify universality would be the acceptance of human rights as natural rights that anyone could deduce from the nature of humankind or human society.

However, an atheistic critique of divine moral standards is just as telling when applied to rights derived from human nature. The God or human nature that is said to be the source of human rights may be nothing more than an invention of the human mind, an invention that may vary according to whoever is reflecting on the issue. A less astringent argument is still just as damning. Even if one accepts that there is a God or a core human nature, there is no definitive way to sort out differing visions that people have of God or human nature. The universal authority of any particular view is initially endorsed only by the adherents of that view. Nevertheless it is possible for human rights to have their genesis in religion or the prerequisites of human society.

Even if human rights start within a specific religious or societal tradition, they could acquire universality as other people come to agree. It is also possible for human rights to become globally recognised because several different approaches may reach the same conclusion. For instance, atheistic natural rights theorists, Christians, and Muslims, may all eventually agree for quite different reasons on a number of ways in which people should be treated; these then can form the basis of human rights standards. However, the different paths to that agreement only lead to an agreement on the benefits, not necessarily on their origin, justification, or application.

Human rights standards could be created in a variety of ways. In one method, a gradual growth of consensus builds around norms of behaviour that eventually acquire an obligatory character. It may be difficult to trace the epistemological origins of this consensus, but the end result is a broad base of agreement that human beings should be treated in certain ways. In another method, there may be a conscious attempt to create binding rules of behaviour in a more contractarian manner. A certain group of individuals or state governments may lead the development of international agreements on human rights. And, as more states join in these agreements, the moral and legal force of the international accords become stronger and stronger. In both approaches to the creation of human rights, the motivation may be principled or consequentialist.

Not everyone will share the same motivation or inspiration for human rights. At a very basic level, the proclamation and acceptance of human rights norms inherently involves majoritarian morality. Human rights are agreed to exist because a majority says they do. Specific goods and benefits are treated as human rights because a majority says they do. With either an invented or natural genesis, human rights are meant to protect some aspect of humanity. Human rights may be those entitlements that we have by virtue of being human, but there are real difficulties in determining which attributes of human life require protection under human rights standards. Basic human traits are determined by both physical attributes and the activities undertaken by a human. The most obvious physical qualities encompass gender, race, size, shape, and health, including disabilities.

Among human activities, one can distinguish between those necessary for sustaining life and those which fill that life. The requirements for sustaining life include nourishment, shelter, clothing, and sleep. Proper health care is needed for human life to be sustained in the long term. And the human species can only survive with procreation. But most humans do not merely exist, they fill their lives with myriad activities. Perhaps the most important activity is that which is usually referred to in order to distinguish humans from all other animals: humans have a creative imagination that provides higher forms of thought that lead to intellectual inquiry and spirituality.

Humans also communicate constantly the results of their thinking. Physical movement from one place to another is another continuous activity of all but the most disabled humans. Human beings are in essence very social animals and much of our activities take place through associating with other humans. In some instances this association is the special intimacy of kinship or close friendships.

Most humans live within readily identifiable social units, such as family, tribal, or national groups, that fundamentally shape the manner in which an individual's most basic characteristics are manifested. These social groupings determine what languages one learns to speak, the style of dress, acceptable foods, religion, form of communication and etiquette, sense of physical beauty and ugliness, the kind of shelter, and the notion of division of roles within one's social groupings. These are not simply superficial differences. While some individuals willingly adopt new life-styles, many believe that their lives can only be satisfying by maintaining their traditional ways. For some, indeed, styles of dress, food, and behaviour are inextricably linked to deep religious beliefs. One group's delicacies or even staples may be quite unacceptable to others. There may be just disdain or revulsion, such as the reaction of many people to eating raw fish, or there may be a strong, religious offence taken to certain foods.

While one could identify various qualities of human life that are universal, there is tremendous variation in the manner in which those qualities are realised. These acquired societal values pose difficulties when they define, or even conflict with, the basic attributes of human life listed earlier. Individual societies develop particular conceptions of what constitutes a dignified life, the essential needs of humans, as well as the relationship between individuals and their community. Particularly complex issues arise when there is a clash between conflicting spiritual and temporal values within or between societies. These difficulties come to the forefront when one tries to ascertain whether global standards can be set by human rights on the treatment that must be given to all human beings.

## REFERENCES

Bentham, Jeremy, "Anarchical Fallacies; being an examination of the Declaration of Rights issues during the French Revolution", Jeremy Waldron (ed.), *Nonsense Upon Stilts: Bentham, Burke and Marx on the Rights of Man*, New York: Methuen, 1987.

Binion, Gayle, "Human Rights: A Feminist Perspective", *Human Rights Quarterly*, 1995.

Donnelly, Jack, *Universal Human Rights in Theory and Practice*, Ithaca: Cornell University Press, 1989.

Gewirth, Allan, "Why There Are Human Rights", *Social Theory and Practice*, 1985.

Husak, Douglas, "The Motivation for Human Rights", *Social Theory and Practice*, 1985.

O'Manique, John, "Universal and Inalienable Human Rights: A Search for Foundations", *Human Rights Quarterly*, 1990.

Paine, Thomas, *The Rights of Man*, New York: Penguin Books, 1985.

# 3

# Universal Declaration of Human Rights

***ADOPTED BY GENERAL ASSEMBLY RESOLUTION 217 A (III) OF 10 DECEMBER 1948***

It is essential, if man is not to be compelled to have recourse, as a last resort, to rebellion against tyranny and oppression, that human rights should be protected by the rule of law.

The importance of ensuring that human rights are protected under the rule of law has been emphasised by the United Nations since the drafting of the Universal Declaration of Human Rights, and has guided the Organisation in its activities for the promotion and protection of human rights ever since. This is most evident in the work of the United Nations Programme of Advisory Services and Technical Cooperation in the Field of Human Rights. This programme, as described below, has been engaged since 1955 in assisting states, at their request, in the building and strengthening of national structures which have a direct impact on the overall observance of human rights and the maintenance of the rule of law.

A decade after the entry into force of the Charter of the United Nations, and after some early *ad hoc* human rights assistance activities, the General Assembly officially established the United Nations Programme of Advisory Services in the Field of Human Rights (resolution 926 (X) of 14

December 1955). Thereby, the General Assembly specifically authorised the Secretary-General to make provision, at the request of governments, for assistance in the field of human rights, including advisory services of experts, fellowships and scholarships, and seminars. Subsequently, the General Assembly increased the services available under the programme to include regional and national human rights training courses. On the basis of these resolutions, activities under the programme have been carried out in numerous countries in each of the world's regions for some 40 years.

The programme was further strengthened when the Voluntary Fund for Advisory Services and Technical Assistance in the Field of Human Rights (subsequently renamed Voluntary Fund for Technical Cooperation in the Field of Human Rights) was established by the Secretary-General in November 1987 pursuant to the Commission on Human Rights resolution 1987/38 of 10 March 1987 and the Economic and Social Council decision 1987/147 of 29 May 1987. The objective of the trust fund is to provide additional financial support for practical activities focused on the implementation of international conventions and other international instruments on human rights promulgated by the United Nations, its specialised agencies or regional organisations.

In accordance with relevant Commission on Human Rights resolutions, practical activities to be financed by the Voluntary Fund include:

a) support for international cooperation aimed at establishing and strengthening national and regional institutions and infrastructures which will have a long-term impact on improved implementation of international conventions and other international instruments on human rights promulgated by the United Nations, its specialised agencies or regional organisations;

b) expert and technical assistance to governments with a view to creating and developing the necessary infrastructures to meet international human rights standards;

c) projects and programmes that can play a catalytic role in the practical realisation of internationally recognised human rights standards;

d) projects for legal protection and strengthening of the independence of the judiciary;

e) comprehensive needs assessments and overall country programmes, including specific projects aimed at strengthening the human rights infrastructure of a country.

The technical assistance programme financed under the Voluntary Fund is therefore a comprehensive programme providing practical assistance for the building of national and regional human rights infrastructures. Programme components focus on the incorporation of international human rights standards into national laws and policies, and on the establishment or strengthening of national institutions capable of promoting and protecting human rights and democracy under the rule of law. Such assistance now takes the form of expert advisory services, training courses, workshops and seminars, fellowships, grants, the provision of information and documentation and the assessment of domestic human rights needs.

For its part, the World Conference on Human Rights, throughout the Vienna Declaration and Programme of Action which it adopted in June 1993, recognised the importance of advisory services and technical assistance for human rights and called for enhancement of the programme.

With regard to technical cooperation, for example, the Declaration and Programme of Action calls for the implementation of plans of action at the national level for the promotion and protection of human rights through the establishment of a comprehensive United Nations programme (part II, paras. 68-69). The Technical Cooperation Programme, according to the Declaration, should be strengthened. The Declaration further states that the Centre for Human Rights should make available to states, upon request, technical and financial assistance, in particular for the elaboration and implementation of coherent and comprehensive plans of action. These plans of action would integrate activities aimed at:

i) strengthening the institutions of human rights and democracy;
ii) reforming penal and correctional establishments;
iii) the legal protection of human rights;
iv) education and training of officials, lawyers, judges, security forces and others in human rights;
v) broad-based education and public information for promoting respect for human rights; and
vi) other means of promoting the good functioning of the rule of law.

## FUNDING AND ADMINISTRATION OF THE TECHNICAL COOPERATION PROGRAMME

The Programme of Technical Cooperation in the Field of Human Rights is funded from the regular budget of the United Nations and from the United Nations Voluntary Fund for Technical Cooperation in the Field of Human Rights, which began operating in 1988 and to date has received more than US$ 19 million in pledges and contributions. In addition to financing from the regular budget and the Voluntary Fund, specific projects are sometimes funded by partners of the Centre for Human Rights in the United Nations system.

Whatever the source of funding, projects are implemented within the common context of a single, unified and comprehensive programme, administered by the Centre for Human Rights. While, consistent with resolutions of the Commission on Human Rights, a distinction is maintained between projects financed under the regular budget and those financed by the Voluntary Fund for purposes of accountability, reporting and budgetary information, the common substance and policy of the programme remain.

Programme development, implementation, support and follow-up are carried out by the Technical Cooperation Branch of the Centre for Human Rights, under the direction of the Assistant Secretary-General for Human Rights. The United Nations High Commissioner for Human Rights holds overall responsibility for the programme, under the authority of the Secretary-General. The High Commissioner is mandated, under General Assembly resolution 48/141 of 20 December 1993, to provide, through the Centre for Human Rights, advisory services and technical assistance at the request of states and, where appropriate, regional human rights organisations, with a view to supporting actions and programmes in the field of human rights. He is also responsible, *inter alia*, for coordinating human rights promotion and protection activities throughout the United Nations system.

In a further important development, the Commission on Human Rights, in its resolution 1993/87 of 10 March 1993 (para. 18), requested the Secretary-General to appoint a board of trustees to assume the administration of the Voluntary Fund. The board of trustees was established in December 1993.

## THE PROGRAMME APPROACH

Technical cooperation activities are seen by the United Nations as a complement to, but never a substitute for, the monitoring and investigating activities of the human rights programme. As emphasised in various reports of the Secretary-General on the subject, and in Commission on Human Rights resolution 1995/53 of 3 March 1995 (preamble), the provision of advisory services and technical assistance does not reduce a government's responsibility to account for the human rights situation and, whenever applicable, would not exempt it from monitoring through the various procedures established by the United Nations. Indeed, action by special rapporteurs of the Commission on Human Rights often takes place in parallel with projects of advisory services and technical assistance.

While the Technical Cooperation Programme occasionally provides grants in support of projects initiated by non-governmental organisations, governments and regional human rights organisations, it is not, in the first instance, a funding source for projects developed outside the Centre for Human Rights. Rather, it is a source of substantive advice and assistance in the field of human rights, within the framework of a comprehensive programme which cooperates with governments, at their request, through Centre-generated needs assessments and projects designed in cooperation with recipient countries.

The Centre for Human Rights, in most cases, responds to a government'srequest by conducting a careful assessment of the country's particular human rights assistance needs. Assistance programmes are then designed to address these needs in a comprehensive and coordinated way. The Centre directly implements all projects for which it has unique or specific competence, drawing on the considerable expertise developed by its staff in the relevant areas, and serves as a focal point and coordinator for other programme elements relating to the human rights needs of the country concerned. This comprehensive approach was first described in the 1993 report of the Secretary-General on advisory services in the field of human rights, and was further elaborated in his 1994 report.

## CONTENT OF THE PROGRAMME

Guided by successive General Assembly and Commission on Human Rights resolutions, and by the nature of state requests themselves, the Technical Cooperation Programme gradually developed capacities for assistance in a range of areas, which now provide a useful framework for national efforts directed at strengthening human rights and the rule of law. Thus the Centre for Human Rights now adopts a comprehensive approach to human rights institution building, which sees as fundamental the following constituent elements for national efforts to secure the protection of human rights under the rule of law:

a) a strong Constitution, which, as the highest law of the land, *inter alia*:

   i) incorporates internationally recognised human rights and fundamental freedoms, as enumerated in the International Bill of Human Rights;

   ii) establishes effective and justifiable remedies at law for violations of those rights;

   iii) empowers an independent judiciary, consistent with the Basic Principles on the Independence of the Judiciary;

   iv) provides for non-discrimination on the basis of race, colour, gender, language, religion, political or other opinion, national or social origin, property, birth or other status and which protects national minorities;

   v) establishes national human rights institutions, such as an office of the ombudsman or an independent human rights commission, consistent with the United Nations Principles relating to the status of national institutions;

vi) provides for the applicability of international human rights treaty obligations in domestic law;

vii) defines and limits the powers of government and its various branches, *vis-a-vis* each other and the people.

b) a strong electoral system, which, *inter alia*:

i) assures that the will of the people is the basis of the authority of government;

ii) assures the right of everyone to take part in the government of his or her country, either directly or through freely chosen representatives;

iii) assures equal access to public service, including elective public service;

iv) provides for periodic and genuine elections;

v) guarantees universal and equal suffrage;

vi) guarantees the secrecy of the ballot;

vii) secures an electoral atmosphere which is free of intimidation and respectful of certain prerequisite rights, such as freedom of opinion, expression, information, assembly and association;

viii) provides for non-discrimination in the area of political rights;

ix) provides for independent review of alleged irregularities;

x) provides for objective, unbiased and independent electoral administration;

xi) provides for the transfer of power to victorious parties and candidates under the law.

c) a strong legal framework, under the Constitution, which protects human rights and democracy and provides for effective redress in all key areas, including, *inter alia*:

i) fair immigration, nationality and asylum laws which are consistent with relevant international standards;

ii) penal laws and laws of criminal procedure which respect and uphold international standards for human rights in the administration of justice;

iii) electoral laws which take account of the above concerns;

iv) prison laws and regulations which are consistent with the Standard Minimum Rules for the Treatment of Prisoners and other relevant international instruments;

v) laws for the protection of minorities, women, children, indigenous people and other vulnerable groups, which take into account their special status and international standards for their protection, and which outlaw and address the effects of discrimination,

vi) laws protecting free association and assembly;

vii) security legislation which is consistent with international standards, and which protects non-derogable human rights;

viii) laws on the judiciary, on legal practice and on prosecution which reflect the standards embodied in the Basic Principles on the Independence of the Judiciary, the Basic Principles on the Role of Lawyers, the Guidelines on the Role of Prosecutors and other United Nations standards on the administration of justice;

ix) laws, guidelines and directives which govern the conduct of police and other security forces, consistent with the Code of Conduct for Law Enforcement Officials, the Basic Principles on the Use of Force and Firearms by Law Enforcement Officials and other relevant international standards;

x) fair procedures for the settlement of civil disputes under the law, and fair administrative laws, procedures and institutions, consistent with international human rights standards;

xi) any other laws which may have a direct impact on the realisation of internationally guaranteed human rights.

d) strong national human rights institutions, including independent commissions on human rights and ombudsman offices, with structures and functions consistent with the United Nations Principles relating to the status of national institutions, as well as strong national human rights research and training institutes;

e) a strong judiciary, which is independent, adequately empowered, adequately financed, adequately equipped, and adequately trained to uphold human rights in the administration of justice;

f) a military which has ultimate allegiance to the Constitution and laws of the land, and to the democratic government, and which is trained in and committed to the principles of human rights and humanitarian law attending legitimate military duties;

g) effective and accessible mechanisms for the resolution of conflicts between and among citizens and groups in society and state organs;

h) full incorporation into the international human rights system, including through ratification of or accession to international human rights treaties and training of government officials in implementing and reporting under those treaties;

i) a society which is educated in its rights and responsibilities, including through national human rights curricula in primary, secondary and post-secondary education, and teachers trained in education for human rights and democracy;

j) a strong civil society, including adequately trained, equipped, financed and organised non-governmental human rights organisations, women's groups, labour unions and community organisations.

Taken together, these essential elements provide for a legal and institutional framework which will best serve to entrench the rule of law in society and thereby secure the effective enjoyment of human rights and democracy. In recognition of this, the Technical Cooperation Programme of the Centre for Human Rights, in partnership with other United Nations organs, governments and non-governmental organisations, offers support to states seeking to strengthen these elements. As already indicated, such support takes the form of comprehensive country programmes and targeted projects, in the form of advisory services of experts, training courses, workshops and seminars, information and documentation projects, fellowships and some forms of financial assistance, in the substantive areas described below:

## 1. National Plans of Action

In the Vienna Declaration and Programme of Action which it adopted in June 1993, the World Conference on Human Rights recommended that the Centre for Human Rights, through its advisory services and technical assistance activities, assist States in the preparation of plans of action at the national level. In accordance with that recommendation, the Technical Cooperation Programme can make available expert assistance in the elaboration of such plans, and in their implementation.

## 2. Constitutional Assistance

Under this programme component, the Centre for Human Rights provides assistance for the inclusion of human rights norms in national constitutions, and can play a facilitative role in encouraging national consensus on the elements to be incorporated in those constitutions. Assistance for these purposes may take the form of advisory services of experts, the organisation of conferences, provision of human rights information and documentation, or support for public information campaigns to ensure the involvement of all sectors of society.

Issues addressed in the Centre's constitutional activities include legislative drafting and constitutional law; the drafting of bills of rights; the provision of justifiable remedies under the law; options for the allocation and separation of governmental powers; the independence of the judiciary; and the role of the judiciary in overseeing the police and prison systems.

## 3. Electoral Assistance

The Centre for Human Rights has been involved in electoral assistance, through its Technical Cooperation Programme, for more than five years. Since 1990, the Centre has provided electoral assistance to Romania (1990-1992), Albania (1991), Lesotho (1991-1993), Eritrea (1992), Angola (1992), Cambodia (1992), Malawi (1992-1993) and South Africa (1993). In addition, the Centre has prepared guidelines for analysis of electoral laws and procedures, published a handbook on human rights and elections, developed draft guidelines for human rights assessments of requests for electoral assistance, and carried out a number of public information activities relating to human rights and elections.

## 4. Legislative Reform Assistance

As a further component of the Technical Cooperation Programme, the Centre for Human Rights makes available international experts and specialised staff to assist governments in the reform of legislation which has a clear impact on human rights and fundamental freedoms. The goal of such assistance is to bring such laws into conformity with international standards, as identified in United Nations and regional human rights instruments. The Centre provides comments on drafts provided by the requesting government, as well as drafting recommendations, which may include comparative reference to similar laws in other jurisdictions.

Appropriate subjects under this programme component include penal codes, codes of criminal procedure, prison regulations, laws regarding minority protection, laws affecting freedom of expression, association and assembly, immigration and nationality laws, laws on the judiciary and legal practice, security legislation, and, in general, any law which might have an impact, directly or indirectly, on the realisation of internationally protected human rights.

## 5. Assistance in the Establishment and Strengthening of National Institutions

As its role has been defined by the Commission on Human Rights, a central objective of the Technical Cooperation Programme is to consolidate and strengthen the role which national institutions can play in the promotion and protection of human rights. Assistance to national institutions under the programme takes several forms. The Centre for Human Rights offers its services to governments which are considering or in the process of establishing a national human rights institution.

Other activities relating to national institutions under the programme are not oriented towards a particular country or institution but are, instead, aimed at promoting the concept of national human rights institutions and encouraging their development. To this end, the Centre has produced information materials and a practical manual for those involved in the establishment and administration of national institutions. The Centre has also conducted a number of seminars and workshops to provide government officials with both information and expertise in the structure and functioning of such bodies. These events have also served as useful forums in which to promote the exchange of information and experience concerning the establishment and operation of national institutions.

The Centre for Human Rights has developed a comprehensive programme of action for technical assistance to national institutions which now guides the elaboration and implementation of all assistance projects to national institutions. In developing this programme, the Centre was guided by the Principles relating to the status of national institutions endorsed by the Commission on Human Rights in its resolution 1992/54 of 3 March 1992 and subsequently by the General Assembly in its resolution 48/134 of 20 December 1993. The programme of action sets out four specific objectives: to promote the concept of national human rights institutions; to assist in the creation of effective institutions; to assist in the strengthening of existing institutions; and to foster cooperation between institutions.

Assistance provided by the Centre for strengthening national institutions may include training of staff; advice on the domestic implementation of international human rights instruments; training and assistance in the drafting of reports to United Nations treaty bodies; training and information on the effective investigation of human rights violations; training in conflict resolution; assistance in the establishment of cooperative relationships with appropriate partners; information on obtaining and managing resources; assistance in conducting reviews and evaluations; and the provision of human rights fellowships for members and staff of national institutions.

## 6. Administration of Justice: Judges, Magistrates, Lawyers, Prosecutors, Police and Prison Officials

The Centre for Human Rights, through its Technical Cooperation Programme, has been involved for many years in the training of judges, lawyers, prosecutors, police officers and prison personnel in the area of human rights in the administration of justice.

The purposes of these courses are to familiarise participants with international standards for human rights in the administration of justice; to facilitate examination of humane and effective techniques for the performance of law enforcement, penal and judicial functions in a democratic society; and to prepare participants to include this information in their own training activities.

This approach to professional training for human rights in the administration of justice has, for three years, been undergoing in-field testing by the Centre in its technical cooperation activities in a number of countries, and has been subjected to a series of revisions on the basis of that experience.

### *a) Law enforcement officials*

The Centre's courses for law enforcement officials cover a variety of topics, including the following: international sources, systems and standards for human rights in the administration of criminal justice; the duties and guiding principles of ethical police conduct in democracies; the use of force and firearms in law enforcement; the crime of torture; effective methods of legal and ethical interviewing; human rights during arrest and pre-trial detention; and the legal status and rights of the accused.

### *b) Prison officials*

Course topics in this category include: minimum standards for facilities for prisoners and detainees; prison health issues, including AIDS and the HIV virus; and special categories of prisoners and detainees, including juveniles and women.

### c) *Judges, magistrates, lawyers and prosecutors*

Topics offered in courses for this group include: international sources, systems and standards for human rights in the administration of justice; human rights during criminal investigations, arrest and pre-trial detention; the independence of judges and lawyers; the elements of a fair trial; juvenile justice; protection of the rights of women in the administration of justice; and human rights under states of emergency.

## 7. Human Rights Training for the Armed Forces

It is essential for the good functioning of the rule of law that the armed forces be bound by the Constitution and other laws of the land, that they answer to the democratic government and that they are trained in and committed to the principles of human rights and humanitarian law attending their legitimate functions in society. The Centre for Human Rights has carried out a number of training activities for military officers.

Certainly, traditional military training has included, in many cases, some attention to the laws of war, including the four Geneva Conventions of 12 August 1949. Human rights training *per se*, however, has been conspicuously absent. Indeed, not uncommon in some military circles is the notion that human rights training and sensitisation are inconsistent with effective military training. Soldiers, for this way of thinking, are warriors, and the waging of war is, by its very nature, contrary to human rights. The Centre's approach to military training takes issue with this notion for two reasons. First, international human rights standards, including but not always limited to humanitarian law, do apply in situations of armed conflict. Secondly, the duties of modern professional soldiers are not limited to the waging of war. Rather, increasingly, they include civil policing duties, the maintenance of order and public safety under states of emergency, and assignment to international peace-keeping operations. The effective, professional and humane performance of these duties requires a knowledge of and sensitisation to human rights standards, as well as the skills to apply them in the daily work of the military.

## 8. Human Rights Support to Parliaments

National parliaments have, under the Technical Cooperation Programme, received direct training and other support designed to assist them in carrying out their important human rights functions. This programme component addresses a variety of crucial issues, including information on national human rights legislation, parliamentary human rights committees, ratifications of and accessions to international human rights instruments, and, in general, the role of parliament in promoting and protecting human rights.

## 9. Curriculum Development and Education for Human Rights

The Centre for Human Rights is in the process of developing curricula for education on human rights for the primary, secondary and university levels, and for non-formal levels of education. These activities are intended to assist in the building of a human rights culture by encouraging the inclusion of human rights concepts in existing programmes; assisting in the adaptation or modification of curricula where necessary; and providing instruction and assistance to those persons centrally involved in the human rights education process.

There are several means by which these objectives are pursued. The first is teacher training, whereby the Centre offers programmes of training for both primary and secondary school teachers. Courses can also be constructed to accommodate other groups in a position to promote human rights education and sensitise others in this field, such as teacher trainers, directors of schools or teacher-resource centres, and inspectors and teachers within the ministry concerned with curriculum development and education.

## 10. Treaty Reporting and International Obligations and Training of Government Officials

The Centre for Human Rights regularly organises training activities to enable government officials to prepare properly reports required under the various international human rights treaties to which their State is a party. In some cases, courses in reporting obligations are offered at the national or regional level. In others, the Centre provides fellowships for government officials to travel to Geneva, where training courses for several countries are held. During these courses, participants are able to take part in workshops with experts from the various treaty-monitoring committees, as well as with relevant staff of the Centre. In some cases, they are given the opportunity to sit as observers during meetings of the treaty bodies themselves. In every case, participants are provided with a copy of the Centre's *Manual on Human Rights Reporting*.

In accordance with the Centre's standard approach to training, course participants are engaged in practical exercises, which allow them to test the drafting skills imparted during the course. Separate course segments are offered for the International Covenant on Civil and Political Rights; the International Covenant on Economic, Social and Cultural Rights; the Convention on the Rights of the Child; the Convention against Torture and Other Cruel, Inhuman or Degrading Treatment or Punishment; the International

Convention on the Elimination of All Forms of Racial Discrimination; the Convention on the Elimination of All Forms of Discrimination against Women; and the International Convention on the Protection of the Rights of All Migrant Workers and Members of Their Families.

## 11. Support to NGOs and Civil Society

National and international non-governmental human rights organisations (NGOs) are key actors in the Technical Cooperation Programme. NGOs both assist in the delivery of assistance, and benefit as recipients of it. Thus, in furthering the programme's goal of strengthening civil society, the Centre for Human Rights is increasingly being called upon by governments and others to provide assistance to national NGOs, in the context of its country activities, by soliciting their input, including them as invitees in seminars and training courses, and supporting appropriate projects developed by them.

## 12. Information and Documentation Projects

The Technical Cooperation Programme also provides assistance in the form of provision of human rights information and documentation, and the building of capacity to utilise and manage such materials properly. This includes direct provision of documentation, translated where necessary into local languages; training in human rights informatics; and assistance in computerisation of national and regional human rights offices. Assistance can also be provided to national libraries in acquiring human rights books and documentation, and support can be given for the establishment and functioning of national or regional human rights documentation centres.

## 13. Regional Institutions and Activities

The Technical Cooperation Programme also focuses on the development of human rights infrastructures at the regional level. This is done primarily through the organisation of regional workshops and seminars, and through support to regional human rights institutions.

The Centre for Human Rights also provides support, through the Voluntary Fund for Technical Cooperation in the Field of Human Rights, for regional human rights institutions involved in educational activities, including direct support to the African Commission on Human and Peoples' Rights, the Arab Institute of Human Rights and the African Centre for Democracy and Human Rights Studies.

## 14. Peace-keeping and Training of International Civil Servants

The Technical Cooperation Programme has recently expanded its activities, in accordance with the Vienna Declaration and Programme of Action adopted by the World Conference on Human Rights in June 1993, to include human rights support within the United Nations system. In the area of peace-keeping, for example, the programme has already provided various forms of assistance to major United Nations missions in Cambodia, Eritrea, Mozambique, Haiti, South Africa, the countries of the former Yugoslavia and Angola. Such assistance has included, variously, the provision of human rights information, legislative analysis, training and advisory services. Efforts are currently under way to conclude a series of agreements with a number of United Nations specialised agencies, the outcome of which is expected to be an increased level of cooperation between the programme and other United Nations organs engaged in human rights-related activities, for example through the provision of human rights training to staff of those agencies.

## 15. Needs Assessments for Human Rights, Democracy and the Rule of Law

Under the programme approach of the Centre for Human Rights to the provision of technical assistance, discussed above, the Centre responds to most government requests by conducting a careful assessment of the country's particular human rights assistance needs. Assistance programmes are then designed to address those needs in a comprehensive and coordinated way.

Needs-assessment missions conducted by the Centre are typically composed of carefully selected international experts, accompanied by staff of the Technical Cooperation Branch. During such missions, a wide range of parties are consulted in the country, including both governmental and non governmental organisations and individuals.

The Centre also carries out periodic and post-implementation evaluations of country programmes, in order that their effect may be gauged and follow-up plans developed. These activities are seen by the Centre as crucial to ongoing efforts to strengthen and improve the Technical Cooperation Programme.

## 16. Human Rights Fellowships

The General Assembly resolution 926 (X) of 14 December 1955, which officially established the advisory services programme, made direct provision for human rights fellowships. Under the programme, fellowships are awarded only to candidates nominated by their governments, and are financed under the regular budget for advisory services.

The Secretary-General annually sends out invitations to member states to submit nominations for fellowships. Governments are reminded that nominees should be directly involved in functions affecting human rights, particularly in the administration of justice. The Secretary-General also draws their attention to concerns expressed by the General Assembly, in many of its resolutions, with regard to the rights of women, and encourages the nomination of women candidates. The principle of equitable geographical distribution is taken into account and priority is given to candidates from states which have never benefited from the fellowship programme, or which have not done so in recent years.

Participants receive intensive training in a variety of human rights issues. They are encouraged to exchange experience among themselves, and are requested to evaluate the fellowship programme, to present individual oral reports, and to prepare recommendations for their superiors on the basis of information acquired during the programme. Finally, in accordance with the policy and procedure governing the administration of United Nations fellowships, each participant is required to submit a comprehensive final report to the Centre for Human Rights on subjects directly related to their field of activity.

## SYSTEM-WIDE COOPERATION

The Technical Cooperation Programme enjoys close cooperation with non-governmental organisations, regional institutions, universities, and a number of United Nations specialised agencies and human rights treaty and Charter-based bodies, as well as with the International Committee of the Red Cross. This cooperation has been further enhanced by the new approach of the Centre for Human Rights to needs assessment and project formulation, which involves the full partnership of all organisations and states engaged in human rights assistance. In pursuing an integrated and coordinated approach to human rights, the programme has sought to solidify a cooperative framework which includes the sharing of expertise and resources from all available sources.

Under the United Nations programme approach, the Centre works closely with other United Nations agencies and programmes active in the country concerned, cooperating with the Organisation's Resident Coordinator in ensuring that the Centre's contribution is part of a coordinated United Nations-system intervention and complementary to the projects of other actors in support of the government's goals, programmes and plans of action. The Centre's technical cooperation activities are therefore placed in the context of a single, unified pursuit of national development objectives through cohesive national programmes which merge United Nations-system inputs with national inputs and those of other actors to achieve government objectives for the promotion and protection of human rights. In every case, the focus is on capacity building, aimed at sustained development progress and the eventual obsolescence of external assistance.

The Technical Cooperation Programme is a vital element within the United Nations system of comprehensive assistance for the strengthening of the rule of law, on the basis of relevant United Nations standards embodied in half a century of human rights standard setting by the Organisation.

The Centre for Human Rights, which develops and implements the programme under the overall direction of the High Commissioner for Human Rights, is the only unit within the United Nations system which is specifically and exclusively charged with institutional responsibility for human rights. This includes gathering and analysing information on the human rights situation in all countries and (through the various official human rights bodies) keeping such situations under periodic review; providing substantive services to United Nations bodies in the development of international human rights standards; assessing the human rights needs, including institutional needs, of individual member states; developing technical cooperation programmes aimed at building and strengthening national human rights and legal infrastructures; and producing human rights information and training materials.

In addition, in connection with its mandated functions, the Centre for Human Rights continually gathers information and materials on the human rights activities of member states, inter-governmental and non-governmental organisations, specialised institutions and other United Nations actors.

All these capacities are the bases for the Centre's Technical Cooperation Programme and for its efforts to assist states in strengthening the rule of law in their respective jurisdictions.

# 4

# Vienna Declaration and Programme of Action

International human rights law has been designed to protect the full range of human rights required for people to have a full, free, safe, secure and healthy life. The right to live a dignified life can never be attained unless all basic necessities of life—work, food, housing, health care, education and culture—are adequately and equitably available to everyone. Based squarely on this fundamental principle of the global human rights system, international human rights law has established individual and group rights relating to the civil, cultural, economic, political and social spheres.

The primary basis of United Nations' activities to promote, protect and monitor human rights and fundamental freedoms is the International Bill of Human Rights. The Bill comprises three texts: the Universal Declaration of Human Rights (1948), the International Covenant on Economic, Social and Cultural Rights (1966), and the International Covenant on Civil and Political Rights (1966) and its two optional protocols.

These instruments enshrine global human rights standards and have been the inspiration for more than 50 supplemental United Nations human rights conventions, declarations and bodies of international minimum rules and other universally recognised principles. These additional standards have further refined international legal norms relating to a very wide range of issues, including women's rights, protection against racial discrimination, protection of migrant workers, the rights of children, and many others.

The two Covenants are international legal instruments. Thus, when member and non-member states of the United Nations ratify a Covenant and become a 'State Party' to it, they are wilfully accepting a series of legal obligations to uphold the rights and provisions established under the text in question.

When a state ratifies one of the Covenants, it accepts a solemn responsibility to apply each of the obligations embodied therein and to ensure the compatibility of their national laws with their international duties, in a spirit of good faith. Through the ratification of human rights treaties, therefore, states become accountable to the international community, to other States which have ratified the same texts, and to their own citizens and others resident in their territories.

This Fact Sheet examines many of the key issues relating to the International Covenant on Economic, Social and Cultural Rights, as well as the work of the Committee on Economic, Social and Cultural Rights which has been entrusted by the international community with monitoring compliance by States Parties with the provisions of the Covenant. It is designed to provide a general overview of the Covenant and the Committee in order to assist with the continued strengthening of the enjoyment of economic, social and cultural rights for everyone, everywhere.

## THE INDIVISIBILITY AND INTERDEPENDENCE OF ALL HUMAN RIGHTS

Under international human rights law (as well as in terms of its application at the national level), civil and political rights have, in many respects, received more attention, legal codification and judicial interpretation, and have been instilled in public consciousness to a far greater degree, than economic, social and cultural rights. It is, therefore, sometimes wrongly presumed that only civil and political rights (right to a fair trial, right to equality of treatment, right to life, right to vote, right to be free from discrimination, etc.) can be subject to violation, measures of redress and international legal scrutiny. Economic, social and cultural rights are often viewed as effectively 'second-class rights' unenforceable, non-justifiable, only to be fulfilled 'progressively' over time.

Such perspectives, however, overlook a postulate of the global human rights system formulated as long ago as 1948 with the adoption of the Universal Declaration of Human Rights, namely, that the indivisibility and interdependence of civil and political rights and economic, social and cultural rights are fundamental tenets of international human rights law. This point of view was repeatedly reaffirmed at the World Conference on Human Rights in 1993.

Economic, social and cultural rights are fully recognised by the international community and throughout international human rights law. Although these rights have received less attention than civil and political rights, far more serious consideration than ever before is currently being devoted to them. The question is not whether these rights are basic human rights, but rather what entitlements they imply and the legal nature of the obligations of states to realise them.

Economic, social and cultural rights are designed to ensure the protection of people as full persons, based on a perspective in which people can enjoy rights, freedoms and social justice simultaneously. In a world where, according to the United Nations Development Programme (UNDP), "a fifth of the developing world's population goes hungry every night, a quarter lacks access to even a basic necessity like safe drinking water, and a third lives in a state of abject poverty at such a margin of human existence that words simply fail to describe it", the importance of renewed attention and commitment to the full realisation of economic, social and cultural rights is self-evident.

Despite significant progress since the establishment of the United Nations in addressing problems of human deprivation, well over one billion people live in circumstances of extreme poverty, homelessness, hunger and malnutrition, unemployment, illiteracy and chronic ill-health. More than 1.5 billion people lack access to clean drinking-water and sanitation, some 500 million children don't have access to even primary education; and more than one billion adults cannot read and write. This massive scale of marginalisation, in spite of continued global economic growth and development, raises serious questions, not only of development, but also of basic human rights.

Of all global human rights standards, the International Covenant on Economic, Social and Cultural Rights provides the most important international legal framework for protecting these basic human rights.

## INTERNATIONAL COVENANT ON ECONOMIC, SOCIAL AND CULTURAL RIGHTS

The International Covenant on Economic, Social and Cultural Rights was adopted and opened for signature, ratification and accession by General Assembly resolution 2200 A (XXI) of 16 December 1966, following almost 20 years of drafting debates. It finally gained the force of law a decade later, entering into force on 3 January 1976.

The Covenant contains some of the most significant international legal provisions establishing economic, social and cultural rights, including rights relating to work in just and favourable conditions, to social protection, to an adequate standard of living, to the highest attainable standards of physical and mental health, to education and to enjoyment of the benefits of cultural freedom and scientific progress.

As on 12 April 1996, 133 states had ratified the Covenant, thereby voluntarily undertaking to implement its norms and provisions.

Compliance by States Parties with their obligations under the Covenant and the level of implementation of the rights and duties in question is monitored by the Committee on Economic, Social and Cultural Rights.

The Committee works on the basis of many sources of information, including reports submitted by States Parties and information from United Nations specialised agencies—International Labour Organisation, United Nations Educational, Scientific and Cultural Organisation, World Health Organisation, Food and Agriculture Organisation of the United Nations—from the Office of the United Nations High Commissioner for Refugees, and from the United Nations Centre for Human Settlements (Habitat) and others. It also receives information from non-governmental and community-based organisations working in states which have ratified the Covenant, from international human rights and other non-governmental organisations, from other United Nations treaty bodies, and from generally available literature.

## Substantive Provisions of the International Covenant on Economic, Social and Cultural Rights Self-Determination

### *Article 1*

1. All peoples have the right of self-determination. By virtue of that right they freely determine their political status and freely pursue their economic, social and cultural development.
2. All peoples may, for their own ends, freely dispose of their natural wealth and resources without prejudice to any obligations arising out of international economic cooperation, based upon the principle of mutual benefit, and international law. In no case may a people be deprived of its own means of subsistence.
3. The States Parties to the present Covenant, including those having responsibility for the administration of

Non-Self-Governing and Trust Territories, shall promote the realisation of the right of self-determination, and shall respect that right, in conformity with the provisions of the Charter of the United Nations.

Article 1 of the Covenant is worded in precisely the same terminology as article one of its sister text, the International Covenant on Civil and Political Rights. The self-determination provisions in common Article 1 are particularly important because the realisation of this right is a fundamental prerequisite for the effective guarantee and observance of individual human rights and is pivotal in securing and strengthening human rights protection measures.

The right to self-determination is a cornerstone of the international legal system, and has been a premier concern of the international community since the creation of the United Nations in 1945, particularly in regard to issues such as independence, non-interference and democracy. This right has both external and internal dimensions and has been the subject of some controversy in recent years, as it is increasingly asserted by groups within countries, as distinct from ex-colonies and occupied countries.

As far as the rights contained in the Covenant are concerned, the right of peoples freely to pursue their economic, social and cultural development includes freedom to carry on economic, social and cultural activities.

## Obligations of States Parties

### *Article 2*

1. Each State Party to the present Covenant undertakes to take steps, individually and through international assistance and cooperation, especially economic and technical, to the maximum of its available resources, with a view to achieving progressively the full realisation of the rights recognised in the present Covenant by all

appropriate means, including particularly the adoption of legislative measures.

2. The States Parties to the present Covenant undertake to guarantee that the rights enunciated in the present Covenant will be exercised without discrimination of any kind as to race, colour, sex, language, religion, political or other opinion, national or social origin, property, birth or other status.

3. Developing countries, with due regard to human rights and their national economy, may determine to what extent they would guarantee the economic rights recognised in the present Covenant to non-nationals.

Article 2 is one of the most important articles of the Covenant because it outlines the nature of States Parties' legal obligations under the Covenant and determines how they must approach the implementation of the substantive rights contained in Articles 6 to 15.

Any analysis of obligations relating to economic, social and cultural rights cannot be isolated from the obligations inherent in securing the individual entitlements of the beneficiaries of the right(s) in question. Most frequently, obligations are divided into 'layers' reflecting duties to (a) respect, (b) protect, (c) promote, and (d) fulfil each of the rights contained in the Covenant. Each of these legal responsibilities can take on more specific obligations of 'conduct' (e.g., action or inaction) and obligations of 'result' (e.g., ends).

The provision from Article 2, paragraph 1, requires all States Parties to begin immediately to take measures towards the full enjoyment by everyone of all the rights in the Covenant. The adoption of legislation will, in many cases, be indispensable if economic, social and cultural rights are to be made real, but laws alone are not a sufficient response at the national level. Administrative, judicial, policy, economic, social and educational measures and many other steps will be required by governments in order to ensure these rights to all.

Under Article 2, paragraph 1, States Parties are legally obliged to undertake legislative action in some instances, particularly when existing laws are clearly incompatible with the obligations assumed under the Covenant. This would be the case when, for instance, a law in a given country was patently discriminatory or had the express effect of preventing the enjoyment of any of the rights in the Covenant, or when legislation allowed the violation of rights, especially in terms of negative duties of states. Laws allowing governments forcibly to remove people from their homes, evicting them without due process of law, would have to be amended in order to bring domestic legislation into conformity with the Covenant.

The 'progressive obligation' component of the Covenant is often mistakenly taken to imply that only once a state reaches a certain level of economic development must the rights established under the Covenant be realised. This is not the intent of this clause. Rather, the duty in question obliges all States Parties, notwithstanding their level of national wealth, to move immediately and as quickly as possible towards the realisation of economic, social and cultural rights. This clause should never be interpreted as allowing states to defer indefinitely efforts to ensure the enjoyment of the rights laid down in the Covenant.

Whereas certain rights, by their nature, may be more apt to be implemented in terms of the 'progressive obligation' rule, many obligations under the Covenant are clearly required to be implemented immediately. This would apply especially to non-discrimination provisions and to the obligation of States Parties to refrain from actively violating economic, social and cultural rights or withdrawing legal and other protection relating to those rights.

The Committee on Economic, Social and Cultural Rights has asserted that this duty exists independently of an increase in available resources and thus recognises that all existing resources must be devoted in the most effective way possible to the realisation of the rights enshrined in the Covenant. Like the 'progressive realisation' provision, this standard is also used to justify the non-enjoyment of rights. However, as recognised in the Limburg Principles on the Implementation of the International Covenant on Economic, Social and Cultural Rights, this requirement obliges States Parties to ensure minimum subsistence rights for everyone, regardless of the level of economic development in a given country.

The term 'available resources' applies both to domestic resources and to any international economic or technical assistance or cooperation available to a State Party. In the use of available resources, due priority should be given to the realisation of rights recognised in the Covenant, considering the need to assure to everyone the satisfaction of subsistence requirements, as well as the provision of essential services.

Importantly, the grounds of discrimination mentioned in this provision are not exhaustive and thus certain other forms of unfair discrimination negatively affecting the enjoyment of the rights enunciated in the Covenant (for instance, on the basis of sexual orientation) must be prevented.

According to the Limburg Principles, special measures taken for the sole purpose of securing adequate advancement of certain groups or individuals requiring protection in order to ensure their equal enjoyment of economic, social and cultural rights are not considered discrimination, provided that such measures do not lead to the maintenance of separate rights for different groups and are not continued after their objectives have been achieved. This applies, for example, to affirmative-action programme.

This provision not only obliges governments to desist from discriminatory behaviour and to alter laws and practices which allow discrimination, it also applies to the duty of States Parties to prohibit private persons and bodies (third parties) from practising discrimination in any field of public life.

## Equal Rights for Men and Women

### *Article 3*

The States Parties to the present Covenant undertake to ensure the equal right of men and women to the enjoyment of all economic, social and cultural rights set forth in the present Covenant.

Women often suffer substantial and disproportionate difficulties in securing human rights, including economic, social and cultural rights. Article 3 guarantees that men and women possess precisely the same legal entitlement to the rights set forth in the Covenant and that, if necessary, special measures will be employed by States Parties to ensure that this position of equality is attained.

The Covenant provides a framework for instigating progressive and immediate measures such that women may enjoy on an equal footing rights which have often been denied them. For instance, the housing rights provisions in article 11, paragraph 1, of the Covenant must apply to men and women equally, and thus women must be accorded equal rights to housing inheritance—something which is still not the case in many countries. Together, Article 3 and Article 2, paragraph 2, thus provide significant legal protection against all forms of discrimination in the pursuit of economic, social and cultural rights.

## Limitations

### *Article 4*

The States Parties to the present Covenant recognise that, in the enjoyment of those rights provided by the state in conformity with the present Covenant, the state may subject such rights only to such limitations as are determined by law only in so far as this may be compatible with the nature of these rights and solely for the purpose of promoting the general welfare in a democratic society.

*Article 5*

1. Nothing in the present Covenant may be interpreted as implying for any state group or person any right to engage in any activity or to perform any act aimed at the destruction of any of the rights or freedoms recognised herein, or at their limitation to a greater extent than is provided for in the present Covenant.
2. No restriction upon or derogation from any of the fundamental human rights recognised or existing in any country in virtue of law, conventions, regulations or custom shall be admitted on the pretext that the present Covenant does not recognise such rights or that it recognises them to a lesser extent.

Articles 4 and 5 were not intended by the drafters of the Covenant to be overly permissive of the imposition of limitations by the state on the rights provided for. Rather, these provisions are formulated in such a manner as to be protective of the rights of individuals. They are also not designed to introduce limitations on rights affecting the subsistence or survival of the individual or the integrity of the person.

If a State Party finds it necessary to invoke the provisions of these articles, it may do so only if this is provided for by law and only if the measures in question are consistent with the Covenant. Such measures cannot be applied in an arbitrary, unreasonable or discriminatory way. Moreover, individuals should have legal safeguards and effective remedies against illegal or abusive imposition of limitations on economic, social and cultural rights.

The term 'democratic society' (Art. 4) further restricts the imposition of limitations under the Covenant and thus the burden rests on the state to prove that any limitations do not impair the democratic functioning of society.

None of the provisions in the law relating to any limitation may be interpreted in such a way as to nullify any of the rights or freedoms recognised in the Covenant. The main purpose of Article 5, paragraph 2, is to ensure that no provision of the Covenant is interpreted so as to prejudice provisions of domestic law or any other legal instrument already in force, or which may come into force, under which more favourable treatment would be accorded to persons protected.

## The Right to Work

### *Article 6*

1. The States Parties to the present Covenant recognise the right to work, which includes the right of everyone to the opportunity to gain his living by work which he freely chooses or accepts, and will take appropriate steps to safeguard this right.
2. The steps to be taken by a State Party to the present Covenant to achieve the full realisation of this right shall include technical and vocational guidance and training programmes, policies and techniques to achieve steady economic, social and cultural development and full and productive employment under conditions safeguarding, fundamental political and economic freedoms to the individual.

Freely chosen work remains an essential part of being human. For many people, whether employed in the formal or informal sectors, work represents the primary source of income on which subsistence, survival and life depend. The right to work is fundamental to the enjoyment of certain subsistence and livelihood rights such as food, clothing, housing, etc. Moreover, one's working status may easily affect the enjoyment of other rights relating to health and education. The right to work is increasingly important as governments the world over continue to withdraw from the provision of basic services, leaving these to market forces and non-governmental actors.

The right to work is fundamental to ensuring the dignity and self-respect of the beneficiaries of the rights contained in the Covenant. Article 6 obliges States Parties to refrain from instigating or allowing forced labour. The Committee on Economic, Social and Cultural Rights has examined this article in terms of the implementation of policies and measures aimed at securing work for all who are available to work. This right encompasses, therefore, both the right to enter into employment and the right not to be unjustly deprived of work. Although unemployment persists in all States Parties, these States must apply the basic principles set out in Article 2 for ensuring the full realisation of the right to work.

## The Right to just and Favourable Conditions of Work

### *Article 7*

The States Parties to the present Covenant recognise the right of everyone to the enjoyment of just and favourable conditions of work which ensure, in particular:

a) Remuneration which provides all workers, as a minimum, with:
   i) Fair wages and equal remuneration for work of equal value without distinction of any kind, in particular women being guaranteed conditions of work not inferior to those enjoyed by men, with equal pay for equal work;
   ii) A decent living for themselves and their families in accordance with the provisions of the present Covenant.

b) Safe and healthy working conditions;

c) Equal opportunity for everyone to be promoted in his employment to an appropriate higher level, subject to no considerations other than those of seniority and competence;

d) Rest, leisure and reasonable limitation of working hours and periodic holidays with pay, as well as remuneration for public holidays.

Article 7 establishes a right to a minimum remuneration for employment, stipulating fair wages sufficient to guarantee a decent living, as well as working conditions that are just and favourable. Wages must be equitable and just in order to be considered fair.

This article relates closely to a large number of conventions adopted by the International Labour Organisation, including the Minimum Wage Fixing Convention (No. 131, 1970) and the Equal Remuneration Convention (No. 100, 1951).

People must be afforded minimum conditions of occupational health and safety, and States Parties are responsible for adopting policies and laws to that end. A coherent national policy in this regard is incumbent on all States Parties.

The standards laid down in article 7 also relate to the duties of States Parties to reduce the working week in a progressive manner and to ensure that workers enjoy adequate rest and holidays. For all aspects of this article, States Parties must establish a baseline or minimum standard below which the working conditions of no worker should be allowed to fall; they must also develop enforcement measures guaranteeing these rights.

## The Right to Form and Join Trade Unions

### *Article 8*

1. The States Parties to the present Covenant undertake to ensure:

   a) The right of everyone to form trade unions and join the trade union of his choice, subject only to the rules of the organisation concerned, for the promotion and protection of his economic and social interests. No restrictions may be placed on the exercise of this right other than those prescribed by law and which are necessary in a democratic society in the interests of national security or public order or for the protection of the rights and freedoms of others;

b) The right of trade unions to establish national federations or confederations and the right of the latter to form or join international trade-union organisations;

c) The right of trade unions to function freely subject to no limitations other than those prescribed by law and which are necessary in a democratic society in the interests of national security or public order or for the protection of the rights and freedoms of others;

d) The right to strike, provided that it is exercised in conformity with the laws of the particular country.

2. This article shall not prevent the imposition of lawful restrictions on the exercise of these rights by members of the armed forces or of the police or of the administration of the state.

3. Nothing in this article shall authorise States Parties to the International Labour Organisation Convention of 1948 concerning Freedom of Association and Protection of the Right to Organise to take legislative measures which would prejudice, or apply the law in such a manner as would prejudice, the guarantees provided for in that Convention.

The right to form and join trade unions is closely linked to the right to freedom of association, which is widely recognised throughout international human rights law. These rights, combined with the right to strike, are fundamental if the rights of workers and other citizens under the Covenant are to be implemented.

Article 8 provides for a right not to be compelled to join a particular trade union, in accordance with the term 'of his choice' (para. 1(a)). It also includes the right to federate or confederate, which should not be subject to state control. The right to collective bargaining, the right to protection from dissolution or suspension and the right to strike are also protected.

States Parties are allowed some measure of discretion concerning the implementation of Article 8, as evidenced by the language concerning limitations in the interests of national security, public order and the rights and freedoms of others. These grounds for exemption, however, must be interpreted narrowly by States Parties seeking to invoke them.

With regard to national security concerns, for instance, the Limburg Principles on the Implementation of the International Covenant on Economic, Social and Cultural Rights stress that the systematic violation of economic, social and cultural rights undermines true national security and may jeopardise international peace and security. A state responsible for such violation shall not invoke national security as a justification for measures aimed at suppressing opposition to such violation or at perpetrating repressive practices against its population.

## The Right to Social Security and Social Insurance

### *Article 9*

The States Parties to the present Covenant recognise the right of everyone to social security, including social insurance.

A large number of states do not maintain adequate social security or social insurance provisions under domestic laws protecting people in circumstances such as old age, disability, ill-health or other situations not allowing them to earn a decent living. At the same time, many countries which do provide such protection are beginning to transfer responsibility for these matters from the state to the private sector. These issues raise serious concerns regarding enjoyment of the rights contained in the Covenant.

The Committee on Economic, Social and Cultural Rights specifically asks States Parties whether they maintain social security schemes in the following areas: medical care, cash sickness benefits, maternity benefits, old-age benefits, invalidity benefits, survivors' benefits, employment injury benefits, unemployment benefits and family benefits.

The Committee has devoted particular attention to enjoyment of the rights provided for in Article 9 by women, older persons (General Comment No. 6 (1995)), and persons with disabilities (General Comment No. 5 (1994)).

## Protection and Assistance for the Family

### *Article 10*

The States Parties to the present Covenant recognise that:

1. The widest possible protection and assistance should be accorded to the family, which is the natural and fundamental group unit of society, particularly for its establishment, and while it is responsible for the care and education of dependent children. Marriage must be entered into with the free consent of the intending spouses.
2. Special protection should be accorded to mothers during a reasonable period before and after childbirth. During such period working mothers should be accorded paid leave or leave with adequate social security benefits.
3. Special measures of protection and assistance should be taken on behalf of all children and young persons without any discrimination for reasons of parentage or other conditions. Children and young persons should be

protected from economic and social exploitation. Their employment in work harmful to their morals or health or dangerous to life or likely to hamper their normal development should be punishable by law. States should also set age limits below which the paid employment of child labour should be prohibited and punishable by law.

Article 10 provides protection for the family, mothers and children. It includes the right to enter freely into marriage, raising doubts as to the situation in countries where marriage occurs without the free and informed consent of one or another spouse, almost invariably the woman. Mothers are to be accorded substantial protection before and after childbirth. The Committee on Economic, Social and Cultural Rights regularly requests information from States Parties as to whether any particular groups of women lack such protection.

The Committee has not spent a great deal of time examining situations relating to family rights, but has devoted increased attention to the rights of the child as they are established under Article 10, paragraph 3. It has paid particular attention to child labour and the living conditions of children. The most intensive work within the United Nations system on children's rights is carried out by the Committee on the Rights of the Child, with which the Committee on Economic, Social and Cultural Rights works closely.

## The Right to an Adequate Standard of Living

### *Article 11*

1. The States Parties to the present Covenant recognise the right of everyone to an adequate standard of living for himself and his family, including adequate food, clothing and housing, and to the continuous improvement of living conditions. The States Parties will take

appropriate steps to ensure the realisation of this right, recognising to this effects the essential importance of international cooperation based on free consent.

2. The States Parties to the present Covenant, recognising the fundamental right of everyone to be free from hunger, shall take, individually and through international cooperation, the measures, including specific programmes, which are needed:

   a) To improve methods of production, conservation and distribution of food by making full use of technical and scientific knowledge, by disseminating knowledge of the principles of nutrition and by developing or reforming agrarian systems in such a way as to achieve the most efficient development and utilisation of natural resources;

   b) Taking into account the problems of both food-importing and food-exporting countries, to ensure an equitable distribution of world food supplies in relation to need.

Article 11 incorporates a broad range of concerns relating to the lives and livelihoods of residents of States Parties, in particular, food, clothing and housing. The Committee on Economic, Social and Cultural Rights has devoted extensive attention to this article, particularly as it relates to the human right to adequate housing. To date, the right to adequate housing is the only right in the Covenant which has had an entire general comment devoted to it (General Comment No. 4 (1991)).

General Comment No. 4 reveals the extensive nature of the protection included under Article 11 and elaborates legal interpretations of the right to adequate housing which go far beyond restricted visions of this right as simply a right to shelter. In it, the Committee, which has given more attention to the right to housing than to any other right under the Covenant, states:

> . . . the right to housing, should not be interpreted in a narrower restrictive sense which equates it with, for example, the shelter provided by merely having a roof over one's head . . . Rather it should be seen as the right to live somewhere in security, peace and dignity . . . . (Para. 7.)

The Committee has defined the term 'adequate housing' to comprise security of tenure, availability of services, affordability, habitability, accessibility, location and cultural adequacy.

Article 11 does not imply a stagnant state of affairs, but also includes a right 'to the continuous improvement of living conditions' (para. 1) and the possibilities associated with international cooperation in the event of States Parties being unable to guarantee the rights in question. This is particularly relevant in times of food crises or famine.

The Committee has decided on several occasions that certain States Parties had violated provisions of Article 11, particularly as a result of the practice of forced evictions. This is indicative of the seriousness which the Committee accords Article 11.

## The Right to the Highest Attainable Standard of Physical and Mental Health

### *Article 12*

1. The States Parties to the present Covenant recognise the right of everyone to the enjoyment of the highest attainable standard of physical and mental health.
2. The steps to be taken by the States Parties to the present Covenant to achieve the full realisation of this right shall include those necessary for:

a) The provision for the reduction of the stillbirth-rate and of infant mortality and for the healthy development of the child;
b) The improvement of all aspects of environmental and industrial hygiene;
c) The prevention, treatment and control of epidemic, endemic, occupational and other diseases;
d) The creation of conditions which would assure to all medical service and medical attention in the event of sickness.

Recognition of the right to health obviously does not mean that beneficiaries of this right have a right to be healthy. Rather, the Covenant stresses the obligation of States Parties to ensure for their citizens "the highest attainable standard of....health"

Article 12 therefore places emphasis on equal access to health care and minimum guarantees of health care in the event of sickness.

The Committee on Economic, Social and Cultural Rights has spent increasing energy on clarifying and monitoring health rights, having held a general discussion on the topic and adopted a general comment on the rights of persons with disabilities (General Comment No. 5 (1994)). The rights of people with HIV/AIDS have also received increasing attention from the Committee in recent years.

## The Right to Education

### *Article 13*

1. The States Parties to the present Covenant recognise the right of everyone to education. They agree that education shall be directed to the full development of the human personality and the sense of its dignity, and shall strengthen the respect for human rights and

fundamental freedoms. They further agree that education shall enable all persons to participate effectively in a free society, promote understanding, tolerance and friendship among all nations and all racial, ethnic or religious groups, and further the activities of the United Nations for the maintenance of peace.

2. The States Parties to the present Covenant recognise that, with a view to achieving the full realisation of this right:

   a) Primary education shall be compulsory and available free to all;

   b) Secondary education in its different forms, including technical and vocational secondary education, shall be made generally available and accessible to all by every appropriate means, and in particular by the progressive introduction of free education;

   c) Higher education shall be made equally accessible to all, on the basis of capacity, by every appropriate means, and in particular by the progressive introduction of free education;

   d) Fundamental education shall be encouraged or intensified as far as possible for those persons who have not received or completed the whole period of their primary education;

   e) The development of a system of schools at all levels shall be actively pursued, an adequate fellowship system shall be established, and the material conditions of teaching staff shall be continuously improved.

3. The States Parties to the present Covenant undertake to have respect for the liberty of parents and, when applicable, legal guardians to choose for their children schools, other than those established by the public authorities, which conform to such minimum

educational standards as may be laid down or approved by the state and to ensure the religious and moral education of their children in conformity with their own convictions.

4. No part of this article shall be construed so as to interfere with the liberty of individuals and bodies to establish and direct educational institutions, subject always to the observance of the principles set forth in paragraph one of this article and to the requirement that the education given in such institutions shall conform to such minimum standards as may be laid down by the State.

## Compulsory and Free Primary Education

### *Article 14*

Each State Party to the present Covenant which, at the time of becoming a party, has not been able to secure in its metropolitan territory or other territories under its jurisdiction compulsory primary education, free of charge, undertakes within two years, to work out and adopt a detailed plan of action for the progressive implementation, within a reasonable number of years, to be fixed in the plan, of the principle of compulsory education free of charge for all.

Articles 13 and 14 recognise that education is a fundamental precondition for the enjoyment and assertion of human rights and that education strengthens human rights and basic democratic principles. The international community has long recognised these basic truths and has proclaimed the decade 1995-2004 as the United Nations Decade for Human Rights Education. The Committee on Economic, Social and Cultural Rights held a general discussion on this topic in 1994.

These two articles guarantee all children a right to free and compulsory primary education, wherever they may live. They also enshrine the right to equal access to education and equal enjoyment of education facilities; the freedom to choose education and to establish educational institutions; the protection of pupils against inhuman disciplinary measures and academic freedom.

## The Right to Culture and to Benefit from Scientific Progress

### *Article 15*

1. The States Parties to the present Covenant recognise the right of everyone:

   a) To take part in cultural life;

   b) To enjoy the benefits of scientific progress and its applications;

   c) To benefit from the protection of moral and material interests resulting from any scientific, literary or artistic production of which he is the author.

2. The steps to be taken by the States Parties to the present Covenant to achieve the full realisation of this right shall include those necessary for the conservation, the development and the diffusion of science and culture.

3. The States Parties to the present Covenant undertake to respect the freedom indispensable for scientific research and creative activity.

4. The States Parties to the present Covenant recognise the benefits to be derived from the encouragement and development of international contacts and cooperation in the scientific and cultural fields.

The rights to enjoy culture, to participate in cultural life and to benefit from technological and scientific progress form the foundation of Article 15. Although these issues may not seem to be matters of human rights, they are of fundamental importance to the principles of equality of treatment, freedom of expression, the right to receive and impart information, and the right to the full development of the human personality.

Cultural attributes can often be attacked or derided by states in attempts to favour one national, racial or ethnic group over another, to cite but one example of how important the rights in question are. Moreover, these rights include the right to participate in the life of society, giving a wide reading to the term 'culture'.

The right to benefit from scientific progress and its applications is designed to ensure that everyone in society can enjoy advances in this regard, in particular, disadvantaged groups. It includes the right of everyone to seek and receive information about such advances resulting from new scientific insights and to have access to any developments which could enhance their enjoyment of the rights contained in the Covenant.

## VIENNA DECLARATION AND PROGRAMME OF ACTION

Although the Committee on Economic, Social and Cultural Rights can assist in the implementation of the Covenant from an international perspective, the ultimate effectiveness of this instrument is contingent on the measures taken by governments to give actual effect to their international legal obligations. In this regard, the Committee has recognised the essential importance of the adoption by states of appropriate legislative measures and the provision of judicial remedies, indicating the very real legal nature of economic, social and cultural rights.

The necessity of implementing the provisions of the Covenant through domestic legislation is consistent with Article 27 of the 1969 Vienna Convention on the Law of Treaties, which states that "a party may not invoke the provisions of its internal law as justification for its failure to perform a treaty." Indeed, the Covenant often requires legislative action to be taken in cases where existing legislation is in violation of the obligations assumed under the Covenant.

The Limburg Principles on the Implementation of the International Covenant on Economic, Social and Cultural Rights emphasise that "States Parties shall provide for effective remedies, including, where appropriate, judicial remedies" (Principle 19). Since there does not yet exist an individual complaints procedure under the Covenant, the full implementation of the rights which this instrument contains is all the more dependent on the provision of appropriate laws and remedies at the national level.

At minimum, the national and local judiciaries of States Parties must consider international human rights laws such as the Covenant an interpretative aid to domestic law and ensure that domestic law is interpreted and applied in a manner consistent with the provisions of international human rights instruments ratified by the state. From the perspective of international law, the underlying principle is that courts should avoid placing their government in violation of the terms of an international treaty which it has ratified.

Regarding the justifiability of the rights contained in the Covenant—i.e., the possibility of their being subjected to judicial review—the Committee has stated in its General Comment No. 3 (1990):

> Among, the measures which might be considered appropriate, in addition to legislation, is the provision of judicial remedies with respect to rights which may, in accordance with the national legal system, be considered justifiable . . . (Para. 5.)

In this regard, the Committee has indicated that a number of articles in the Covenant are capable of immediate implementation, including Article 3, Article 7, subparagraph

(a) (i), Article 8, Article 10, paragraph 3, Article 13, paragraphs 2 (a), 3 and 4, and Article 15, paragraph 3. It has also stressed, with respect to the right to adequate housing, for example, that "instances of forced eviction are *prima facie* incompatible with the requirements of the Covenant and can only be justified in the most exceptional circumstances, and in accordance with the relevant principles of international law." In order to put such obligations into effect domestically, national courts would obviously have an important role to play in ensuring respect for the rights in question.

## Monitoring the Implementation of the Covenant: the Committee on Economic, Social and Cultural Rights

### *Creation and composition of the committee*

Unlike the five other human rights treaty bodies, the Committee on Economic, Social and Cultural Rights was not established by its corresponding instrument. Rather, the Economic and Social Council (ECOSOC) created the Committee, following the less than ideal performance of two previous bodies entrusted with monitoring the Covenant.

The Committee was established in 1985, met for the first time in 1987 and has to date held 14 sessions. Meeting initially on an annual basis, the Committee currently convenes twice a year, holding two three-week sessions, generally in May and November/December. It holds all its meetings at the United Nations Office at Geneva.

The Committee comprises 18 members who are experts with recognised competence in the field of human rights. Members of the Committee are independent and serve in their personal capacity, not as representatives of Governments. At present, the Committee is made up of 13 men and five women. The Committee itself selects its chairperson, three vice-chairpersons and rapporteur.

Members of the Committee are elected by ECOSOC for four-year terms, and are eligible for re-election if renominated. The Committee is thus a subsidiary organ of ECOSOC and derives its formal authority from that body. Elections take place in a secret ballot from a list of nominees proposed by States Parties to the Covenant. States which have not ratified the Covenant cannot, therefore, nominate their own nationals for positions on the Committee. The principles of equitable geographical distribution and the representation of different social and legal systems guide the selection process. The Committee is serviced by the United Nations Centre for Human Rights.

The primary function of the Committee is to monitor the implementation of the Covenant by States Parties. It strives to develop a constructive dialogue with States Parties and seeks to determine through a variety of means whether or not the norms contained in the Covenant are being adequately applied in States Parties and how the implementation and enforcement of the Covenant could be improved so that all people who are entitled to the rights enshrined in the Covenant can actually enjoy them in full.

Drawing on the legal and practical expertise of its members, the Committee can also assist governments in fulfilling their obligations under the Covenant by issuing specific legislative, policy and other suggestions and recommendations such that economic, social and cultural rights are more effectively secured.

## How do States Parties Report to the Committee?

Under Articles 16 and 17 of the Covenant, States Parties undertake to submit periodic reports to the Committee within two years of the entry into force of the Covenant for a particular State Party, and thereafter once every five years—outlining the legislative, judicial, policy and other measures which they have taken to ensure the enjoyment of the rights contained in the Covenant. States Parties are also requested to provide detailed data on the degree to which the rights are implemented and areas where particular difficulties have been faced in this respect.

The Committee has assisted the reporting process by providing States Parties with a detailed 22-page set of reporting guidelines specifying the types of information the Committee requires in order to monitor compliance with the Covenant effectively.

The reporting requirement is much more than simply a formalistic commitment. Although the reporting process is imbued with a number of difficulties, not the least of which are the non-submission of reports by a large number of States Parties and problems relating to resource constraints of states, this mechanism has a number of important functions. Among these are the initial review function, the monitoring function, the policy formulation function, the public scrutiny function, the evaluation function, the function of acknowledging problems and the information-exchange function.

The Committee has emphasised that reporting obligations under the Covenant fulfil seven key objectives. In its General Comment No. 1 (1989), the Committee stated these objectives as follows:

1. to ensure that a State Party undertakes a comprehensive review of national legislation, administrative rules and procedures, and practices in order to assure the fullest possible conformity with the Covenant;
2. to ensure that the State Party regularly monitors the actual situation with respect to each of the enumerated rights in order to assess the extent to which the various rights are being enjoyed by all individuals within the country;

3. to provide a basis for government elaboration of clearly stated and carefully targeted policies for implementing the Covenant;
4. to facilitate public scrutiny of government policies with respect to the Covenant's implementation, and to encourage the involvement of the various sectors of society in the formulation, implementation and review of relevant policies;
5. to provide a basis on which both the State Party and the Committee can effectively evaluate progress towards the realisation of the obligations contained in the Covenant;
6. to enable the State Party to develop a better understanding of problems and shortcomings impeding the realisation of economic, social and cultural rights;
7. to facilitate the exchange of information among States Parties and to help develop a fuller appreciation of both common problems and possible solutions in the realisation of each of the rights contained in the Covenant.

The Committee typically considers some five or six reports of States Parties during any given session. If a State Party which has submitted a report that is scheduled for the Committee's consideration at a given session seeks to defer the presentation of the report at the last minute, the Committee does not grant such a request, and proceeds with its consideration, even in the absence of a State Party representative.

The Committee has also had to grapple with problems relating to the non-submission of reports and reports which are considerably overdue. In response to such situations, the Committee has notified States Parties whose reports are long overdue of its intention to consider these reports at specified future sessions. If no report is forthcoming, the Committee then proceeds to consider the status of economic, social and cultural rights in the states concerned in the light of all available information.

## Submission of Reports and the Pre-sessional Working Group

When States Parties submit their reports, a standard procedure of consideration is followed by the Committee. Once received, processed and translated by the Secretariat, States Parties' reports are initially reviewed by the Committee's five-person pre-sessional working group, which meets six months prior to a report being considered by the full Committee. The pre-sessional working group gives a preliminary consideration to the report, appoints one member to give particular consideration to each report, and develops written lists of questions based on disparities found in the reports which are submitted to the States Parties concerned. The States Parties are then required to reply in writing to these questions prior to their appearance before the Committee.

## Presentation of Reports

Representatives of reporting states are strongly encouraged to be present at meetings when the Committee considers their reports. Such delegations are virtually always present during this process, which is generally carried out over a two-day period. Delegations first provide introductory comments and responses to the pre-sessional working group's written questions. This is followed by the provision of information by the United Nations specialised agencies relevant to the report under consideration. Committee members then put questions and observations to the State Party appearing before it. A further period of time is then allowed for representatives of States Parties to respond, generally not on the same day, to the questions and views put to them, as precisely as possible. If the questions cannot be adequately dealt with, the Committee often requests a State Party to provide it with additional information for its consideration at forthcoming sessions.

## Concluding Observations: The Committee Decides

Upon completion by the Committee of its analysis of reports and the appearance by States Parties, the Committee concludes its consideration of States Parties' reports by issuing 'concluding observations', which constitute the decision of the Committee regarding the status of the Covenant in a given State Party. Concluding observations are divided into five sections: (a) introduction; (b) positive aspects; (c) factors and difficulties impeding the implementation of the Covenant; (d) principal subjects of concern; and (e) suggestions and recommendations. Concluding observations are adopted in private session, and are released to the public on the final day of each session.

On a number of occasions, the Committee has concluded that violations of the Covenant had taken place, and subsequently urged States Parties to desist from any further infringements of the rights in question.

All human rights are subject to violation, and economic, social and cultural rights are no exception. The Limburg Principles on the Implementation of the International Covenant on Economic, Social and Cultural Rights list the following circumstances amounting to violations of the Covenant by a State Party (principle 72): (a) it fails to take a step which the Covenant requires it to take; (b) it fails to remove promptly obstacles which it is obligated to remove to permit the immediate fulfilment of a right; (c) it fails to implement without delay a right which the Covenant requires it to provide immediately; (d) it wilfully fails to meet a generally accepted international minimum standard of achievement, which is within its powers to meet; (e) it applies a limitation to a right recognised in the Covenant in a manner not in accordance with the Covenant; (f) it deliberately retards or halts the progressive realisation of a right, unless it is acting within a limitation permitted by the Covenant or it does so because of a lack of available resources; and (g) it fails to submit reports as required under the Covenant.

While the Committee's concluding observations, in particular suggestions and recommendations, may not carry legally binding status, they are indicative of the opinion of the only expert body entrusted with and capable of making such pronouncements. Consequently, for States Parties to ignore or not act on such views would be to show bad faith in implementing their Covenant-based obligations. In a number of instances, changes in policy, practice and law have been registered at least partly in response to the Committee's concluding observations.

In addition to concluding observations, letters from the chairperson are occasionally addressed to States Parties informing them of the Committee's concerns.

The Committee also adopts draft decisions for eventual adoption by ECOSOC, when such approval is required. This is generally the case when the Committee requests a State Party to issue it with an invitation to visit the country and provide the government with technical and other assistance which it may require in order to implement more fully and enforce the norms of the Covenant. The Committee has to date twice requested invitations to visit the territories of States Parties (Dominican Republic and Panama). Only in one of these instances (Panama), however, did the state issue the requisite invitation, and a mission took place in April 1995.

## Generating Interpretative Clarity

### a) General comments

The Committee decided in 1988 to begin preparing 'general comments' on the rights and provisions contained in the Covenant with a view to assisting States Parties in fulfilling their reporting obligations and to provide greater interpretative clarity as to the intent, meaning and content of the Covenant. The Committee further views the adoption of general comments as a means of promoting the implementation of the Covenant, by drawing the attention of States Parties to insufficiencies disclosed by a large number of States Parties' reports, and by inducing renewed attention to particular provisions of the Covenant on the part of States Parties, United Nations agencies and others with a view to achieving progressively the full realisation of the rights established under the Covenant.

General comments are a crucial means of generating jurisprudence, providing a method by which members of the Committee may come to an agreement by consensus regarding the interpretation of norms embodied in the Covenant.

As of April 1996, the Committee has adopted six general comments. These are:

- — General Comment No. 1 (1989) on reporting by States Parties;
- — General Comment No. 2 (1990) on international technical assistance measures (art. 22);
- — General Comment No. 3 (1990) on the nature of States Parties' obligations (art. 2, para. 1, of the Covenant);
- — General Comment No. 4 (1991) on the right to adequate housing (art. 11, para. 1, of the Covenant);
- — General Comment No. 5 (1994) on persons with disabilities;
- — General Comment No. 6 (1995) on the economic, social and cultural rights of older persons.

It is likely that the Committee will consider the adoption of additional general comments in the near future on issues such as the right to health; the domestic application of the

Covenant; forced evictions and the Covenant; the non-discrimination clauses of the Covenant (Art. 2, para. 2); the right to food; and others.

### *b) General discussions*

At each of its sessions, the Committee holds a 'day of general discussion' on particular provisions of the Covenant, particular human rights or other themes of direct relevance to the Committee in order to develop its understanding of the issues concerned. The Committee has sought to draw on a wide range of expertise during these discussions and has, therefore, engaged in dialogue with United Nations special rapporteurs, experts from relevant non-governmental organisations and representatives of United Nations specialised agencies.

General discussions to date have been held on the right to food (1989); the right to housing (1990); economic and social indicators (1991); the right to take part in cultural life (1992); the rights of the ageing and elderly (1993); the right to health (1993); the role of social safety nets as a means of protecting economic, social and cultural rights, with particular reference to situations involving major structural adjustment and/or transition to a free market economy (1994); human rights education (1994); the interpretation and practical application of the obligations incumbent on States Parties (1995); and a draft optional protocol to the Covenant (1995).

## Civil Society and the Work of the Committee

The World Conference on Human Rights affirms that extreme poverty and social exclusion constitute a violation of human dignity and that urgent steps are necessary to achieve better knowledge of extreme poverty and its causes, including those related to the problem of development, in order to promote the human rights of the poorest, and to put an end to extreme poverty and social exclusion and to promote the enjoyment of the fruits of social progress. It is essential for states to foster participation by the poorest people in the decision-making process and the community in which they live, the promotion of human rights and efforts to combat extreme poverty.

## RELEVANCE OF NGOS AND CBOS

The Committee has long recognised the important contribution which can be made by civil society in the provision of information concerning the status of the Covenant within States Parties. The Committee was the first treaty body to provide non-governmental organisations (NGOs) with the opportunity to submit written statements and make oral submissions dealing with issues relating to the enjoyment or non-enjoyment of the rights contained in the Covenant in specific countries.

On the first day of each session of the Committee, the afternoon meeting is set aside to give international and national NGOs and community-based organisations (CBOs) an opportunity to express their views about how the Covenant is or is not implemented by States Parties. The Committee will receive oral testimony from NGOs as long as the information focuses specifically on the provisions of the Covenant, it is of direct relevance to matters under consideration by the Committee, is reliable, and is not abusive. In recent years, NGOs and CBOs have taken increased advantage of this procedure and provided the Committee with written, audio and video materials alleging the non-enjoyment of economic, social and cultural rights in States Parties.

The Committee has indicated that the purposes of the NGO procedure are to enable it to inform itself as fully as possible, to examine the accuracy and pertinence of information which would most probably be available to it anyway, and to put the process of receiving NGO information on a more transparent basis. NGOs and CBOs wishing to provide reliable and new information to the Committee may write to the secretariat of the Committee several months prior to the beginning of a particular session, with a specific request to intervene during the NGO procedure. Groups with written materials may also send these to the secretariat, and may attend Committee sessions. NGOs in consultative status with the United Nations or other groups which have relations with such NGOs also may attend Committee sessions. NGOs with consultative status may, in accordance with the relevant ECOSOC resolutions, submit written submissions to the Committee at any time. Committee sessions are generally held in public, with the exception of meetings at which it prepares its concluding observations, which are held privately.

The active participation of NGOs in the work of the Committee has also proven fundamental in ensuring the wide distribution of information about the Covenant and the Committee at the national and local levels. In many instances, these organisations have generated substantial media attention in their countries following the adoption of concluding observations regarding the states in question.

## Towards a Formal Complaints Procedure (Optional Protocol)

At present it is not possible for individuals or groups who feel that their rights under the Covenant have been violated to submit formal complaints to the Committee. The absence of such procedure places significant constraints on the ability of the Committee to develop jurisprudence or case-law and, of course, greatly limits the chances of victims of abuses of the Covenant obtaining international redress.

There are numerous arguments supporting the adoption of a complaints procedure under the Covenant. These include the improved enjoyment by people of economic, social and cultural rights; a strengthening of international accountability of States Parties; increased congruence in the legal standing and seriousness accorded to both international covenants; a refinement of the rights and duties emerging from the provisions of the International Covenant on Economic, Social and Cultural Rights; and a structural and concrete affirmation of the indivisibility and interdependence of all human rights. It is also argued that such a procedure would encourage States Parties to provide similar remedies at the local and national levels.

The Committee has devoted increasing attention to the possibility of elaborating such an optional protocol since 1990 and has discussed the issue at length on several occasions. At its sixth session, in 1991, the Committee supported the drafting of an optional protocol "since that would enhance the practical implementation of the Covenant as well as the dialogue with States Parties and would make it possible to focus the attention of public opinion to a greater extent on economic, social and cultural rights."

The World Conference on Human Rights, held at Vienna in June 1993, gave added impetus to this initiative by asserting, in the Vienna Declaration and Programme of Action which it adopted, that the Committee should continue its efforts towards this end. The Committee has prepared a draft optional protocol, but it has yet to be officially adopted by the relevant United Nations organs.

Many other initiatives have also addressed the desirability of including a complaints procedure under the International Covenant on Economic, Social and Cultural Rights, and these have given added support to this means of strengthening this pivotal human rights treaty.

Pending the addition of an optional protocol, beneficiaries of the rights contained in the Covenant may still have recourse to the general procedures of the Committee, and may utilise what has been called "an unofficial petition procedure" based on the modalities of the Committee.

### *NGO participation in the activities of the Committee on Economic, Social and Cultural Rights*

At its eighth session, in May 1993, the Committee adopted the following procedure regarding the participation of non-governmental organisations in its activities:

*A. Written Information*

1. The Committee reiterates its long-standing invitation to NGOs to submit to it in writing, at any time, information regarding any aspect of its work.

*B. Oral Information*

2. In addition to the receipt of written information, a short period of time will be made available at the beginning of each session of the pre-sessional working group to provide NGOs with an opportunity to submit relevant oral information to the members of the working group.
3. Furthermore, the Committee will set aside part of the first afternoon at each of its sessions to enable it to receive oral information provided by NGOs. Such information should: (a) focus specifically on the provisions of the International Covenant on Economic, Social and Cultural Rights; (b) be of direct relevance to matters under consideration by the Committee; (c) be reliable; (d) not be abusive. The relevant meeting, will be open and will be provided with interpretation services, but will not be covered by summary records. The purposes are: to enable the Committee to inform itself as fully as possible; to probe the accuracy and pertinence of information which would most probably be available to it

anyway; and to put the process of receiving NGO information on a more transparent and open basis than is permitted by the current approach.

4. NGOs wishing to present oral information should inform the Committee in advance. In cases in which the Committee receives more expressions of interest than can be dealt with in the limited time available, the Chairperson of the Committee, in consultation with the Bureau, shall determine on an objective basis which NGOs will be invited to make an oral presentation.

5. To the extent that information provided to the Committee in writing, under these procedures is referred to by any member of the Committee in questions posed to the State Party, the relevant information should be available for consultation by the government concerned and all other interested parties.

6. The Committee requests its chairperson, in conjunction with the secretariat, to make these procedures as widely known as possible.

# 5
# Sustainable Human Development

Human rights are essential to the well-being of every man, woman and child. They are based on respect for the dignity and worth of all human beings and seek to ensure freedom from fear and want. They are rooted in ethical principles and usually inscribed in a country's constitutional and legal framework. Premised on fundamental and inviolable standards, they are universal and inalienable. What is the best way to ensure the progressive realisation of human rights? One way is the 'violations approach', whereby human rights are closely monitored to publicise abuses and hold states accountable for upholding the law and implementing their international human rights commitments. A second way, which can often complement the first, emphasises on a comprehensive view of human rights, stressing both the protection and promotion of rights. While securing the rule and enforcement of the law is crucial, so too is adopting measures that enable people to exercise their rights under the law.

The sustainable human development aims to eliminate poverty, promote human dignity and rights, and provide equitable opportunities for all through good governance, thereby promoting the realisation of all human rights—economic, social, cultural, civil and political. The promotion of human rights is of particular relevance in the context of globalisation and its potential for excluding and marginalising weak members of the international community and people with limited resources.

Development is unsustainable where the rule of law and equity do not exist; where ethnic, religious or sexual discrimination are rampant; where there are restrictions on free speech, free association and the media; or where large numbers of people live in abject and degrading poverty. The 1986 UN Declaration on the Right to Development states that development is a human right to be aware of and claim their rights. Sustainable human development and human rights will be undone in a repressive environment where threat or disease prevails, and both are better able to promote human choices in a peaceful and pluralistic society.

It is the responsibility of every individual and every organ of society to promote respect for human rights and to secure their universal recognition and observance. All human beings should act towards one another in a spirit of brotherhood. The Article 29 of Universal Declaration states: Everyone has duties to the community in which alone the free and full development of his personality is possible. These concepts from the Universal Declaration are important in the context of sustainable human development; social capital is a critical factor for development.

The UN Declaration on the Right to Development (1986) states that development is a human right. That proclamation was strengthened by the Declaration of the 1993 UN World Conference on Human Rights, which says that the right to development is an inalienable human right and an integral part of fundamental human freedoms. This view was confirmed at the UN global conferences on population and development (Cairo) and women (Beijing) and at the World Summit on Social Development (Copenhagen).

The UN Working Group on the Right to Development (October 1995), states that the right to development is multidimensional, integrated, dynamic and progressive. Its realisation involves the full observance of economic, social, cultural, civil and political rights. It further embraces the different concepts of development of all development sectors, namely, sustainable development, human development and the concept of indivisibility, interdependence and universality of all human rights.

Under the UN Charter the international community recognises that all human beings have equal, inalienable rights. With the Charter and the subsequent Universal Declaration of Human Rights, those rights were codified and acquired legal status. The preamble of the Charter states that the UN was formed:

> to reaffirm faith in fundamental human rights, in the dignity and worth of the human person, in the equal rights of men and women; . . . to establish conditions under which justice and respect for the obligations arising from treaties and other sources of international law can be maintained; and to promote social progress and better standards of life in larger freedom.

## UNDP AND HUMAN RIGHTS

UNDP plays an important role in the protection and promotion of human rights, both in its country activities and through its participation in national, international and multilateral meetings and conferences. Its programme is an application of the right to development and addresses primarily the economic, social and cultural rights of citizens. In some countries the programme has expanded into civil and political rights. There is a need, however, to more systematically address and focus the programme's human rights content and dimensions.

The emphasis on one aspect of human rights cannot be used to detract from the promotion of any other aspect. The United Nations Development Programme (UNDP) approaches this commitment to human rights at three levels. They are:

i) UNDP works for the full realisation of the right to development. UNDP's mandate for the eradication of poverty can be understood in this light. Poverty is a brutal denial of human rights. Thus by working to eradicate poverty, by supporting the anti-poverty capacity of governments and civil society organisations, and by ensuring that United Nations operational activities for development are fully coordinated for the eradication of poverty, UNDP is fostering the implementation of the right to development.

ii) UNDP advocates the realisation of human rights as part of sustainable human development, an approach that places people at the centre of all development activities. The central purpose is to create an enabling environment in which all human beings lead secure and creative lives. Sustainable human development is thus directed towards the promotion of human dignity and the realisation of all kinds of human rights.

iii) UNDP is devoting more of its programming activities to good governance. At the request of governments, UNDP is implementing programmes aimed at reforming legislatures, increasing the efficiency of the executive and strengthening the judiciary. These activities promote the quality of governance and the rule of law. They also promote transparency, accountability and decentralisation. In addition, UNDP governance programmes strengthen participation in decision-making at the national and local levels. In many of these activities, UNDP works with national authorities and civil society organisations to promote civil and political rights.

By protecting human rights, we can help prevent the many conflicts based on poverty, discrimination and exclusion that continue to plague humanity and destroy decades of development efforts. The vicious circle of human rights violations that lead to conflicts—which in turn lead to more violations—must be broken. The 1993 World Conference on Human Rights and the 1995 World Summit for Social

Development highlighted the importance of an integrated approach to social advancement. Lasting progress depends on respect for human rights and effective participation of citizens in public affairs.

Democracy and human rights will prove elusive without social justice and sustainable development. Poverty deprives millions of their fundamental rights. Societies, in turn, are deprived of these people's contributions. Achieving sustainable progress requires recognising the interdependence between respect for human rights, sustainable development and democracy.

Human rights requires the ceaseless efforts of thousands of dedicated human rights advocates, including international civil servants. Their work, particularly at the country level, is essential. UNDP Resident Representatives can play in helping governments and civil society to establish systems through which human rights become ingrained in the life of the community. Daunting challenges must be overcome for the full realisation of all human rights for all people.

United Nations (UN) global conferences—from Rio in 1992 to Rome in 1996—have highlighted the crucial links between the three key goals of the UN Charter: peace, development and human rights. At the same time, increased importance has been given to linking development and human rights. Development is a comprehensive process directed towards the full realisation of all human rights and fundamental freedoms. As the UN global conferences have reaffirmed, development is an inalienable human right and an integral part of fundamental human freedoms. The sustainable human development paradigm is a holistic strategy for development that embraces all human rights—economic, social, cultural, civil and political.

UNDP should develop a human rights-based framework in its anti-poverty, pro-sustainable human development work. It should focus on promoting human rights, primarily through support for the development of national capacity in the programming countries and through sustainable human development activities. The approach should be holistic and multidimensional, recognising the mutual dependency and complementarity of sustainable human development and social, economic, cultural, civil and political rights.

The UNDP development strategies have the following relevance for human rights:

i) Sustainable human development programming with a focus on eliminating poverty.
ii) Targeting disadvantaged or excluded groups (women, children, minorities, migrant workers, people with HIV/AIDS), thereby linking social justice, discrimination and development.
iii) Promoting partnerships with NGOs and civil society organisations, thereby encouraging people's participation at all stages of programme initiation, formulation and design, implementation and evaluation.
iv) Addressing governance issues (such as corruption, the rule of law, participation, democratisation and accountability) in which human rights have been integral but, all too often, not explicitly spelled out.
v) Strengthening institutions of governance and developing human rights capacity within such institutions.

In the past few years there has been an increase in programmes and projects that focus on protecting civil and political rights. A recently completed study of these activities found that in 1994-95 more than $44 million was allocated to 59 activities focusing on civil and political rights. This represents almost 13 per cent of UNDP funding for governance in 1994-95 and 11 per cent of the number of projects. Activities were concentrated in Latin America and the Caribbean (29 projects) and Africa (20 projects). Five projects were supported in Asia and five in Europe and the Commonwealth of Independent States, but none in the Arab States.

Since 1996 activities have increased substantially, with seven additional projects approved in Asia, six in Latin America and Africa, five in Europe and the Commonwealth of Independent States and one in the Arab States. UNDP activities have tended to fall under three broad categories: electoral assistance, democratic institution-building and peace-building and political transition.

UNDP's four main areas of sustainable human development programming:

i) eliminating poverty and sustaining livelihoods,
ii) promoting the advancement of women,
iii) protecting and regenerating the environment, and
iv) developing capacity for good governance.

All have dimensions pivotal to human rights.

## Poverty Elimination

Poverty and inequality can undermine human rights by fuelling social unrest and violence and increasing the precariousness of social, economic and political rights. Likewise, people's access to and control over productive resources is often determined by a country's legal framework and institutions.

Like human rights, poverty and sustainable livelihoods are multifaceted and complex, involving both material factors (meeting basic needs) and non-material ones (rights, participation, human dignity and security). Due to these links, programming in poverty and sustainable livelihoods can benefit from broadening the focus to include human rights.

Civic and social education will help people better understand their rights and increase their choices and income-earning capacity. At the same time, developing and implementing equal opportunity laws will empower people to gain more equitable access to productive resources. Poverty elimination is a core UNDP goal and a prime objective of its sustainable human development paradigm.

The right to an adequate standard of living, ensuring freedom from want, is an integral and inalienable human right affirmed in the Universal Declaration on Human Rights, the International Covenant on Economic, Social and Cultural Rights, the Convention on the Elimination of All Forms of Racial Discrimination, the Convention on the Elimination of All Forms of Discrimination against Women, and the Convention on the Rights of the Child. Adopting a human rights approach to its work on poverty elimination is crucial as UNDP moves towards strengthening its promotion and protection of economic, social and cultural rights and the right to development.

## Promotion of Women's Advancement

Legal rights can enhance women's living conditions by legislating against gender bias in employment, discrimination in pay and incentives, and violence and harassment. They can contribute towards increasing women's capabilities by giving them property and inheritance rights, better access to credit and other productive resources, and increased political participation and representation. UNDP's sustainable human development efforts must work to eliminate discrimination against women through programmes and processes that help governments:

- i) Reform legal systems and outlaw discrimination in employment, education, family affairs, land rights, credit services and other entitlements.
- ii) Redress the effects of past discrimination.
- iii) Educate and empower women and enable their effective participation in development.

## Protection of Environment

Environmental laws can help protect and renew the environment for current and future generations. In developing countries especially, such laws can be crucial in ensuring the survival of millions of people whose lives and livelihoods depend on their natural surroundings. Thus, like poverty and gender, the environment has crucial human rights dimensions that a human rights approach can help address. Development must be concerned with protecting and rehabilitating environments and must be environmentally sustainable. From a human rights perspective this would require:

— Conserving ecosystems and natural resources for future generations.

— Assessing the environmental and social impacts of development activities, and setting and enforcing standards to govern them.

— Providing environmental education.

— Encouraging free and meaningful participation in these activities.

## Development of Good Governance

The UNDP policy document 'Governance for Sustainable Human Development' defines governance as:

> the exercise of economic, political and administrative authority to manage a country's affairs at all levels. . . . Good governance is, among other things, participatory, transparent and accountable. It is also effective and equitable. And it promotes the rule of law. Good governance ensures that political, social and economic priorities are based on broad consensus in society and that the voices of the poorest and the most vulnerable are heard in decision-making over the allocation of development resources.

The preamble of the Universal Declaration also enunciates the relationship between human rights and governance:

> it is essential, if man is not to be compelled to have recourse, as a last resort, to rebellion against tyranny and oppression, that human rights should be protected by the rule of law.

Concern for human rights and good governance is reflected in public management programmes, which address such issues as accountability, transparency, participation, decentralisation, legislative capacity and judicial independence. UNDP's governance programme identifies three domains—the state, the private sector and civil society—each of which has a unique role in promoting sustainable human development. Like human rights, governance impinges on each of UNDP's other focus areas for sustainable human development—poverty and livelihoods, gender and the environment.

Strengthening human rights within governance activities will, by extension, help strengthen programming in each of the other focus areas—UNDP's mandate, mission, comparative advantage, constraints and limitations.

*Mandate*: A human rights approach will help fulfil UNDP's responsibilities to integrate human rights with its activities. It will also strengthen its ability to implement declarations and agreements reached at UN global conferences, many of which have human rights content.

*Mission*: To promote sustainable human development, which will reinforce the realisation of human rights.

*Comparative advantage*: UNDP has many strengths that distinguish it from other international and multilateral partners engaged in human rights. Due to its multilateral status, UNDP can work as an impartial agent of change for all actors-a crucial feature in human rights.

*Constraints and limitations*: At the country level, almost all UNDP activities require an official government request. UNDP cannot work directly with NGOs and civil society organisations without government approval. This is a serious limitation in countries where human rights abuses are serious or where authoritarian governments are intolerant of participation.

UNDP may be called on to support several types of human rights programmes. Three focus areas for human rights have been identified to best achieve the agency's goals. The first is providing support for institutions of governance, with an emphasis on building the human rights capacity of these institutions and providing direct support to human rights institutions. The second is developing a human rights approach to sustainable human development. The third is contributing to the human rights policy dialogue and UN conference follow-up.

National governance institutions such as legislatures, executives and judiciaries are crucial to establishing enabling environments for eliminating poverty, promoting equality and protecting the environment. Strengthening governance through human rights-related capacity development will help achieve these goals. Governance institutions are responsible for respecting, protecting and promoting human rights. But they are not the only ones involved in human rights and sustainable human development. Of equal importance are the civil society organisations—human rights and other law-related NGOs, socioeconomic NGOs, community organisations, schools, indigenous people's organisations, women's advocacy groups and the media—that play a crucial role in monitoring, protecting and promoting human rights.

Civil society organisations can monitor human rights even under extreme or authoritarian political conditions. They also protect and promote human rights, often complementing government efforts. Their expertise, experience and resources are invaluable given current resource scarcity and deficit cutting. These organisations face many of the same institutional and capacity constraints as governments, however. Helping both sets of institutions address these constraints will greatly enhance the vital contribution they make to human rights.

Judiciaries, legislatures and electoral bodies are crucial to the protection and promotion of human rights. They can ensure the rule and enforcement of the law, helping to establish anti-discriminatory practices and achieve socioeconomic, political and cultural equality. An effective executive branch can provide leadership in promoting legislation and implementing human rights laws and programmes. Civil service reform can help better formulate governance strategies, procedures and rules, contributing to more effective human rights programming.

Decentralisation, local governance and support to civil society organisations can empower people and local organisations to claim and exercise their rights or carry out human rights advocacy, outreach and networking.

Both governmental and non-governmental institutions benefit from comprehensive and coherent legislation or constitutions guaranteeing basic rights and protecting the rights of minorities, women, children and other disadvantaged groups. They will also benefit from building their expertise and knowledge on specific rights legislation.

Doing so will provide clarity on international commitments and obligations, on the distinction between public and private human rights violations, and on the consequences for human rights of government and development programmes and NGO actions. Capacity development will help these institutions build more sustainable organisational cultures by sensitising them to human rights issues.

Where human rights institutions do not exist, UNDP support will help build them or design programmes geared towards promoting human rights. Where human rights institutions do exist, support will help them become more independent, transparent, effective, accessible, legally secure and institutionally linked to other national and international organisations.

Humanitarian emergencies are accompanied by widespread disregard for fundamental human rights. UNDP's large field presence puts its country offices at the forefront of response to such emergencies. These crises provoke massive internal displacements, undermine coping capacities, destroy economic infrastructure, devastate the environment and often neutralise legitimate political systems and governance institutions. They also can threaten regional and international peace and security. Any effective development strategy for responding to these emergencies and their aftermath must address their root causes. Development can play a preventive role by addressing the social, economic, cultural and political causes of armed conflicts, which are often manifested by human rights denials and violations.

A better understanding of the interdependence between the strengthening of democratic governance institutions, respect for human rights, participation in sustainable human development and peace-building can prevent renewed conflict. In the aftermath of conflict, development programmes can address the social and economic rights of former combatants, displaced persons and returning refugees.

Any society emerging from conflict must have an independent judiciary, including a functioning criminal justice system that maintains order while respecting human rights, and a well-trained and impartial civilian police force and detention facilities under modern penal administration.

In most cases these institutions will have been limited before the conflict and militarised, polarised or destroyed during it. Yet criminality is likely to be serious in a society unable to fully integrate former combatants. It is also important to help build national human rights institutions established by governments and parliaments and to support the role of civil society in promoting and protecting human rights.

Governmental and non-governmental efforts to build a culture of human rights require assistance. Dealing with the legacy of past human rights violations may pose daunting challenges to a country's justice systems. UNDP has a key role to play in providing technical assistance and coordinating the contributions of multilateral and bilateral donors and UN specialised agencies.

## UNDP's Approach to Sustainable Human Development

UNDP is a development agency, special attention will be paid to economic, social and cultural rights and to the human right to development. Special attention will also be paid to ensuring that civil and political rights are fully respected in UNDP's sustainable human development programming and implementation. UNDP's approach to human rights will be developed in close consultation and cooperation with the High Commissioner for Human Rights.

UNDP's human rights approach to poverty alleviation will emphasise empowerment, participation and nondiscrimination and address vulnerability, marginalisation and exclusion.

UNDP's approach will also reflect its capacity-building mandate. Capacity-building initiatives will seek to enhance the realisation of human rights through UNDP's sustainable human development programming, UNDP funds and manages the Resident Coordinator system, which is responsible for coordinating the operational activities of the UN system in programme countries. This responsibility will be exercised in a way that supplements and complements the mandate of the High Commissioner for Human Rights for system-wide coordination on all matters related to human rights, democracy and rule of law. This approach will be reiterated in the Memorandum of Understanding being finalised between UNDP and the Office of the High Commissioner.

Developing UNDP's human rights approach to sustainable human development will be a dynamic process, undertaken in close cooperation with the High Commissioner for Human Rights and other UN agencies. The process will inevitably focus on the rights most frequently encountered in UNDP's sustainable human development activities, including:

i) *Rights of participation*: Fundamental freedoms include rights of people to meet with others, organise assemblies and speak freely. These are universal rights, and their exercise is essential in securing all other rights in development processes, as well as crucial in building civil society in social, economic, political and legal terms.

ii) *Rights to food, health, habitat and economic security*: It is the legal obligation of all states and of UN agencies such as the Food and Agriculture Organisation, the World Health Organisation, the International Labour Organisation and UNDP to promote the progressive realisation of these rights through development efforts. Since these are human rights, as well as government obligations, they empower people.

iii) *Rights to education*: This covers not only formal schooling but also access to civic knowledge and training that facilitate people's awareness and exercise of other rights and their effective participation in development.

iv) *Rights to work*: This imposes obligations on development planners to promote opportunities for productive employment, reduce risks to people from policies that create unemployment and adopt training programs that help people become qualified for productive work in a world of changing technologies and economic activities.

v) *Rights of children*: These reaffirm the right to life and protection against violence, abuse and neglect; the right to health and social security, education, and rest and leisure; freedom from trafficking in children and protection against child prostitution; and freedom from torture and cruel, inhuman or degrading treatment.

vi) *Rights of workers*: These include rights to organise and bargain over terms of employment and rights to adequate remuneration and a safe workplace.

vii) *Rights of minorities and indigenous peoples*: These include rights to maintain languages and cultures and rights of distinct peoples living in distinct regions to self-determined development and control of ancestral lands. These are often the basis of community organisation, culture and ways of life.

viii) *Rights to land*: Protection of the rights of those who depend on their lands for their livelihood. These rights are often grounded in customary law, and special processes may be needed to protect them.

ix) *Rights to equality*: This ensures freedom from discrimination against enjoying the above rights and empowerment of women and marginalised groups to organise and demand removal of customs and practices that inhibit equal opportunities to realise the benefits of development.

x) *Rights to environmental protection*: Rights to food, health, habitat and livelihood depend on environmental protection and the complementary relationships between promoting and protecting human rights and promoting and protecting environments.

xi) *Rights to administrative due process*: These include rights of access to officials responsible for designing or administering development activities; of access to information and to a fair hearing for people who claim to be threatened or harmed by development projects; and to redress and impose accountability on development actors who disregard the rights of affected people.

xii) *Rights to the rule of law*: These include the rules, procedures and institutions that enable people to secure enforcement of all their rights.

UNDP already engages in national, regional and global human rights policy discussions. It can benefit greatly from a more active role. Substantive human rights debates are taking place on the right to development and the way to make that right operational at the international and national levels, on the role of technical cooperation and capacity development in human rights, and on the intended and, more important, the unintended effects on human rights of development programming by multilateral and bilateral development assistance agencies, international finance and trade institutions, and governments and NGOs.

Sustainable human development provides a unique and holistic paradigm from which to integrate human rights and development and hence a unique platform for global advocacy. UNDP's general and human rights programming will also gain from donor policy coordination and dialogue to avoid duplication in programming, gain better focus and pool scarce resources, improve policy and programme coherence, share experience and knowledge and, where possible, engage in joint programming. UNDP can benefit from better integrating human rights follow-up from the major UN global conferences of the 1990s—especially from the World Conference on Children, the Earth Summit, the Social Summit, the Fourth World Conference on Women, the Education for All Conference, the Human Rights Conference, the Population and Development Conference, Habitat II and the World Food Summit. This integration of follow-up activities will provide valuable insights and benchmarks for UNDP's current and future programmes.

The implementation process of UNDP's human rights approach to sustainable human development involves several steps:

i) Taking country conditions into account, strengthening UNDP capacity in human rights.
ii) Working with the High Commissioner for Human Rights.
iii) Strengthening human rights at the national level.
iv) Building partnerships.
v) Dividing responsibilities.

UNDP support for human rights will respond to national needs and priorities, recognising that human rights issues and conditions vary greatly within and between countries. In all cases UNDP's approach will be flexible enough to address different country needs and priorities. The starting point for programming will be each country's human and institutional capacities, local human rights conditions, and local values and culture. Indeed, cultural differences are of crucial importance.

As the Vienna Declaration of the UN World Conference on Human Rights stresses, while the significance of national and regional particularities and various historical, cultural and religious backgrounds must be borne in mind, it is the duty of states, regardless of their political, economic and social systems, to promote and protect all human rights and fundamental freedoms. UNDP will need to develop strategies for countries with a difficult human rights environment.

UNDP must develop a firm policy to ensure that its development programmes do not become vehicles for human rights abuses—for example, in a country that excludes women, indigenous people or ethnic minorities from the benefits of development. In such countries economic, social and cultural rights provide the obvious entry point for human rights-based sustainable human development programming. But UNDP will have to guard against neglecting political and civil rights—and difficult questions of how to incorporate them in programmes in such countries will have to be addressed.

Cooperation with the Office of the High Commissioner for Human Rights will be vital for UNDP's human rights support. A Memorandum of Understanding on such cooperation is being finalised. UNDP's role will be to support the Office of the High Commissioner, which has an expressly designated mandate and leading role in human rights for the entire UN system.

The programme for Human Rights Strengthening is intended to help countries build and strengthen national capacities to protect and promote human rights in the light of international treaty commitments. The programme will also support efforts to integrate human rights concerns with broader governance programmes supported by UNDP. Implementation will be closely linked to advocacy for human rights in policy dialogues with governments. The programme will focus on:

i) Developing national strategies for human rights treaty ratification and implementation.

ii) Collecting, measuring, monitoring and reporting data on human rights.

iii) Supporting the development of public and non-governmental human rights institutions, national commissions for human rights and ombudsmen.

iv) Documenting and analysing UNDP experience and best practices.

UNDP builds partnerships and ensure the full involvement of major stakeholders. These partnerships will help build consensus, coordinate and share expertise and best practices, and establish a policy dialogue, ensuring the sustainability of UNDP's human rights support.

The most important partners will be the programme countries of UNDP and UN agencies involved in human rights. UNDP will also work with regional organisations like the Organisation of African Unity and bilateral donors and international institutions. And UNDP will continue to build partnerships with human rights and other NGOs and networks inside and outside the UN system.

Leadership by country offices is crucial because most of UNDP's resources and capacity are at the country level. Vital tasks for the country offices include identifying entry points and programme partners and designing and monitoring programmes and projects.

Subregional resource facilities will build capacity to support country operations. Human rights-related regional programmes, among others, can help share experiences, establish regional networks and centres of excellence, and undertake regional studies of trends.

The Bureau for Development Policy's Management Development and Governance Division is the UNDP's focal point for human rights at the global level, with three main responsibilities related to human rights—developing policies, tools and methodologies and documenting and disseminating best practices based on country experiences.

UN Secretary-General, Kofi Annan, in his report to the General Assembly, 'Renewing the United Nations: A Programme for Reform', states,

> Developments in the present decade have underscored that human rights are inherent to the promotion of peace, security, economic prosperity and social equity. . . . A major task for the future will be to enhance the human rights programme and integrate it into the broad range of the Organisation's activities, including in the development and humanitarian affairs areas."

The issue of human rights has been designated as cutting across the four substantive fields of the secretariat's work programme and will need to be integrated with all aspects of development cooperation.

## REFERENCES

Donnelly, Jack, *Universal Human Rights in Theory and Practice*, Ithaca: Cornell University Press, 1989.

Paine, Thomas, *The Rights of Man*, New York: Penguin Books, 1985.

Leonardo Despouy, *Conflict Prevention and Poverty Alleviation*, 1996.

'Governance for Sustainable Human Development', *Policy document*, 1997.

*Report on Conference on Governance, Leadership and Poverty Eradication*, Ougodougou, Burkina Faso, 1996.

*Report on International Conference for Sustainable Growth and Equity*, New York, 28-30, July 1997.

*Report on the Regional Conference on Governance and Social Development*, Beirut, Lebanon, 1997.

*Report on the Third International Conference of the New and Restored Democracies on Democracy and Development*, Bucharest, Romania, 2-4, September 1997.

*Report on the Third International Human Rights Conference*, Riga, Latvia, 1997.

*Survey of UNDP Activities in the Field of Human Rights*, 1997.

# 6
# Religion and Human Rights

The concept of human rights stands in the modern world as a set of universalistic ethical norms that state ideals for all human societies. They identify first principles and goals by which the community of nations may legitimate or delegitimate various legal systems or cultural practices and limit the use of state power against persons and groups. The very idea of universalistic norms is viewed by some as nothing more than the imposition of some particular set of religiocultural values on the other peoples of the world. That is due to the fact that in most of human history and in much of the world still today, ethical norms are rooted in religious orientations that seldom embrace human rights except in-so-far as they advance the particular religion.

The idea of ethical principles standing beyond religions, cultures, and societies, and able to evaluate and alter them, is to many a strange and hostile notion. Such an understanding of ethics requires that we tie thought and faith together in a philosophical theology, which is able to defend itself in public discourse, critically evaluate the relative adequacy of various religions on key questions, and provide the deep guidance system for complex societies and cultures. Modern articulations of human rights were born out of the attempt to constrain the great barbarisms of the twentieth century. In this context, ancient insights, which had been obscured or suppressed, were retrieved and made the basis for what is today called human rights. For the most part, the surge of interest in human rights that occurred after World War II turned to the formulations of human rights and democracy that grew out of the Enlightenment. However, it was only sometimes noted that these developments were themselves rooted in previously established theological assumptions that derive from antiquity—which the Enlightenment had claimed to overcome. While the great thinkers of the Enlightenment were familiar with the ancient sources, their heirs were not.

Hence, the interpretations of human rights that have come to triumph in the West are both derived from and opposed to their deeper religious roots. They nearly always ignore the greatest contribution of faith to human rights: namely, that some religious positions in alliance with selected philosophical traditions developed a transcendental view of the world and began to conceive of it as a whole, and thus to recognise that there is a perspective which is beyond time and space, culture and society, religion and morality which we inhabit when we imagine the unity.

At the close of the second millennium, the world is torn by crisis and tumult by a moral Armageddon, if not a military one. With the memories of world wars, gulags, and the Holocaust still fresh in our minds, we see the bloody slaughter of Rwanda and the Sudan, the tragic genocide of the Balkans, the massive unrest of the Middle East, Western Africa, Latin America, and the former Soviet bloc. On every continent, we see clashes between movements of incremental political unification and radical balkanisation, gentle religious ecumenicism and radical fundamentalism, sensitive cultural integration and rabid diversification, sensible moral pluralisation and shocking moral relativism. Even in the ostensibly peaceful societies of the West, bitter culture wars have aligned defenders of various old orders against an array of social, legal, and cultural deconstructionists.

It is time for us to take religious rights seriously to shake off our political indifference and parochial self-interest and to address the plight and protection of people of all faiths. It is time to exorcise the demons of religious intolerance that have beset both religious and non-religious peoples around the world and to exercise the golden rules of religious rights, doing unto other religious believers and beliefs what we would have done to us and ours. Human rights norms provide no panacea to the world crisis, but they are a critical part of any solution. Religions are not easy allies to engage, but the struggle for human rights cannot be won without them. For human rights norms are inherently abstract ideals, universal statements of the good life and the good society. They depend upon the visions of human communities and institutions to give them content and coherence, to provide the scale of values governing the exercise and concrete manifestation.

Religion is an ineradicable condition of human lives and communities; religions invariably provide universal sources and scales of values by which many persons and communities govern themselves. Religions must thus be seen as indispensable allies in the modern struggle for human rights. To exclude them from the struggle is impossible, and indeed catastrophic. To include them to enlist their unique resources and to protect their unique rights is vital to enhancing and advancing the regime of human rights.

If the world is a unity, and we can conceive of if as a whole—this, of course, means that we transcend it in some degree and do not simply live within it, trapped by its horizons—then we begin to suspect that it is governed by a unified moral law, even though the customs and habits of many people in the world and their ways of modelling the whole differ. Further, these customs, habits, and models can be altered according to a more ultimate and reliable pattern. The most pertinent developments of modernity, in this view, have to do with the recovery, radicalisation, propagation, and relative institution-alisation of an ethical vision of this sort.

Human rights provisions are now built into the constitutions of more peoples than any previous civilisation could have imagined, and are among the decisive criteria as to whether a religion, a culture, a regime, or a society should be honoured or altered, isolated or revolutionised.

However, this has also been the century in which we have faced dramatic challenges to these ideas. These challenges have taken and continue to take many forms—most notably the quests for the solidarity of a particular community against such universal and transcendental claims. Indeed, the greatest struggles of the twentieth century are of this order, one against the pagan anti-modernism of Hitlerian-Fascist National Socialism, another against the secularist hyper-modernism of Marxist Leninist Proletarian Socialism. Each manifested itself in massive political military movements that became the chief threats to human rights and to modernity in this century. Both have, in substantive measure, been defeated, although, like all great terrors, they writhe in their bonds and threaten to reappear from their graves in new forms.

A direct challenge to human rights from these defeated forces appeared in new conspiracy of anti-modernists and hyper-modernists who, while having apparently abandoned the Nazism of Hitler's politics and Communism of Stalinist economics, now join the internal entrepreneurs of Asia's liberalising economic policies and the business interests of the West who want access to Asia's cheap labour and vast markets to echo the defeated arguments.

In 1993, China led a coalition of nations, including Indonesia, Vietnam, Burma, Syria, and Iran that posed concepts of national sovereignty and state-supported development against democracy and human rights, as stated in the Bangkok Declaration, which became the basis for their postures in the UN conference on human rights in Vienna. The triumph of these developments in the long run is unlikely, unless the fundamental conception of human rights itself begins to collapse. The maledictive of political or economic gain may be decisive in many matters of indeterminate policy, but the deeper theological and ethical influences shape determinate matters of polity, and over time polity guides, leavens, and sets boundaries for policy.

The more profound threat to the idea of human rights as a determinate of polity, thus, is an attack from both its detractors and, unwittingly, from many of its defenders. A number of contemporary philosophers, social theorists, and religious thinkers of note have begun to doubt that there are such things as human rights, or have attempted to defend them in such terms as to make them impossible to sustain.

In perhaps the most famous absolutist denial of the validity of human rights, one of the premier philosophers of our day, Alasdair MacIntyre, wrote that the concept has no meaning at all:

> [T]he truth is plain: there are no such rights, and belief in them is one with belief in witches and unicorns.... The best reason for asserting so bluntly that there are no such rights is [the same]... reason for asserting that there are no witches.... [E]very attempt to give good reasons for believing that there are such rights has failed.... Natural or human rights... are fictions.

Leo Strauss, the widely regarded political philosopher who taught at Chicago for many years, has convinced a generation of young minds to become neo-conservative on the grounds that the classical ethical notion of natural rights and the proper exercise of virtue especially of prudence are subverted by this modern ideology of rights.

A major attempt to defend human rights from a liberal point of view has been advanced by Rhoda E. Howard and Jack Donnelly. They use sociological and anthropological theory to argue that human rights involve the affirmation of the autonomy and equality of every individual, in contrast to all the tribalisms, feudalisms, socialisms, communisms, and Communitarianisms, old and new, that view the individual as a part of a whole. They argue that the idea of rights is rooted in structural changes that began to emerge in late medieval and early modern Europe, gained particular force in the eighteenth and nineteenth centuries, and today are increasingly the norm throughout the world.

Human rights are seen to be an historical artifact, pertinent only in-so-far as social conditions stand at a particular stage of development, and subject to disappearance if those conditions do not obtain or eventually pass away. These philosophical and sociological views would be a great comfort to those in closed societies who use torture as a policy of governance or allow slave labour, for they can claim that they are at a particular stage of development. And neither are these scholars alone.

Literally hundreds of social commentators and clergy share this understanding of morality, even if they read the signs of the times of societal evolution differently. What is missing in these philosophical and sociological views is an account of why such matters as human rights, which cannot be derived from the empirical analysis of the world, prudentially or socio-historically, are plausible or why people should be committed to them, since it is empirically obvious that human rights are violated often and not everyone believes in them.

Human rights are based on nothing less than decisive theological convictions, distinct from but incorporating and utilising some of the best insights of philosophy and social theory. The challenges to human rights today, thus, are more subtle than the threats of Nazism and of Communism, for what we face is not likely to be overcome so quickly as these rose and fell—in a mere century or so.

The three great challenges for human rights in the next century are:

i) the decay of philosophy, and the consequent suspicion of any onto-theological account of how things are;

ii) the attempt to establish normative principles for civil society on the basis of social description alone—the sadly unfulfilled promise of the social sciences; and

iii) the power of resurgent, ancient religions, particularly Islam and Hinduism, which do have a normative metaphysical-moral vision and which have shown their capacity to organise complex and vast civilisations over long periods of time.

In their present forms, it is doubtful that any one of these three can sustain the idea of human rights in the long run—although it may turn out that Islam and Hinduism, or at least key strands of them, like key strands of Christianity critically refined by theology, will come closer than philosophy and sociology insofar as these try to remain detached from religion and theology.

To be sure, all of these are potential companions of the kind of ethic that could sustain human rights, if and when they develop a public theology in the sense that they seek to discern, under God, the moral and spiritual architecture whereby just and humane civilisations can be constructed. But it is also the case that if any one of them should become the dominant view without substantial reform, human rights are likely to be subordinated or lost.

## ISSUES OF RELIGION AND HUMAN RIGHTS

We cannot say that all religious orientations are good or equal or supportive of human rights. Some religions are quite destructive of all that human rights stands for, and the very intensity and potency of religion makes the destructiveness all the more vicious. It therefore makes a good deal of difference what sort of religion is at hand.

Such intensity and potency has at times been supportive and even generative of human rights, and that the commitment to a moral substratum which can guide the common life seems to appear most strongly in those societies informed by certain kinds of religious influence, and to be least vigorous in those societies shaped by other religious traditions or by anti-religion. We have a situation, thus, in which the freedom and vitality of religion at one level appears to depend on human rights, but in which the intensity and viability of human rights in society at another level seems to depend on the extent of certain kinds of religious influence.

Although there is considerable evidence that human rights are deeply and fundamentally dependent on religion and specifically on certain kinds of theological issues, it is equally clear that not all are convinced of this rather substantive point. Indeed, it is probable that for human rights to be recognised and sustained in the common life, two things are necessary: a theological understanding of normative reality, and a set of concrete institutional channels to actualise these normative visions in society and make them accessible in a civilisation.

The challenges to human rights are based upon doubts about the nature of theology as well as the confusion between confessionalism and theology. Religion is often treated as a strictly personal, cultural, or historical experience, and theology is understood to be its formal, dogmatic articulation. Thus, to root human rights in religion or theology is seen as a form of personal, cultural, or historical imperialism. Further, since we have come to wider awareness of the variety of religions in the world, it is hard for some to imagine that not all the religions contribute equally to moral matters.

Although the world religions have been around for centuries, they did not seem to many to be present as living options or necessarily related to human rights. The deep roots of human rights ideals are rooted nowhere else than in the biblical tradition, for it is here that we find the decisive unveiling of a perspective in which moral first principles demanding the respect for the neighbour are made known to humanity by a reality that is universal and absolute. This reality, which the Western traditions call 'God', is neither a figment of human imagination, a projection of our personal needs or tribal consciousness, nor a product of human creativity. Nor is this God morally neutral. This is an ethical God, the source and norm of a kind of justice and righteousness and contends against what we often find as we look around the world.

Christianity arose and radicalised the prophetic point of view, carried it into the Graeco-Roman world, and linked it to philosophical and jurisprudential theories that, on quite other grounds, also had begun to articulate a notion of a universal normative moral order. This interaction of faith and philosophy created theology and ethics as basic modes of discourse to guide thought and action on the most universalistic bases possible. These developments remained a minority tradition for centuries, and were often suppressed by pagan tendencies, power interests, and forms of myth and magic that could not be said to be universalistic, moral, faithful, or philosophically sound.

But periodically this tradition was retrieved and made central, to attempts to reform life, and to establish it on a more universalistic, more humane, and more godly foundation. This we can see in the revolutionary transformations of law and society so central to the history of the West, in the theological theories of conciliarism that anticipated and approximated constitutional democracy and especially in parts of the reformation that influenced the modern formation of human rights. However, it was periodically the case that precisely this tradition was distorted by both the ideological use of religion at the hands of political power to legitimate its interests, and the betrayal of the rational and ethical character of theology by religious leaders who made Christianity into a series of arbitrary dogmas to be accepted on blind faith, without intellectual justification, moral rigour, or a sense of what it meant to be for all peoples.

When the wars of religion of early modern Europe combined these perversions, the heritage was discredited in the eyes of the people. All sorts of post-Christian views of human moral *a priori*, self-evident truths and natural rights were developed to attempt to guide and strain political authority without religion, and to develop a cosmopolitan ethic that would allow the various obscurantist religions to hold their own dogmas albeit only as private preferences. Theology, in a public sense, was destroyed in favour of apolitical or pietistic feudalism, on one side, and an ontologically free-floating rationality, on the other. The destruction was called

Enlightenment. However, the Enlightenment could not carry the full load of what it attempted, and its rational fruits became instruments of oppression, even as it struggled to establish and maintain a sense of universal moral order. Its godless foundations could not bear the weight of all that the Enlightenment philosophers confidently placed upon them. The Enlightenment's initial success depended upon the deeper, but hidden, foundations which had been laid by theology.

We need to get and keep our history straight, although that would be a very good idea. It is quite possible for an idea that is generated out of one context to be found valid in another, and to become contextualised in forms of thought and life in ways that enhance possibilities within those adopted forms of thought and life that were only latently central to the new host. This, of course, produces revisionist history in the secondary tradition as happened to Greek philosophy and Roman law when they were wedded to biblical insights to form a theology which surpassed these original sources. Today human rights can best be seen as a part of the process of the recognition of the validity of decisive ethical concepts that, while offered and made actual by a particular tradition, are recognisably valid for all people and are essentially true for the world.

Human rights are a modern way of speaking about cross cultural ethical concepts that actualise certain valid theological presuppositions and in turn legitimates constraints on what humans or states can do to each other, where theology is understood to be the critically examined and systematically stated interpretation of what humanity is—sinful creatures not driven entirely by nature and nurture, that know we live under God who establishes moral laws and ends and contexts of life we cannot attain alone. Theology, in this view, is not merely the rationalised form of a social or cultural view legitimated by a privileged religion. It is also a necessary partner of philosophy and the social sciences, and a critic of religions, in clarifying, and establishing universal and valid ethical norms for an emerging global civilisation. Theology tells us whether this or that religion, our own or someone else's, is valid or whether it ought to be challenged on the grounds of its truth or its justice. This hypothesis then bears within it an ironic implication: it suggests the likelihood of religious, philosophical, and social conflict, for not all religions are equally capable of developing or sustaining a theology that can generate a universalistic ethic of jurisprudential importance.

It is doubtful whether human rights can be sustained without a theology that has certain definable characteristics, which we will attempt to indicate. Yet, as the threats of the anti-modernists on the right and the hyper-modernists on the left fade, increasingly frequent attacks are made upon the theological genealogy of human rights and the very possibility of anything being universal especially anything with normative content. A new surge of pragmatic anti-Enlightenment and anti-theological philosophy has attempted to deconstruct all aspects of culture, including language, with the reductive techniques of the social sciences, and to view the great world religions as evidence against the possibility of developing and sustaining a universalistic theological ethic.

Human rights would be on a more secure footing if we could place them on a foundation that has both a sustainable normativity and a concrete, institutional footing. The theological ethical considerations of the world religions bring these concerns together, because all of the axial religions express metaphysical-moral visions that entail normativity, and their civilisational expansiveness verifies their sustainability.

In many classic societies, religion is identified with one or more of these social structures, so that it is not strange to speak of a tribal, clan, or caste religion, an imperial, political or civic religion, a religion focused around the hunt, the harvest, or a religion of a cultural-linguistic grouping. In some societies, however, where religion is focused upon a culture-transcending, ethical reality, it becomes distinguished from these so that it is not to be identified with any one of them. There, quite often, we find the formation of voluntary associations—centres of bonding and meaning that are intentionally not tied to any of these, even if these associations continue to influence any or all of them. When this begins to happen, we find also the emergence of other independent institutions of society—law, science, medicine, and business—which also segregate particular activities into distinctive institutions.

Certain kinds of traditions have spawned voluntary associations, and thereby it is in institutional pluralism, nearly always populated by minorities at the outset, that we find the most promising institutional focus for the creedal recognition, affirmation, and nurture of human rights. Such associations are primarily called into existence by proselytising, ethical religions, where these transcend family, governments, special economic of cultural interests and try to influence them to approximate justice. These associations are also created in secular forms, once the space is established and rationalised by religious groups, and these associations can transmit the ethical ideas in routine institutions, quite often in forms which are not recognised as religious.

The world's major civilisational religions are, to use post-modernism's contemptuous phrase, totalising theories. God's covenant with Israel, commissions it to be a prophet to the nations. The Christian gospel is to be taken into all the world. The *Quran* is the Arabic words of Allah. The sounds of the Sanskrit words preexist the cosmos itself.

The world religions are allies in identifying a fundamental need to transform reality as we now find it, and together they form a cluster of formal deontological claims that categorically address all humans and all human societies. Every religion has something like universal moral laws that condemn murder, rape, lying, stealing, dishonouring religion and proper authority, and commanding truth-telling, promise-keeping, and upright living. Members of the religions can agree with each other, and often with philosophies that also seek to know the right order of things, and can cooperate on these bases about many matters concerning human rights.

All the great religious traditions have a way of interpreting and guiding the social context of life. They become attached to a socially and historically conditioned ideal, which determines what the most fitting context of life ought to be, and what kinds of concrete social arrangements best allow the right order of things to be actuated.

Every society has to have a way of dealing with familial, political, economic, and cultural matters; if the societies are complex, they must also have independent institutions for law, science, medicine, and business. Religious institutions and loyalties have been, and presumably always will be, closely allied with these, but how that connection is made from the standpoint of the religion will be decisive for the actual functioning of the first principles of right and wrong, including the ways in which human rights operate. If we look at Islam and Hinduism, we can see important elements of this dimension of religious ethics that bear upon human rights.

Islam, the religion founded by Prophet Mohammed, who was the mediator of the *Quran* and the first judge in legal cases, established a direct and immediate connection between faith and political and legal rule. It would, indeed, be very strange if religious organisations in that tradition did not draw a close connection between political, military, and legal principles, especially as they dealt with property, trade, and agreements among the heads of households, clans, tribes, and nations. Over the centuries, that has been quite characteristic, from the rise of the Caliphate, to the Iranian Revolution, to the new militancy nearly every Islamic country is now facing. Religion encouraged political and military expansion and thereby the establishment of the *Shari'a* and of trade When political and military expansion went well, religion flourished, marked by wider establishment of the sacred law and commercial success.

There have been grand moments in the history of Islam, when issues of cultural and philosophical genius, medicine, science, commercial fairness, and generosity to the poor have surpassed most other civilisations, and these arenas of life remain highly regarded by many devotees of the tradition. Of course, Islam, has quite distinctive teachings about family life, presumably born out of the political, military, and legal history of the faith, and quite supportive of an ethic which nourished their common life.

In the case of Hinduism which is organised by a priestly caste, it is viewed as superior to the military-political-legal custodians of public order, and they, in turn, are superior to those given to commerce and production. The fact that priestly domination triumphed over political and military rule in India is of basic significance; the priests have first-order contact with the first principles of morality, in a way that no other vocational group does. A caste hierarchy, determined by birth, sets the extended familial patterns at the core of religious association in a way that has no real analogy in Islam or Christianity.

Both Islam and Hinduism have elements of transcendence, of the dignity of the human soul, and of the necessity of legal protections for life. But neither has developed a general theory of human rights. However, these deeply embedded social orders are not beyond change, any more than the imperial and feudal structures of medieval Christianity were. Further, once the concept of human rights is presented to these traditions, and once the possibilities of a pluralistic and open civil society becomes accessible to them, and people within these faiths begin to adopt patterns of organisation that are neither totally given to political-legal militancy or to familiar-dynastic hierarchy, elements in their own traditions can be found that support the notion of human rights.

Religious traditions can alter and reform themselves in the light of new ideas and circumstances. Gandhi is the great symbol of what that kind of transformation might look like in Hinduism, and present debates in Islam suggest that some changes in a comparable direction are available to Islam. Great traditions change only uneasily, and some traditions get lost or simply become minority themes in other grand traditions as the history of Hinduism poignantly suggests, but as is also evident in the heterodox sects of Islam. Even more important is how the religions react to cosmopolitan, inter-cultural, and inter-religious contact—a crisis that is currently confronting Islam, Hinduism, and Christianity. To be sure, the direction of change is not fully predictable, and it is ambiguous whether these will bring about recognition of human rights.

The world religions offer constructive, forward-looking visions or teleologies, that is, guidance about how to discern good from evil consequences of our actions by considering them in reference to ultimate aims. This teleological dimension of ethical discourse is rather decisive in this process of selective adoption. As the traditions now stand, they have deeply formed, rich contexts, and these make the deontological and teleological conceptions concretely available to people.

While all the religions deconstruct the world with the absolute spectre of religious criticism and the call to transformation, they all also reconstruct it through imagination, doctrine, practice, and ritual so as to redeem or sanctify the world realities.

All the world religions also know that without a vision the people perish. Here, however, no hasty synthesis is possible: the Kingdom of God is neither *nirvana* nor the Paradise of the *Quran*, and liberation in Latin America means something quite different than the *moksha* and *bhakti*.

Thus human rights find possible support in the metaphysical moral visions of the world religions, though these are indigenised in various contexts, sometimes in ways that suppress the deontological insights. But what shall be made of the world is not so clear. It may well be the case, as many human rights advocates argue, that a high degree of agreement and clarity exists about the possible cooperation of religious believers on some matters bearing on human rights. Most also agree that contexts should be treated with care, although some appeals to context become contextualist ideologies of identity and pluralism that effectively resist every call to transform society toward greater justice.

On the question of teleology, however, there is neither agreement nor clarity. Often the role played by teleology in human rights is ignored, and when it is treated, it usually compromises the deontological character of rights. Undoubtedly this is partly the case because of the conflict between communitarians and universalists. We can invoke the *dharma*, the *dhamma*, the Mosaic law, the *Quran*, the Holy Spirit, and, in times past, the proletariat against the injustices we perceive in the world. We must also speak about what we and the various constituencies of the world's religions are for. And that moves us into an area where many are not comfortable—an area where one must not only be against the injustices of the world, but also ready to claim that some teleologies see farther and more than others.

## RELIGIOUS APPROACH TO RELIGIOUS RIGHTS

Among all the other ways to explore the situation of rights, one has been neglected but, if recovered, it should contribute to understanding and action. This is what we might call a religious approach to discussion of religious human rights. There are religious dimensions to struggles over religious human rights, and that religious studies in their many forms can illumine the inquiry. Such a proposal and understanding does not require every religious phenomenon to be the subject of reductionism, as currently is often the case. When reductionism is privileged, religious issues simply and quickly get translated to psychological, anthropological, sociological, or economic and political factors.

The quest for religious human rights in such cases is reduced to nothing. This reduction would lead to a situation in which when one hears the voice of the religious there is a temptation to say, this concern for religious rights is nothing but a power move by dissenters who want to be victorious insiders. Religious approaches would find scholars and diplomats suspending disbelief in the presence of homo-religious. They would take seriously the claims of individuals and groups to be grounded in ultimate concern, and see their individual and group identity issuing from response to myths and symbols, rites and ceremonies, metaphysical claims and behavioural correlates of that concern.

Religions' organisations do not respect the rights of its employees to bargain collectively and form unions, even while their leaders are occupied with advocacy for such unionising and bargaining rights in other spheres of employment. A teacher in a church-related college is threatened with loss of tenure, shunned, and virtually or actually driven out because academic rights are always secondary to religious claims as these are being guarded and professed by the momentarily-in-power leaders of that religion who support and represent the authority but never freedom in such a college. The child of Christian Scientists, Jehovah's Witnesses, or one or another of the small healing sects is deprived of the rights to life and health, thanks to the parental obedience to churchly teaching that is disrespectful of such rights.

In many countries members of religious groups are virtually, bound by authority so that they cannot challenge their own communities' prohibitions against birth control at United Nations conferences on the subject. Native Americans get reservated, and few non-Indians pay attention to their needs, including their need to defend rights to practice tribal rites of a sacred character and to do this apart from the superimposition of the will of their conquerors and reservators. A special challenge presents itself in all such cases when religious problems suggest religious addresses, if not always solutions.

What business does one religion or set of religious leaders have intruding on the religious practices of another group? When is such intrusion appropriate and when is it not? What rights do religionists have to protect themselves from efforts to convert them, especially when this is done by the use of instruments of power or deception? What rights do people have to impose their views on those who practise rites that are offensive to others? A vivid example is female circumcision. Many cultural relativists who fight for the right of other religions simply to be themselves find that there are boundaries beyond which such defence will not go. Thus they find religiously legitimated practices like female circumcision offensive and, on grounds alien to the practitioners of such a rite, want it stopped.

The introduction of specifically religious voices into religious and other rights talk makes the speakers and what they say both less comprehensible to outsiders and more vivid and satisfying to insiders in the particular traditions and communities. People of various faith communities live in and develop what phenomenologist Alfred Schutz calls different universes of discourse. These might include universes related to race, ethnicity, tribe, gender, class, culture, aesthetics, or national experience. Religious experience connected with any of these raises everything to a new plane of complication or to a new depth of understanding.

Family quarrels within religions often lead to suppression of rights. Islamic fundamentalist groups, by insisting on literal application of *Shari'a*, religious law, often embarrass, inconvenience, and thwart more moderate Muslim leaders and citizens, for example, in the matter of the rights of women.

The winners and losers in the Southern Baptist Convention or Missouri Synod Lutheran fights make appeals to the same primal texts and long elaborative traditions. But their interpretations vary, and the winners find the losers *de trop* and expel them from responsible positions or respectability within the denomination. Both Pope John Paul II and dissenting theologians appeal to biblical texts, but the Pope holds the power to take away the licence to teach priests if he disagrees with the theologians, whose resort to arguments for academic freedom and the accuracy of their interpretations of the Catholic tradition go unheeded and are ineffectual in the power situation.

When one introduces religious concerns to rights, the talk comes when a mediator seeks some sort of common ground. This is done so that there can be meaningful conversation across the boundaries of these separate universes of discourse or family conflicts. The cultural absolutist has it easy: my religion is the only right one, the only one that assures and deserves rights; others are all wrong. They have no rights, or at least can make no compelling case for expressing and defending them. The cultural relativist seems to have an equal advantage, though probably at the expense of any satisfactory outcome when there is conflict. Such a relativist says that anthro-pologists can always find somewhere, in some tribe or communion, a religiously-certified practice that violates any conception of common grounding, natural law, or whatever.

In many inquiries, the pro-community voices often speak up in terms that are disturbing to advocates of individual rights. Thus we can see that human rights are a product of modern, post-Enlightenment, liberal, secular humanism. This is a religiously alienating humanism because it elevates the individual to the point that the group is forgotten—yet it is precisely the group that makes the strongest religious claims. Conversation across the boundaries of debate over rights of individuals over groups versus rights of groups is always more difficult.

If religion is so complicating, so difficult, why deal with it? Why not be content with casual recourse or wilful reversion to non- or anti-religious arguments derived from Enlightenment era understandings of secular reasoning? In 1945 and 1948, it helped United Nations come to sufficient consensus or sufficient assertion of persuasive power that there could even be a UN Charter. Such an approach made it possible for the nations to speak of faith in fundamental human rights and to produce a Universal Declaration of Human Rights. On its grounds, the UN could produce contentions like these:

> Everyone has the right to education, and education should promote understanding, tolerance and friendship among all nations, racial or religious groups. . . .

The world community deals with religion because it is there and will not go away. If some forms of faith and institutions have dwindled, cooled, or even disappeared in the northern spiritual ice belt, there are temperate and tropical zones of spirituality where religion prospers. There it is the main motivator in the discussion of rights or their limits. The scholar or the adjudicator deals with religion because its professor claims that its impulses have derived from the vertical dimensions of experience. They issue from God or the heavens before respondents connect them with the horizontal elements. On that secondary plane, humans interact with each other both within and beyond the boundaries of religious communities.

The issue of human rights in religion has not been perceived as being clearly anticipated or enjoined in ancient sacred texts. The writers of these texts, in response to revelation or transcendent experience, had what to them were wider, deeper, and longer interests.

Religious cultures evolve, just as the ancient texts are rarely rich in the use of explicit rights language, so they do not freeze traditions, even those that claim to be frozen in literalist interpretations. They all belong to history, and they experience inevitable cultural change.

Most religious groups, whether they immediately supported the new talk or were dragged screaming into the sphere that it defined and illuminated, soon found it congenial and began to make claims that promoting such rights was their impulse all along. Hannah Arendt, among many others, noted how almost all the religions liked to claim that they were present at the creation of such rights-frameworks. She suggested that such religious spokespersons might at least send a card of thanks to modernity, to the Enlightenment, for having led them to the delayed discovery of the latent pro-human rights, pro-religious rights, elements in their treasury.

According to James Madison and Baptist elder and rights advocate John Leland, religion can help assure the rights of others. This assurance, say some advocates, need not result because of the obscuring or muting of religious concerns. It is not necessary to reduce them to only highly noncommittal, low-conviction, tolerant forms of faith in order to make them ready to be brought to bear on the issue.

Indeed, properly understood and cultivated, it might well yet turn out to be the case that it is now often the religions of deep commitment and high conviction that are of greatest aid. In that case, it is not the corrupted heir of eighteenth-century Enlightenment philosophy that best promotes tolerance by arguing that all beliefs have the same claims and quality all others.

How might one best defend the rights of those who serve as the other within a religious community? On what grounds should one urge the toleration of those people, with their rights, across the boundaries of community? Make it sound personal: How can I assure you that I will defend your rights and tolerate you despite our differences?

Gabriel Marcel argues that toleration (translated here to include the concept of defending the rights of someone within and between religious communities) is only a psychological reality, but must be approached phenomenologically. One is always tolerant, he argues, with respect to something. Tolerance is not mere non-prevention, non-prohibition, which in our case would mean not merely an attempt to prevent deprivation of the rights of another or to prevent a religion from ruling in prohibitive ways. The truly tolerant one is concerned to do more than support our human rights.

Thus tolerance is ultimately the negation of a negation, a counter-intolerance; it seems difficult for tolerance to be manifested before intolerance; tolerance is not primitive; it is to action what reflection is to thought. In any case, it is inconceivable without a certain power which sustains it and to which it is, as it were, attached; the more it is tied to a state of weakness, the less it is itself, the less it is tolerance. It has at least a vestige of a mandate connected with it. One is a steward, one has a trust to be responsible about rights of others; one is not merely psychologically moved to be empathic about one whose rights have been taken away. The accent falls less on the sincerity of the tolerant one than on the way she acts upon something conceived as a mandate.

## REFERENCES


Mayer, Ann, E., *Islam and Human Rights: Tradition and Politics*, 2nd ed., Boulder, CO: Westview Press, 1995.

An-Na'im, Abdullahi, Ahmed, *Toward an Islamic Reformation: Civil Liberties, Human Rights and International Law*, Syracuse University Press, 1990.

Writte, John, Jr., and Johan van der Vyver, eds., *Religious Human Rights in Global Perspectives: Religious Perspectives*, Dordrecht: Martinus Nijhoff, 1966.

Moltmann, Jurgen, The original study paper: a theoretical basis of human rights and of the liberation of human beings, in Allen and Miller (eds.),*A Christian Declaration on Human Rights*, 1977.

Nicholas, J.H., *Democracy and the Churches*, Westminster Press, Philandelphia.

Ichimare S. and B.P. Kirtisinghe, 'Human Rights and the Buddhist Concept of Law and Norm' in A. Adikari (ed.), *Sambbasha, the Mahadodhi Centenary Commemorative Volume*, Ministry of Education & Higher Education, Battaramulla, Sri Lanka, Vol. 1. No. 2, 1991.

# 7

# Children and Human Rights

It is a general belief that childhood as currently understood is a relatively recent creation. In the old days, the life of the young subjects was strictly monitored. The period before puberty was divided into two parts. During infancy, that is to say, up to the age of seven, the child was incapable of reason and could perform no legal act. Thereafter, the *pupillus* was granted a limited capacity, in other words, it could acquire rights but it was not entitled to alienate them, nor to incur duties. The modest objective of this chapter is to discuss the development and scope of human rights of children, an important component of any society.

Socially and physically speaking children represent the weakest pall of society. This situation often favours their exploitation in different areas; tabour, sexual integrity, etc. They depend for their survival on adults. Child abuse and neglect have been defined as the portion of harm to the child that results from human action or inaction, this is prescribed as proximate and preventable. Child abuse is active, neglect passive maltreatment. There are three main causes of child suffering war, poverty and social disruption. They all have a common denominator which is the economic impulse that rules on the rules societies.

The 1989 UNICEF report on the conditions of children in the world reveals that during the 1980s in the 37 poorest countries there has been a cut of 50 per cent on health expenditure and of 25 per cent on education. As a result, the average weight of these children has lessened, the proportion of children between six and 11 years attending school is family. Separation from family, community and the routines of normal life can be devastating to the children.

An idea that may find its realisation through the future Conventions on Right of the Child is that of stigmatising as unlawful forms of neglect that result in an implicit denial of a positive right enshrined by the law.

For instance, it would be illegal to employee a child in a job which would prevent it from attending school, thus affecting its right to education. To meet these ends, on 20th November, 1989, the United Nations General Assembly has adopted by unanimity the Convention on the Rights of the Child which entered into force on second September, 1990.

The expression is a wide consensus upon the opportunity of establishing a binding legal instrument for the global protection of children and it is the goal of an increased awareness concerning the many problems that affect children worldwide.

## CONVENTION ON THE RIGHTS OF THE CHILD*

### Preamble

The States Parties to the present Convention,

Considering that, in accordance with the principles proclaimed in the Charter of the United Nations, recognition of the inherent dignity and of the equal and inalienable rights of all members of the human family is the foundation of freedom, justice and peace in the world,

---

* Adopted by the General Assembly of the United Nations on 20th November 1989.

Bearing in mind that the peoples of the United Nations, have, in the Charter, reaffirmed their faith in fundamental human rights and in the dignity and worth of the human person, and have determined to promote social progress and better standards of life in larger freedom,

Recognising that the United Nations has, in the Universal Declaration of Human Rights and in the International Covenants on Human Rights, proclaimed and agreed that everyone is entitled to all the rights and freedoms set forth therein, without distinction of any kind, such as race, colour, sex, language religion, political or other opinion, national or social origin, property, birth or other status,

Recalling that, in the Universal Declaration of Human Rights, the United Nations has proclaimed that childhood is entitled to special care and assistance,

Convinced that the family, as the fundamental group of society and the natural environment for the growth and well-being of all its members and particularly children, should be afforded the necessary protection and assistance so that it can fully assume its responsibilities within the community,

Recognising that the child, for the full and harmonious development of his or her personality, should grow up in a family environment, in an atmosphere of happiness, love and understanding,

Considering that the child should be fully prepared to live an individual life in society, and brought up in the spirit of the ideals proclaimed in the Charter of the United Nations, and in particular in the spirit of peace, dignity, tolerance, freedom, equality and solidarity,

Bearing in mind the need to extend particular care to the child has been stated in the Geneva Declaration of the Rights of the Child of 1924 and in the Declaration of the Rights of the Child adopted by the General Assembly on 20 November 1959 and recognised in the Universal Declaration of Human Rights, in the International Covenant on Civil and Political Rights (in particular in Articles 23 and 24), in the International Covenant on Economic, Social and Cultural Rights (in particular in Article 10) and in the statutes and relevant instruments of specialised agencies and international organisations concerned with the welfare of children,

Bearing in mind as indicated in the Declaration of the Rights of the Child, "the child, by reason of his physical and mental immaturity, needs special safeguards and care, including appropriate legal protection, before as well as after birth",

Recalling the provisions of the Declaration on Social and Legal Principles relating to Protection and Welfare of Children, with Special Reference to Foster Placement and Adoption Nationally and Internationally; the United Nations Standard Minimum Rules for the Administration of Juvenile Justice (The Beijing Rules); and the Declaration on the Protection of Women and Children in Emergency and Armed Conflict,

Recognising that, in all countries in the world, there are children living in exceptionally difficult conditions, and at such children need special consideration,

Taking due account of the importance of the traditions and cultural values of each people for the protection and harmonious development of the child,

Recognising the importance of international cooperation for improving the living conditions of children in every country, in particular in the developing countries,

Have agreed as follows:

## Part I

### *Article 1*

For the purposes of the present Convention, a child means every human being below the age of eighteen years unless under the law applicable to the child, majority is attained earlier.

### *Article 2*

1. States Parties shall respect and ensure the rights set forth in the present Convention to each child within their jurisdiction without discrimination of any kind, irrespective of the child's or his or her parent's or legal guardian's race, colour, sex, language, religion, political or other opinion, national ethnic or social origin, property, disability, birth or other status.
2. States Parties shall take all appropriate measures to ensure that the child is protected against all forms of discrimination or punishment on the basis of the status, activities, expressed opinions, or beliefs of the child's parents, legal guardians, or family members.

### *Article 3*

1. In all actions concerning children, whether undertaken by public or private social welfare institutions, courts of law, administrative authorities or legislative bodies, the best interests of the child shall be a primary consideration.
2. States Parties undertake to ensure the child such protection and care as is necessary for his or her well-being, taking into account the rights and duties of his or her parents, legal guardians, or other individuals legally responsible for him or her, and to this end, shall take all appropriate legislative and administrative measures.
3. States Parties shall ensure that the institutions, services and facilities responsible for the care or protection of children shall conform with the standards established by competent authorities, particularly in the areas of safety, health, in the number and suitability of their staff, as well as competent supervision.

### *Article 4*

States Parties shall undertake all appropriate legislative, administrative, and other measures for the implementation of the rights recognised in the present Convention. With regard to economic, social and cultural rights, States Parties shall undertake such measures to the maximum extent of their available resources and, where needed, within the framework of international cooperation.

### *Article 5*

States Parties shall respect the responsibilities, rights and duties of parents or, where applicable, the members of the extended family or community as provided for by local custom, legal guardians or other persons legally responsible for the child, to provide, in a manner consistent with the evolving capacities of the child, appropriate direction and guidance in the exercise by the child, appropriate direction and guidance in the exercise by the child of the rights recognised in the present Convention.

### *Article 6*

1. States Parties recognise that every child has the inherent right to life.
2. States Parties shall ensure to the maximum extent possible the survival and development of the child.

### *Article 7*

1. The child shall be registered immediately after birth and shall have the right from birth to a name, the right to acquire a nationality and, as far as possible, the right to know and be cared for by his or her parents.
2. States Parties shall ensure the implementation of these rights in accordance with their national law and their obligations under the relevant international instruments in this field, in particular where the child would otherwise be stateless.

### *Article 8*

1. States Parties undertake to respect the right of the child to preserve his or her identity, including nationality,

name and family relations as recognised by law without unlawful interference.

2. Where a child is illegally deprived of some or all of the elements of his or her identity, States Parties shall provide appropriate assistance and protection, with a view to re-establishing speedily his or her identity.

### *Article 9*

1. States Parties shall ensure that a child shall not be separated from his or her parents against his/her will, except when competent authorities subject to judicial review determine, in accordance with applicable law and procedures, that such separation is necessary for the best interests of the child. Such determination may be necessary in a particular case such as one involving abuse or neglect of the child by the parents, or one where the parents are living separately and a decision must be made as to the child's place of residence.
2. In any proceedings pursuant to paragraph 1 of the present Article, all interested parties shall be given an opportunity to participate in the proceeding and make their views known.
3. States Parties shall respect the right of the child who is separated from one or both parents to maintain personal relations and direct contact with both parents on a regular basis, except if it is contrary to the child's best interests.
4. Where such separation results from any action initiated by a States Party, such as the detention, imprisonment, exile, deportation or death (including death arising from any cause while the person is in the custody of the State) of one or both parents or of the child, that State Party shall, upon request, provide the parents, the child or, if appropriate, another member of the family with the essential information concerning the whereabouts of the absent member(s) of the family unless the provision of

the information would be detrimental to the well-being of the child. States Parties shall further ensure that the submission of such a request shall of itself entail no adverse consequences for the person(s) concerned.

### Article 10

1. In accordance with the obligation of States Parties under article 9, paragraph 1, applications by a child or his or her parents to enter or leave a State Party for the purpose of family reunification shall be dealt with by States Parties in a positive, humane and expeditious manner. States Parties shall further ensure that the submission of such a request shall entail no adverse consequences for the applicants and for the members of their family.
2. A child whose parents reside in different states shall have the right to maintain on a regular basis, save in exceptional circumstances personal relations and direct contacts with both parents. Towards that end and in accordance with the obligation of States Parties under Article 9, paragraph 1, States Parties shall respect the right of the child and his or her parents to leave any country, including their own, and to enter their own country. The right to leave any country shall be subject only to such restrictions as are prescribed by law and which are necessary to protect the national security, public order (order public), public health or morals or the rights and freedoms of others and are consistent with the other rights recognised in the present Convention.

### Article 11

1. States Parties shall take measures to combat the illicit transfer and non-return of children abroad.
2. To this end, States Parties shall promote the conclusion of bilateral or multilateral agreements or accession to existing agreements.

### *Article 12*

1. States Parties shall assure to the child who is capable of forming his or her own views the right to express those views freely in all matters affecting the child, the views of the child being given due weight in accordance with the age and maturity of the child.
2. For this purpose, the child shall in particular be provided the opportunity to be heard in any judicial and administrative proceedings affecting the child, either directly, or through a representative or an appropriate body, in a manner consistent with the procedural rules of national law.

### *Article 13*

1. The child shall have the right to freedom of expression; this right shall include freedom to seek, receive and impart information and ideas of all kinds, regardless of frontiers, either orally, in writing or in print, in the form of art, or through any other media of the child's choice.
2. The exercise of this right may be subject to certain restrictions, but these shall only be such as are provided by law and are necessary:
   a) For respect of the rights or reputations of others, or
   b) For the protection of national security or of public order (order public), or of public health or morals.

### *Article 14*

1. States Parties shall respect the right of the child to freedom of thought, conscience and religion.
2. States Parties shall respect the rights and duties of the parents and when applicable, legal guardians, to provide direction to the child in the exercise of his or her right in a manner consistent with the evolving capacities of the child.
3. Freedom to manifest one's religion or beliefs may be subject only to such limitations as are prescribed by law

and are necessary to protect public safety, order, health or morals, or the fundamental rights and freedoms of others.

### *Article 15*

1. States Parties recognise the rights of the child to freedom of association and to freedom of peaceful assembly.
2. No restrictions may be placed on the exercise of these rights other than those imposed in conformity with the law and which are necessary in a democratic society in the interests of national security or public safety, public order (order public), the protection of public health or morals or the protection of the rights and freedoms of others.

### *Article 16*

1. No child shall be subjected to arbitrary or unlawful interference with his or her privacy, family, home or correspondence, nor to unlawful attacks on his or her honour and reputation;
2. The child has the right to the protection of the law against such interference or attacks.

### *Article 17*

States Parties recognise the important function performed by the mass media and shall ensure that the child has access to information and material from a diversity of national and international sources, especially those aimed at the promotion of his or her social, spiritual and moral well-being and physical and mental health. To this end, States Parties shall:

1. Encourage the mass media to disseminate information and material of social and cultural benefit to the child and in accordance with the spirit of Article 29.
2. Encourage international cooperation in the production, exchange and dissemination of such information and material from a diversity of cultural, national and international sources.

3. Encourage the production and dissemination of children's books.
4. Encourage the mass media to have particular regard to the linguistic needs of the child who belongs to a minority group or who is indigenous.
5. Encourage the development of appropriate guidelines for the protection of the child from information and material injurious to his or her well-being, bearing in mind the provisions of Articles 13 and 18.

### Article 18

1. States Parties shall use their best efforts to ensure recognition of the principles that both parents have common responsibilities for the upbringing and development of the child. Parents or, as the case may be, legal guardians, have the primary responsibility for the upbringing and development of the child. The best interests of the child will be their basic concern.
2. For the purpose of guaranteeing and promoting the rights set forth in the present Convention, States Parties shall render appropriate assistance to parents and legal guardians in the performance of their child-rearing responsibilities and shall ensure the development of institutions, facilities and services of the care of children.
3. States Parties shall take all appropriate measures to ensure that children of working parents have the right to benefit from child-care services and facilities for which they are eligible.

### Article 19

1. States Parties shall take all appropriate legislative, administrative social and educational measures to protect the child from all forms of physical or mental violence, injury or abuse, neglect or negligent treatment, maltreatment or exploitation, including sexual abuse, while in the care of parent(s), legal guardian(s) or any other person who has the care of the child.

2. Such protective measures should, as appropriate, include effective procedures for the establishment of social programmes to provide necessary support for the child and for those who have the care of the child, as well as for other forms of prevention and for identification, reporting, referral, investigation, treatment and follow-up of instances of child maltreatment described heretofore, and, as appropriate, for judicial involvement.

### *Article 20*

1. A child temporarily or permanently deprived of his or her family environment, or in whose own best interests cannot be allowed to remain in that environment shall be entitled to special protection and assistance provided by the State.
2. States Parties shall in accordance with their national laws ensure alternative care for such a child.
3. Such care could include, *inter alia*, foster placement *kafalah of Islamic law*, adoption or if necessary placement in suitable institutions for the care of children. When considering solutions, due regard shall be paid to the desirability of continuity in a child's upbringing and to the child's ethnic, religious, cultural and linguistic background.

### *Article 21*

States Parties that recognise and/or permit the system of adoption shall ensure that the best interests of the child shall be the paramount consideration and they shall:

1. Ensure that the adoption of a child is authorised only by competent authorities who determine, in accordance with applicable law and procedures and on the basis of all pertinent and reliable information, that the adoption is permissible in view of the child's status concerning parents, relatives and legal guardians and that, if required, the persons concerned have given their informed consent to the adoption on the basis of such counselling as may be necessary;

2. Recognised that inter-country adoption may be considered as an alternative means of child's care, if the child cannot be placed in a foster or an adoptive family or cannot in any suitable manner be cared for in the child's country of origin;
3. Ensure that the child concerned by inter-country adoption enjoys safeguards and standards equivalent to those existing in the case of national adoption;
4. Take all appropriate measures to ensure that, in inter-country adoption, the placement does not result in improper financial gain for those involved in it;
5. Promote, where appropriate, the objectives of the present article by concluding bilateral or multilateral arrangements or agreements, and endeavour, within this framework, to ensure that the placement of the child in another country is carried out by competent authorities or organs.

### *Article 22*

1. States Parties shall take appropriate measures to ensure that a child who is seeking refugee status or who is considered a refugee in accordance with applicable international or domestic law and procedures shall, whether unaccompanied or accompanied by his or her parents or by any other person, receive appropriate protection and humanitarian assistance in the enjoyment of applicable rights set forth in the present Convention and in other international human rights or humanitarian instruments to which the said states are parties.
2. For this purpose, States Parties shall provide, as they consider appropriate, co-operation in any efforts by the United Nations and other competent intergovernmental organisations or non-governmental organisations co-operating with the United Nations to protect and assist such a child and to trace the parents or other members of the family of any refugee child in order to obtain

information necessary for reunification with his or her family. In cases where no parents or other members of the family can be found, the child shall be accorded the same protection as any other child permanently or temporarily deprived of his or her family environment for any reason, as set forth in the present Convention.

### Article 23

1. States Parties recognise that a mentally or physically disabled child should enjoy a full and decent life, in conditions which ensure dignity, promote self-reliance and facilitate the child's active participation in the community.
2. States Parties recognise the right of the disabled child to special care and shall encourage and ensure the extension, subject to available resources, to the eligible child and those responsible for his or her care, of assistance for which application is made and which is appropriate to the child's condition and to the circumstances of the parents or others caring for the child.
3. Recognising the special needs of a disabled child, assistances extended in accordance with paragraph 2 of the present article shall be provided free of charge, whenever possible, taking into account the financial resources of the parents or others caring for the child, and shall be designed to ensure that the disabled child has effective access to and receives education, training, health care services, rehabilitation services, preparation for employment and recreation opportunities in a manner conducive to the child's achieving the fullest possible social integration and individual development, including his or her cultural and spiritual development.
4. States Parties shall promote, in the spirit of international cooperation, the exchange of appropriate information in the field of preventive health care and of

medical psychological and functional treatment of disabled children, including dissemination of and access to information concerning methods of rehabilitation, education and vocational services, with the aim of enabling States Parties to improve their capabilities and skills and to widen their experience in these areas. In this regard, particular account shall be taken of the needs of developing countries.

### *Article 24*

1. States Parties recognise the right of the child to the enjoyment of the highest attainable standard of health and to facilities for the treatment of illness and rehabilitation of health. States Parties shall strive to ensure that no child is deprived of his or her right of access to such health care services.
2. States Parties shall pursue full implementation of this right and, in particular, shall take appropriate measures:
   a) To diminish infant and child mortality;
   b) To ensure the provision of necessary medical assistance and health care to all children with emphasis on the development of primary health care;
   c) To combat disease and malnutrition, including within the framework of primary health care, through, *inter alia*, the application of readily available technology and through the provision of adequate nutritious foods and clean drinking water, taking into consideration the dangers and risks of environmental pollution;
   d) To ensure appropriate pre-natal and post-natal health care for mothers;
   e) To ensure that all segments of society, in particular parents and children, are informed, have access to education and are supported in the use of basic knowledge of child health and nutrition, the advantages of breast-feeding, hygiene and environmental sanitation and the prevention of accidents;

f) To develop preventive health care, guidance for parents and family planning education and services.

3. States Parties shall take all effective and appropriate measures with a view to abolishing traditional practices prejudicial to the health of children.
4. States Parties undertake to promote and encourage international cooperation with a view to achieving progressively the full realisation of the right recognised in the present article. In this regard, particular account shall be taken of the needs of developing countries.

### *Article 25*

States Parties recognise the right of a child who has been placed by the competent authorities for the purposes of care, pro-tection or treatment of his or her physical or mental health, to a periodic review of the treatment provided to the child and all other circumstances relevant to his or her placement.

### *Article 26*

1. States Parties shall recognise for every child the right to benefit from social security, including social insurance, and shall take the necessary measures to achieve the full realisation of this right in accordance with their national law.
2. The benefits should, where appropriate, be granted, taking into account the resources and the circumstances of the child and persons having responsibility for the maintenance of the child, as well as any other consideration relevant to an application for benefits made by or on behalf of the child.

### *Article 27*

1. States Parties recognise the right of every child to a standard of living adequate for the child's physical, mental, spiritual, moral and social development.

2. The parent(s) or others responsible for the child have the primary responsibility to secure, within their abilities and financial capacities, the conditions of living necessary for the child's development;
3. States Parties, in accordance with national conditions and within their means, shall take appropriate measures to assist parents and others responsible for the child to implement this right and shall in case of need provide material assistance and support programmes, particularly with regard to nutrition, clothing and housing.
4. States Parties shall take all appropriate measures to secure the recovery of maintenance for the child from the parents of other persons having financial responsibility for the child, both within the State Party and from abroad. In particular, where the person having financial responsibility for the child lives in a state different from that of the child, States Parties shall promote the accession to international agreements of the conclusion of such agreements, as well as the making of other appropriate arrangements.

### *Article 28*

1. States Parties recognise the right of the child to education, and with a view to achieving this right progressively and on the basis of equal opportunity, they shall, in particular:
   a) Make primary education compulsory and available free to all;
   b) Encourage the development of different forms of secondary education, including general and vocational education, make them available and accessible to every child, and take appropriate measures such as the introduction of free education and offering financial assistance in case of need;
   c) Make higher education accessible to all on the basis of capacity by every appropriate means;

d) Make educational and vocational information and guidance available and accessible to all children;

e) Take measures to encourage regular attendance at schools and the reduction of dropout rates.

2. States Parties shall take all appropriate measures to ensure that school discipline is administered in a manner consistent with the child's human dignity and in conformity with the present Convention.

3. States Parties shall promote and encourage international cooperation in matters relating to education, in particular with a view to contributing to the elimination of ignorance and illiteracy throughout the world and facilitating access to scientific and technical knowledge and modern teaching methods. In this regard, particular account shall be taken of the needs of developing countries.

### *Article 29*

1. States Parties agree that the education on the child shall be directed to:

a) The development of the child's personality, talents and mental and physical abilities to their fullest potential.

b) The development of respect for human rights and fundamental freedoms, and for the principles enshrined in the Charter of the United Nations.

c) The development of respect for the child's parents, his or her own cultural identity, language and values, for the national values of the country in which the child is living, the country from which he or she may originate, and for civilisations different from his or her own.

d) The preparation of the child for responsible life in a free society, in the spirit of understanding, peace tolerance equality of sexes, and friendship among all peoples, ethnic, national and religious groups and persons of indigenous origin.

e) The development of respect for the natural environment.

2. No part of the present Article or Article 28 shall be construed so as to interfere with the liberty of individuals and bodies to establish and direct educational institutions, subject always to the observance of the principle set forth in paragraph 1 of the present article and to the requirements that the education given in such institutions shall confirm to such minimum standards as may be laid down by the state.

### *Article 30*

In those states in which ethnic, religious or linguistic minorities or persons of indigenous origin exist, a child belonging to such a minority or who is indigenous shall not be denied the right, in community with other members of his or her group, to enjoy his or her own culture, to profess and practise his or her own religion, or to use his or her own language.

### *Article 31*

1. States Parties recognise the right of the child to rest and leisure, to engage in play and recreational activities appropriate to the age of the child and to participate freely in cultural life and the arts.
2. States Parties shall respect and promote the right of the child to participate fully in cultural and artistic life and shall encourage the provision of appropriate and equal opportunities for cultural, artistic, recreational and leisure activity.

### *Article 32*

1. States Parties recognise the right of the child to be protected from economic exploitation and from per-

forming any work that is likely to be hazardous or to interfere with the child's education, or to be harmful to the child's health or physical, mental, spiritual, moral or social development.

2. States Parties shall take legislative, administrative, social and educational measures to ensure the implementation of the present article. To this end, and having regard to the relevant provisions of other international instruments, States Parties shall in particular:
   a) Provide for a minimum age or minimum ages for admission to employment;
   b) Provide for appropriate regulation of the hours and conditions of employment; and
   c) Provide for appropriate penalties or other sanctions to ensure the effective enforcement of the present article.

### *Article 33*

States Parties shall take all appropriate measures, including legislative, administrative, social and educational measures, to protect children from the illicit use of narcotic drugs and psychotropic substances as defined in the relevant international treaties, and to prevent the use of children in the illicit production and trafficking of such substances.

### *Article 34*

States Parties undertake to protect the child from all forms of sexual exploitation and sexual abuse. For these purposes, States Parties shall in particular take all appropriate national, bilateral and multilateral measures to prevent:

1. The inducement or coercion of a child to engage in any unlawful sexual activity;
2. The exploitative use of children in prostitution or other unlawful sexual practices; and
3. The exploitative use of children in pornographic performances and materials.

### *Article 35*

States Parties shall take all appropriate national, bilateral and multilateral measures to prevent the abduction of the sale of or traffic in children for any purpose or in any form.

### *Article 36*

States Parties shall protect the child against all other forms of exploitation prejudicial to any aspects of the child's welfare.

### *Article 37*

States Parties shall ensure that:

1. No child shall be subjected to torture or other cruel, inhuman or degrading treatment or punishment. Neither capital punishment nor life imprisonment without possibility of release shall be imposed for offences committed by persons below eighteen years of age;
2. No child shall be deprived of his or her liberty unlawfully or arbitrarily. The arrest, detention or imprisonment of a child shall be in conformity with the law and shall be used only as a measure of last resort and for the shortest appropriate period of time;
3. Every child deprived of liberty shall be treated with humanity and respect for the inherent dignity of the human person, and in a manner which takes into account the needs of persons of his or her age. In particular, every child deprived of liberty shall be separated from adults unless it is considered in the child's best interest not to do so and shall have the right to maintain contact with his or her family through correspondence and visits, save in exceptional circumstances; and
4. Every child deprived of his or her liberty shall have the right to prompt access to legal and other appropriate assistance, as well as the right to challenge the legality of the deprivation of his or her liberty before a court or other competent, independent and impartial authority, and to a prompt decision on any such action.

*Article 38*

1. States Parties undertake to respect and to ensure respect for rules of international humanitarian law applicable to them in armed conflicts which are relevant to the child.
2. States Parties shall take all feasible measures to ensure that persons who have not attained the age of fifteen years do not take a direct part in hostilities.
3. States Parties shall refrain from recruiting any person who has not attained the age of fifteen years into their armed forces. In recruiting among those persons who have attained the age of fifteen years but who have not attained the age of eighteen years, States Parties shall endeavour to give priority to those who are oldest.
4. In accordance with their obligations under international humanitarian law to protect the civilian population in armed conflicts, States Parties shall take all feasible measures to ensure protection and care of children who are affected by an armed conflict.

*Article 39*

States Parties shall take all appropriate measures to promote physical and psychological recovery and social reintegration of a child victim of: any form of neglect, exploitation, or abuse; torture or any other form of cruel, inhuman or degrading treatment or punishment; or armed conflicts. Such recovery and reintegration shall take place in an environment which fosters the health, self-respect and dignity of the child.

*Article 40*

1. States Parties recognise the right of every child alleged as, accused of, or recognised as having infringed the penal law to be treated in a manner consistent with the promotion of the child's sense of dignity and worth, which reinforces the child's respect for the human rights and fundamental freedoms of others and which takes into account the child's age and the desirability of

promoting the child's reintegration and the child's assuming a constructive role in society.

2. To this end, and having regard to the relevant provisions of international instruments, States Parties shall, in particular, ensure that:
   a) No child shall be alleged as, be accused of, or recognised as having infringed the penal law by reason of acts or omissions that were not prohibited by national or international law at the time they were committed.
   b) Every child alleged as or accused of having infringed the penal law has at least the following guarantees:
      i) To be presumed innocent until proven guilty according to law;
      ii) To be informed promptly and directly of the charges against him or her, and, if appropriate, through his or her parents of legal guardians, and to have legal or other appropriate assistance in the preparation and presentation of his or her defence.
      iii) To have the matter determined without delay by a competent, independent and impartial authority or judicial body in a fair hearing according to law, in the presence of legal or other appropriate assistance and, unless it is considered not to be in the best interest of the child, in particular, taking into account his or her age or situation, his or her parents or legal guardians.
      iv) Not to be compelled to give testimony or to confess guilt; to examine or have examined adverse witnesses and to obtain the participation and examination of witnesses on his or her behalf under conditions of equality.
      v) If considered to have infringed the penal law to have this decision and any measures imposed in

consequence thereof reviewed by a higher competent, independent and impartial authority or judicial body according to law.

vi) To have the free assistance of an interpreter if the child cannot understand or speak the language used.

vii) To have his or her privacy fully respected at all stages of the proceedings.

3. States Parties shall seek to promote the establishment of laws, procedures, authorities and institutions specifically applicable to children alleged as, accused of or recognised as having infringed the penal law, and, in particular:

a) The establishment of a minimum age below which children shall be presumed not to have the capacity to infringe the penal law; and

b) Whenever appropriate and desirable measures for dealing with such children without resorting to judicial proceedings, providing that human rights and legal safeguards are fully respected.

4. A variety of dispositions, such as care, guidance and supervision orders; counselling; probation; foster care; education and vocational training programmes and other alternatives to institutional care shall be available to ensure that children are dealt with in a manner appropriate to their well being and proportionate both to their circumstances and the offence.

### *Article 41*

Nothing in the present Convention shall affect any provisions which are more conducive to the realisation of the rights of the child and which may be contained in:

1. The law of a State Party; or
2. International law in force for that State.

## Part II

### *Article 42*

States Parties undertake to make the principles and provisions of the Convention widely known, by appropriate and active means, to adults and children alike.

### *Article 43*

1. For the purpose of examining the progress made by States Parties in achieving the realisation of the obligations undertaken in the present Convention, there shall be established a Committee in the Rights of the Child, which shall carry out the functions hereinafter provided.
2. The Committee shall consist of ten experts of high moral standing and recognised competence in the field covered by this Convention. The members of the Committee shall be elected by States Parties from among their nationals and shall serve in their personal capacity, consideration being given to equitable geographical distribution, as well as to the principal legal systems.
3. The members of the Committee shall be elected by secret ballot from a list of persons nominated by States Parties. Each State Party may nominate one person from among its own nationals.
4. The initial election to the Committee shall be held no later than six months after the date of the entry into force of the present Convention and thereafter every second year. At least four months before the date of each election, the Secretary-General of the United Nations shall address a letter to States Parties inviting them to submit their nominations within two months. The Secretary-General shall subsequently prepare a list in alphabetical order of all persons thus nominated, indicating States Parties which have nominated them, and shall submit it to the States Parties to the present Convention.

5. The elections shall be held at meetings of States Parties convened by the Secretary-General at United Nations Headquarters. At those meetings, for which two thirds of States Parties shall constitute a quorum, the persons elected to the Committee shall be those who obtain the largest number of votes and an absolute majority of the votes of the representatives of States Parties present and voting.
6. The members of the Committee shall be elected for a term of four years. They shall be eligible for re-election if renominated. The term of five of the members elected at the first election, shall expire at the end of two years; immediately after the first election the names of these five members shall be chosen by lot by the Chairman of the meeting.
7. If a member of the Committee dies or resigns or declares that for any other cause he or she can no longer perform the duties of the Committee, the State Party which nominated the member shall appoint another expert from among its nationals to serve for the remainder of the term, subject to the approval of the Committee.
8. The Committee shall establish its own rules of procedure.
9. The Committee shall elect its officers for a period of two years.
10. The meetings of the Committee shall normally be held at United Nations Headquarters or at any other convenient place as determined by the Committee. The Committee shall normally meet annually. The duration of the meetings of the Committee shall be determined, and reviewed, subject to the approval of the General Assembly.
11. The Secretary-General of the United Nations shall provide the necessary staff and facilities for the effective performance of the functions of the Committee under the present Convention.

12. With the approval of the General Assembly, the members of the Committee established under the present Convention shall receive emoluments from United Nations resources on such terms and conditions as the Assembly may decide.

### *Article 44*

1. States Parties undertake to submit to the Committee, through the Secretary-General of the United Nations, reports on the measures they have adopted which give effect to the rights recognised herein and on the progress made on the enjoyment of those rights:
   a) Within two years of the entry into force of the Convention for the State Party concerned; and
   b) Thereafter every five years.
2. Reports made under the present article shall indicate factors and difficulties, if any affecting the degree of fulfilment of the obligations under the present Convention. Reports shall also contain sufficient information to provide the Committee with a comprehensive understanding of the implementation of the Convention in the country concerned.
3. A State Party which has submitted a comprehensive initial report to the Committee need not, in its subsequent reports submitted in accordance with paragraph 1 (b) of the present article, repeat basic information previously provided.
4. The Committee may request from States Parties further information relevant to the implementation of the Convention.
5. The Committee shall submit to the General Assembly, through the Economic and Social Council, every two years, reports on its activities.
6. States Parties shall make their reports widely available to the public in their own countries.

### Article 45

In order to foster the effective implementation of the Convention and to encourage international cooperation in the field covered by the Convention:

1. The specialised agencies, the United Nations Children's Fund, and other United Nations organs shall be entitled to be represented at the consideration of the implementation of such provisions of the present Convention as fall within the scope of their mandate. The Committee may invite the specialised agencies, the United Nations Children's Fund and other competent bodies as it may consider appropriate to provide expert advice on the implementation of the Convention in areas falling within the scope of their respective mandates. The Committee may invite the specialised agencies, the United Nations Children's Fund, and other United Nations organs to submit reports on the implementation of the Convention in areas falling within the scope of their activities;
2. The Committee shall transmit, as it may consider appropriate to the specialised agencies, the United Nations Children's Fund and other competent bodies, any reports from States Parties that contain a request, or indicate a need, for technical advice or assistance, along with the Committee's observations and suggestions, if any, on these requests or indications;
3. The Committee may recommend to the General Assembly to request the Secretary-General to undertake on its behalf studies on specific issues relating to the rights of the child;
4. The Committee may make suggestions and general recommendations based on information received pursuant to articles 44 and 45 of the present Convention. Such suggestions and general recommendations shall be transmitted to any State Party concerned and reported to the General Assembly, together with comments, if any, from States Parties.

## Part III

### Article 46

The present Convention shall be open for signature by all States.

### Article 47

The present Convention is subject to ratification. Instruments of ratification shall be deposited with the Secretary-General of the United Nations.

### Article 48

The present Convention shall remain open for accession by any State. The instruments of accession shall be deposited with the Secretary-General of the United Nations.

### Article 49

1. The present Convention shall enter into force on the thirtieth day following the date of deposit with the Secretary-General of the United Nations of the twentieth instrument of ratification or accession.
2. For each State ratifying or acceding to the Convention after the deposit of the twentieth instrument of ratification or accession, the Convention shall enter into force on the thirtieth day after the deposit by such State of its instrument of ratification or accession.

### Article 50

1. Any State Party may propose an amendment and file it with the Secretary-General of the United Nations. The Secretary-General shall thereupon communicate the proposed amendment to States Parties, with a request that they indicate whether they favour a conference of States Parties for the purpose of considering and voting upon the proposal. In the event that, within four months from the date of such communication, at least one-third of the States Parties favour such a conference, the

Secretary-General shall convene the conference under the auspices of the United Nations. Any amendment adopted by a majority of States Parties present and voting at the conference shall be submitted to the General Assembly for approval.

2. An amendment adopted in accordance with paragraph 1 of the present article shall enter into force when it has been approved by the General Assembly of the United Nations and accepted by a two-thirds majority of States Parties.
3. When an amendment enters into force, it shall be binding on those States Parties which have accepted it, other States Parties still being bound by the provisions of the present Convention and any earlier amendments which they have accepted.

### *Article 51*

1. The Secretary-General of the United Nations shall receive and circulate to all States the text of reservations made by States at the time of ratification or accession.
2. A reservation incompatible with the object and purpose of the present Convention shall not be permitted.
3. Reservations may be withdrawn at any time by notification to that effect addressed to the Secretary-General of the United Nations, who shall then inform all states. Such notification shall take effect on the date on which it is received by the Secretary-General.

### *Article 52*

A State Party may denounce the present Convention by written notification to the Secretary-General of the United Nations. Denunciation becomes effective one year after the date of receipt of the notification by the Secretary-General.

### *Article 53*

The Secretary-General of the United Nations is designated as the depository of the present Convention.

### *Article 54*

The original of the present Convention, of which the Arabic, Chinese, English French, Russian and Spanish text are equally authentic, shall be deposited with the Secretary-General of the United Nations.

In Witness Whereof the undersigned plenipotentiaries, being duly authorised thereto by their respective Governments have signed the present Convention.

The inalienable rights of the child are in consonance with the principles and philosophy proclaimed in the United Nations' charter—a document of fundamental significance. For peace, prosperity, and social progress, justice with equity and the building up of a stable peaceful world order, a clear cut recognition of the rights of the child is inevitable. For a proper and balanced development of the child, the state and the society have to create a conductive environment that subsumes happiness, compassion and deep understanding of his psyche. Given the infancy, modern, society has created a plethora of national and international organisations/institutions to safeguard and secure the welfare of children. They need special care and safeguards including appropriate legal protection, further growth, flourishment and contribution to international peace and prosperity. In line with this kind of approach, attempts have been made on a global scale to prevent any discrimination based on caste, class, creed, etc., so that the child's survival and development is secured.

The child's right to freedom of part expression/thought, conscience and religion and peaceful assembly are part of his fundamental human rights. The covenant also enjoins the state to take appropriate administrative, social and educational measures to protect the child from all forms of physical, mental violence, injury or abuse, maltreatment or exploitation including sexual abuse.

In recent years, the child has become the victim of economic exploitation. He has to work in an environment that is not conductive to his health or physical, mental, moral or social development. Hence, the states are enjoined to provide for a minimum age or wages for admission to employment including regulation of the hours and terms and conditions of employment.

The concerns of the rights of the child also provide for rules of international humanitarian law applicable during war or armed hospitalities. The rules are explicit and include among others, the physical and psychological recovery and social integration of the child. For the effective implementation of the provisions of the covenant, the United Nations specialised agencies, the United Nations Children' fund and many NGO's devote considerable time and agency to enable the child to become a major instrumentality or tool for the all-round development of the society eventually contributing to the quality, tenor and substance of contemporary human civilisation.

## EDUCATION FOR THE FUTURE

Education gives shape and structure to children's lives and can instil community values, promote justice and respect for human rights and enhance peace, stability and interdependence. It has a crucial preventive and rehabilitative part to play in fulfilling the needs and rights of children in conflict and post-conflict situations. Unfortunately, not even schools are safe from attack during times of armed conflict. In rural areas the school building may be the only substantial permanent structure, making it highly susceptible to shelling, closure or looting. Often, local teachers are prime targets because they are important community members or because they may hold strong political views.

The destruction of education networks represents one of the greatest developmental setbacks for countries affected by armed conflict. Lost education and vocational skills take years to replace, making the overall task of post-war recovery even more difficult. If countries continue to employ four times as many soldiers as teachers, education and social systems will remain fragile and inadequate, and governments will continue to fail children and break the promises made to them through ratification of the Convention on the Rights of the Child.

During situations of armed conflicts, fear and disruption make it difficult to create an atmosphere conducive to learning, and the morale of both teachers and pupils is likely to be low. As conflicts drag on for months or even years, economic and social conditions suffer and educational opportunities become more limited or even cease to exist altogether. Sometimes, even when educational opportunities exist in war-torn areas, parents may be reluctant to send their children to school. They may be afraid that the children will not be safe while they are on their way to and from school, or during classes.

When children have been forced to leave their homes and are crowded into displaced persons camps, establishing schooling systems as soon as possible reassures everyone by signalling a degree of stability and a return to normal roles and relationships within the family and community. Refugee children can sometimes attend regular schools in host countries, as provided for in international law, though very few get the opportunity to do so. It is important to carry on educating children and young people, no matter how difficult the circumstances. Education promotes their psychosocial and physical well-being. Teachers can recognise signs of stress in children as well as impart vital survival information on issues such as personal safety and health or the dangers of landmines.

Flexible systems of distance learning, home or group study using pre-packaged teaching materials complemented by broadcast and recorded media, are especially valuable for girls when parents are reluctant to have them travel far from home. Education can also be strengthened through a variety of community channels.

When public sector agencies are absent or severely weakened, community groups and non-governmental organisations (NGOs) can support local educational administrators in their efforts to keep children in schools. All states must come together to build ethical frameworks, integrating traditional values of cooperation through religious and community leaders with international legal standards, such as the United Nations Convention on the Rights of the Child. Some of the groundwork for this can be laid in schools. Both the content and the process of education should promote peace, social justice, respect for human rights and the acceptance of responsibility.

## REFERENCES

*A Human Rights Approach to UNICEF Programming for Children and Women*, Part I, C3.

Gomango, S. P., *Child Labour: A Precarious Future*, Authorspress, New Delhi, 2001.

Lee-Wright, P., 1990, *Child Slaves*, London, Eathscan.

Piggozzi, Mary Joy, *Implications of the Convention on the Rights of the Child for Education Activities Supported by UNICEF*, UNICEF, New York, March 1997.

United Nations Commission on Human Rights, *Report of the Working Group on Contemporary Forms of Slavery* (Geneva): Annual Reports, see especially 1985-87.

# 8

# Women and Human Rights

Women's human rights is a revolutionary notion. This radical reclamation of humanity and the corollary insistence that women's rights are human rights have profound transformative potential. The incorporation of women's perspectives and lives into human rights standards and practice forces recognition of the dismal failure of countries worldwide to accord women the human dignity and respect that they deserve simply as human beings. A woman's human rights framework equips women with a way to define, analyse, and articulate their experiences of violence, degradation, and marginality.

During the UN Decade for Women (1976-1985), women from many geographical, racial, religious, cultural, and class backgrounds took up organising to improve the status of women. The United Nations-sponsored women's conferences, which took place in Mexico City in 1975, Copenhagen in 1980, and Nairobi in 1985, were convened to evaluate the status of women and to formulate strategies for women's advancement. These conferences were critical venues at which women came together, debated their differences and discovered their commonalties, and gradually began learning to bridge differences to create a global movement.

In the late eighties and early nineties, women in diverse countries took up the human rights framework and began developing the analytic and political tools that together constitute the ideas and practices of women's human rights.

Taking up the human rights framework has involved a double shift in thinking about human rights and talking about women's lives. Put quite simply, it has entailed examining the human rights framework through a gender lens, and describing women's lives through a human rights framework.

In looking at the human rights framework from women's perspectives, women have shown how current human rights definitions and practices fail to account for the ways in which already recognised human rights abuses often affect women differently because of their gender. This approach acknowledges the importance of the existing concepts and activities, but also points out that there are dimensions within these received definitions that are gender-specific and that need to be addressed if the mechanisms, programmes, and the human rights framework itself are to include and reflect the experiences of the female half of the world's population. When people utilise the human rights framework to articulate the vast array of human rights abuses that women face, they bring clarifying analyses and powerful tools to bear on women's experiences.

This strategy has been pivotal in efforts to draw attention to human rights that are specific to women that heretofore have been seen as women's rights but not recognised as human rights. Take, for example, the issue of violence against women. The Universal Declaration states: "No one shall be subject to torture or to cruel, inhuman or degrading treatment or punishment". This formulation provides a vocabulary for women to define and articulate experiences of violence such as rape, sexual terrorism and domestic violence as violations of the human right not to be subject to torture or to cruel, inhuman or degrading treatment or punishment.

The concept of women's human rights has opened the way for women around the world to ask hard questions about the official inattention and general indifference to the widespread discrimination and violence that women experience everyday. Whether used in political lobbying, in legal cases, in grassroots mobilisation, or in broad-based educational efforts, the idea of women's human rights has been a rallying point for women across many boundaries and has facilitated the creation of collaborative strategies for promoting and protecting the human rights of women. While women have raised questions for a long time about why their rights are seen as ancillary to human rights, a coordinated effort to change this attitude using a human rights framework gained particular momentum in the early part of the 1990s.

The opening of space for new debates afforded by the end of the Cold War facilitated the exchange of ideas and experiences among women around the world that led to strategising about how to make women's human rights perspectives more visible. As women's activities developed globally during and following the United Nations' Decade for Women, more and more women raised the question of why women's rights and women's lives have been deemed secondary to the human rights and lives of men.

Over the past decade, a movement around women's human rights has emerged to challenge limited notions of human rights, and it has focused particularly on violence against women as a prime example of the bias against women in human rights practice and theory. The United Nations World Conference on Human Rights held in Vienna in 1993 was the first such meeting since 1968, and it became a natural vehicle to highlight the new visions of human rights thinking and practice being developed by women.

Since the conference represented an historic reassessment of the status of human rights, it became the unifying public focus of a worldwide Global Campaign for Women's Human Rights—a broad and loose international collaborative effort to advance women's human rights. The campaign launched a petition calling upon the World Conference to comprehensively address women's human rights at every level of its proceedings and to recognise gender violence, a universal phenomenon which takes many forms across culture, race, and class as a violation of human rights requiring immediate action.

The petition was eventually translated into 23 languages, and was used by over 1,000 sponsoring groups who gathered a half million signatures from 124 countries. The petition and its demands instigated discussions about why women's rights, and gender-based violence in particular, were left out of human rights considerations, and served to mobilise women around the World Conference. Women acted to inject issues of women's human rights into the entire pre-conference preparatory process: Women from all regions demanded that women's human rights be discussed at the preparatory meetings held in Tunis, San Jose, and Bangkok, as well as at other non-governmental and national preparatory events.

The idea of women's human rights was a framework for women to articulate and collaborate around broad and similar concerns about the status of women; it also provided women with a way to elaborate on the most pressing human rights issues specific to particular political, geographic, economic, and cultural contexts. By the time the World Conference convened, the idea that women's rights are human rights had become the rallying call of thousands of people all over the world and one of the most discussed new human rights debates.

The Vienna Declaration and Programme of Action, which is the product of the conference and is meant to signal the agreement of the international community on the status of human rights, states unequivocally that:

> The human rights of women and of the girl-child are an inalienable, integral and indivisible part of universal human rights. Vienna Declaration (1,18,1993).

At subsequent United Nations Conferences, women continued to lobby for and gain wider recognition of women's human rights. So, for example, at the International Conference on Population and Development in Cairo in 1994, women's reproductive rights were explicitly recognised as human rights. A particularly significant development was the way in which the Platform for Action at the IV World Conference on Women in Beijing in 1995 became virtually an agenda about the human rights of women. This signalled the successful mainstreaming of women's rights as human rights. The agreements that are produced by such conferences are not legally binding; however, they do have ethical and political weight and can be used to pursue regional, national, or local objectives.

Conference documents can also be used to reinforce and interpret international treaties such as the Covenant on Civil and Political Rights, or the Covenant of Social, Economic and Cultural Rights. These covenants, when signed by a country, do have the status of international law and have been used in courts by lawyers seeking redress for human rights violations. The most important international treaty specifically addressing women's human rights is the Convention on the Elimination of All Forms of Discrimination Against Women (CEDAW) which was initiated during the UN Decade for Women and has been ratified by over 130 countries.

Women's human rights not only teaches women about the range of rights that their governments must honour; it also functions as a kind of gestalt by which to organise analyses of their experiences and plan action for change. The human rights framework creates a space in which the possibility for a different account of women's lives can be developed. What is so useful about this framework is that it provides women with principles by which to develop alternative visions of their lives without suggesting the substance of those visions. The fundamental principles of human rights that accord to each and every person the entitlement to human dignity give women a vocabulary for describing both violations and impediments to the exercise of their human rights. The large body of international covenants, agreements and commitments about human rights gives women political leverage and a tenable point of reference.

In the Fourth World Conference on Women in Beijing in September 1995, the then United Nations Secretary-General, Boutros Boutros Ghali, said that violence against women is a universal problem that must be universally condemned. But he said that the problem continues to grow. The Secretary-General noted that domestic violence alone is on the increase. Studies in 10 countries, he said, have found that between 17 per cent and 38 per cent of women have suffered physical assaults by a partner. In the Platform for Action, the core document of the Beijing Conference, Governments declared that violence against women constitutes a violation of basic human rights and is an obstacle to the achievement of the objectives of equality, development and peace.

Advancement of women's rights has concerned the United Nations since the Organisation's founding. Yet the alarming global dimensions of female-targeted violence were not explicitly acknowledged by the international community until December 1993, when the United Nations General Assembly adopted the Declaration on the Elimination of Violence against Women. Until that point, most governments tended to regard violence against women largely as a private matter between individuals, and not as a pervasive human rights problem requiring state intervention. In view of the alarming growth in the number of cases of violence against women throughout the world, the Commission on Human Rights adopted resolution 1994/45 of 4 March 1994, in which it decided to appoint the Special Rapporteur on violence against women, including its causes and consequences. As a result of these steps, the problem of violence against women has been drawing increasing political attention.

Females fall prey to violence before they are born, when expectant parents abort their unborn daughters, hoping for sons instead. In other societies, girls are subjected to such traditional practices as circumcision, which leave them maimed and traumatised. In others, they are compelled to marry at an early age, before they are physically, mentally or emotionally mature. Women are victims of incest, rape and domestic violence that often lead to trauma, physical handicap or death. And rape is still being used as a weapon of war, a strategy used to subjugate and terrify entire communities.

The Platform for Action adopted at the Fourth World Conference on Women declared that rape in armed conflict is a war crime and could, under certain circumstances, be considered genocide. Secretary-General Boutros-Ghali told the Beijing Conference that more women today were suffering directly from the effects of war and conflict than ever before in history.

The Declaration on the Elimination of Violence against Women is the first international human rights instrument to exclusively and explicitly address the issue of violence against women. It affirms that the phenomenon violates, impairs or nullifies women's human rights and their exercise of fundamental freedoms. The Declaration provides a definition of gender-based abuse, calling it "any act of gender-based violence that results in, or is likely to result in, physical, sexual or psychological harm or suffering to women, including threats of such acts, coercion or arbitrary deprivation of liberty, whether occurring in public or in private life". The definition is amplified in Article 2 of the Declaration, which identifies three areas in which violence commonly takes place:

i) Physical, sexual and psychological violence that occurs in the family, including battering; sexual abuse of female children in the household; dowry-related violence; marital rape; female genital mutilation and other traditional practices harmful to women; non-spousal violence; and violence related to exploitation;
ii) Physical, sexual and psychological violence that occurs within the general community, including rape; sexual abuse; sexual harassment and intimidation at work, in educational institutions and elsewhere; trafficking in women; and forced prostitution; and
iii) Physical, sexual and psychological violence perpetrated or condoned by the state, wherever it occurs.

The importance of the question of violence against women was emphasised over the last decade through the holding of several expert group meetings sponsored by the United Nations to draw attention to the extent and severity of the problem. In September 1992, the United Nations Commission on the Status of Women established a special Working Group and gave it a mandate to draw up a draft declaration on violence against women. The following year, the United Nations Commission for Human Rights, in resolution 1993/46 of 3 March, condemned all forms of violence and violations of human rights directed specifically against women.

The Vienna World Conference on Human Rights laid extensive groundwork for eliminating violence against women. In the Vienna Declaration and Programme of Action, governments declared that the United Nations system and member states should work towards the elimination of violence against women in public and private life; of all forms of sexual harassment, exploitation and trafficking in women; of gender bias in the administration of justice; and of any conflicts arising between the rights of women and the harmful effects of certain traditional or customary practices, cultural prejudices and religious extremism.

## TYPES OF VIOLENCE AGAINST WOMEN

Violence against women takes a dismaying variety of forms, from domestic abuse and rape to child marriages and female circumcision. All are violations of the most fundamental human rights.

### Domestic Violence

Domestic violence against women occurs in developed and developing countries alike. It has long been considered a private matter by bystanders—including neighbours, the community and government. But such private matters have a tendency to become public tragedies. In the United States, a woman is beaten every 18 minutes. Indeed, domestic violence is the leading cause of injury among women of reproductive age in the United States.

Despite governments' promises to guarantee women's equality and full rights under the constitutions of their countries, governments denied women legal freedom to achieve such rights. In many countries statutory restrictions curtailed, among other things, women's ability to inherit property, contract marriage, and seek divorce.

In South Africa, women married under customary law were still considered minors and could not enter into any legal contract without the consent of their husbands or guardians. In India, Syria, and Pakistan women were discriminated against in divorce and inheritance laws.

The Zimbabwe's highest court ruled in February 1999 in *Magaya vs. Magaya* that women were perpetual minors without the legal capacity to inherit property and that it was not contrary to the anti-discrimination clause of the Zimbabwean Constitution to give preference to male heirs in inheritance rights. The Zimbabwean Constitution's anti-discrimination clause did not apply to customary law. This constitutional limitation effectively undercut women's rights and status in the family, especially in instances where customary law governed cases of marriage, divorce, inheritance, and other personal matters. The Magaya case was met with outrage by women's groups in Zimbabwe, who considered it a major setback in their efforts to achieve equal status for women under the law.

Many governments now recognise the importance of protecting victims of domestic abuse and taking action to punish perpetrators. The establishment of structures allowing officials to deal with cases of domestic violence and its consequences is a significant step towards the elimination of violence against women in the family. The Special Rapporteur's report highlights the importance of adopting legislation that provides for prosecution of the offender. It also stresses the importance of specialised training for law enforcement authorities as well as medical and legal professionals, and of the establishment of community support services for victims.

In many countries, women fall victim to traditional practices that violate their human rights. The persistence of the problem has much to do with the fact that most of these physically and psychologically harmful customs are deeply rooted in the tradition and culture of society.

## Female Genital Mutilation

The World Health Organisation (WHO) have reported that 85 million to 115 million girls and women in the population have undergone some form of female genital mutilation and suffer from its adverse health effects. Every year an estimated two million young girls undergo this procedure. Most live in Africa and Asia, but an increasing number can be found among immigrant and refugee families in Western Europe and North America. Indeed, the practice has been outlawed in some European countries. In France, a Malian was convicted in a criminal court after his baby girl died of a female circumcision-related infection. The procedure had been performed on the infant at home. There is a growing consensus that the best way to eliminate these practices is through educational campaigns that emphasise their dangerous health consequences.

## Son Preference

The consequences of son preference can be anything from foetal or female infanticide to neglect of the girl-child over her brother in terms of such essential needs as nutrition, basic health care and education. In China and India, some women choose to terminate their pregnancies when expecting daughters but carry their pregnancies to term when expecting sons. According to reports from India, genetic testing for sex selection has become a booming business, especially in the country's northern regions. Indian gender-detection clinics drew protests from women's groups after the appearance of advertisements suggesting that it was better to spend $38 now to terminate a female foetus than $3,800 later on her dowry.

## Dowry-related Violence

In many countries, weddings are preceded by the payment of an agreed-upon dowry by the bride's family. Failure to pay the dowry can lead to violence. In India, an average of five women a day are burned in dowry-related disputes.

## Early Marriage

Early marriage, especially without the consent of the girl, is another form of human rights violation. Early marriage followed by multiple pregnancies can affect the health of women for life. The report of the Special Rapporteur has documented the destructive effects of marriage of female children under 18 and has urged governments to adopt relevant legislation.

## Rape

Rape occurs in the community, where a woman can fall prey to any abuser. It also occurs in situations of armed conflict and in refugee camps. In the United States, national statistics indicate that a woman is raped every six minutes. In 1995, the case of a Brazilian jogger raped and murdered in New York City's Central Park drew international attention once again to the problem. The incident occurred only a few years after an earlier sensational jogger-assault case in which the victim— an American assaulted in the same general area of the park — barely survived after her assailants left her for dead.

Relations between residents of the Japanese island of Okinawa and American GIs were thrown into turmoil in 1995 after two marines and a sailor allegedly kidnapped and raped a

12-year-old girl. The Special Rapporteur's report underlines the importance of education to sensitise the public about the special horrors of rape, and of sensitivity training for the police and hospital staff who work with victims.

## Sexual Harassments

In many countries sexual assault by a husband on his wife is not considered to be a crime: a wife is expected to submit. It is thus very difficult in practice for a woman to prove that sexual assault has occurred unless she can demonstrate serious injury. The report of the Special Rapporteur noted that light sentences in sexual assault cases send the wrong message to perpetrators and to the public at large: that female sexual victimisation is unimportant.

Sexual harassment in the workplace is a growing concern for women. Employers abuse their authority to seek sexual favours from their female co-workers or subordinates, sometimes promising promotions or other forms of career advancement or simply creating an untenable and hostile work environment. Women who refuse to give in to such unwanted sexual advances often run the risk of anything from demotion to dismissal. But in recent years more women have been coming forward to report such practices.

## Prostitution

Many women are forced into prostitution either by their parents, husbands or boyfriends or as a result of the difficult economic and social conditions in which they find themselves. They are also lured into prostitution, sometimes by 'mail-order bride' agencies that promise to find them a husband or a job in a foreign country. As a result, they very often find themselves illegally confined in brothels in slavery-like conditions where they are physically abused and their passports withheld. Most women initially victimised by sexual traffickers have little inkling of what awaits them. They generally get a very small percentage of what the customer pays to the pimp or the brothel owner. Once they are caught up in the system there is practically no way out, and they find themselves in a very vulnerable situation.

Since prostitution is illegal in many countries, it is difficult for prostitutes to come forward and ask for protection if they become victims of rape or want to escape from brothels. Customers, on the other hand, are rarely the object of penal laws. In Thailand, prostitutes who complain to the police are often arrested and sent back to the brothels upon payment of a fine.

The extent of trafficking in women and girl children has reached alarming proportions, especially in Asian countries. Many women and girl children are trafficked across borders, often with the complicity of border guards. In one incident, five young prostitutes were burned to death in a brothel fire because they had been chained to their beds. At the same time, sex tours of developing countries are a well-organised industry in several European and other industrialised countries. The Special Rapporteur has called on governments to take action to protect young girls from being recruited as prostitutes and to closely monitor recruiting agencies.

## Violence against Women Workers

According to the International Labour Organisation's (ILOs) estimates in ten years 80 per cent of all women in industrialised countries and 70 per cent globally would work outside the home. Human rights violations continued for women trapped in forced labour throughout the world. As the numbers of women in the labour market swelled, their disproportionate responsibility for uncompensated domestic labour did not diminish. On average, in a review of the issue in selected developing countries, the United Nations Development Programme (UNDP) reported that women's work burden was 113 per cent that of men. In industrialised countries, women's share was 105 per cent that of men.

The US government reported that murder continued to be the leading cause of women's death in the workplace. In Mexico, the government side-stepped its duty to protect women in the export-processing sector from corporate discrimination. Human Rights Watch's research in 1998 and 1999 demonstrated that corporations operating in this sector subjected virtually all women applicants to pregnancy exams or other methods of determining pregnancy status as a condition of work; denied employment to those who were pregnant; and put those who became pregnant after being hired at the risk of being fired. These problems continued despite local, national, and international efforts to improve conditions in the *maquiladoras*.

As a part of a Human Rights Watch-initiated review under the labour rights side agreement of the North American Free Trade Agreement (NAFTA), the United States engaged Mexico in ministerial-level consultations on the issue of pregnancy-based sex discrimination against women. One component of the ministerial consultation agreement was a trilateral conference in Merida, Yucatan, in March 1999. At that conference, Mexico continued to vacillate on the issue of women's right to equality in the labour force. Mexican officials avoided the issues under consideration, disseminated misinformation, and denied their labour law obligations. In one such episode, the Mexican government at long last admitted that pre-hire pregnancy testing violated its labour law, but then undermined the significance of its admission by justifying pregnancy testing as long as it was intended to protect the woman's reproductive health or the health of her fetus.

Despite excellent organisation and planning by local women's NGOs, the NAFTA process in this case produced only slim results in 1999. In contrast to the slow progress of the NAFTA process, two days after being sworn in as Mexico City's first female mayor at the end of September 1999, Rosario

Robles signed into force a new law that would punish Mexico City businesses that required women to take a pregnancy test before being hired.

Through coercion, deception, and debt bondage, traffickers held women in involuntary servitude and slavery-like conditions. Trafficking of women from Thailand to Japan remained a large-scale problem in 1999, as thousands of women from Thailand travelled to Japan to work. Although their initial decisions to migrate were voluntary, the vast majority found themselves trapped in debt bondage and forced into prostitution by the agents who facilitated their travel. Recruiters and agents regularly deceived women about the nature of the work, wages, debt amounts, and/or working conditions.

Once in Japan, women were given no choice over their occupation or terms of employment. While in debt, women could not refuse clients or clients' demands and received no compensation for their labour. Agents and traffickers enforced the repayment of debts through abusive tactics such as passport deprivation, illegal confinement, physical violence, and threats of resale into renewed levels of debt. The government of Japan, as in many other destination countries, approached trafficking as an immigration problem, summarily deporting women found working illegally. In rare cases, the Japanese government prosecuted abusive traffickers and agents for employing illegal aliens. But victims of trafficking did not have access to justice or compensation for the severe human rights violations they had suffered while in Japan.

US federal law enforcement officials brought indictments against thirteen ringleaders of a nationwide trafficking network. Federal prosecutors alleged that the traffickers had brought hundreds of young women and girls from Asia to work in forced prostitution in cities throughout the United States. According to press accounts, traffickers held the women in debt bondage, forcing them to perform approximately 600 sex acts without salary before their debt was cleared. In many trafficking cases in the United States, women were arrested, detained, and deported without any opportunity to file charges or demand compensation from employers.

Hundreds of women from the former Soviet Union and Eastern Europe, some of them promised lucrative employment opportunities in West European countries, found themselves sold into slavery-like conditions and held as virtual prisoners in cafe-bars throughout the Federation and Republika Srpska. The women had no legal redress; instead, local law enforcement officials in Bosnia and Herzegovina often forced the women to stand trial, fined them, and deported them across county lines, allowing traffickers to pick them up and sell them to another bar owner.

Women migrant workers themselves fare badly, and sometimes tragically. Many become virtual slaves, subject to abuse and rape by their employers. They typically leave their countries for better living conditions and better pay—but the real benefits accrue to both the host countries and the countries of origin. For home countries, money sent home by migrant workers is an important source of hard currency, while receiving countries are able to find workers for low-paying jobs that might otherwise go unfilled.

In regions of Middle East and Persian Gulf, there are an estimated 1.2 million women, mainly Asians, who are employed as domestic servants. According to the independent human rights group Middle East Watch, female migrant workers in Kuwait often suffer beatings and sexual assaults at the hands of their employers. The police are often of little help. In many cases, women who report being raped by their employers are sent back to the employer or are even assaulted at the police station. Working conditions are often appalling, and employers prevent women from escaping by seizing their passports or identity papers. There are many international instruments that can be used to prevent abuse against migrant women and suggests some measures to protect the human rights of migrant women.

## Violence against Women Refugees

Women and children form the great majority of refugee populations all over the world and are especially vulnerable to violence and exploitation. In refugee camps, they are raped and abused by military and immigration personnel, bandit groups, male refugees and rival ethnic groups. They are also forced into prostitution. The number of refugees and internally displaced persons assisted by United Nations High Commissioner for Refugess (UNHCR) in 1998 exceeded 21 million people. The populations of refugees and displaced persons around the world remained predominantly made up of women and their dependent children.

Women refugees had limited or no legal recourse for sexual and domestic violence, partly as a result of their unfamiliarity with and wariness of local police and judicial authorities and partly because of the lack of proactive, systematic, and sensitive responses by the relevant international and local authorities. In many situations women faced particular protection and security risks in refugee camps, as well as the challenges of heading households while suffering from their disadvantaged status as women.

Refugee women were subjected to rape, sexual assault, and other forms of sexual violence. Levels of domestic violence were also reported to be very high in many refugee communities, perhaps because in the refugee setting, pressures regarding housing, food, security, and resources further strained domestic situations and erupted in violence. Moreover, extended networks of family, neighbours, and community leaders that may have acted as a deterrent to abuse no longer existed in the unfamiliar territory of refugee camps.

## Post-conflict Discrimination

Despite assurances made in 1995 at the UN Conference on Women in Beijing, many governments continued to discriminate against women directly or to allow others to do so unimpeded. When the opportunity arose to remedy this discrimination, particularly during post-conflict reconstruction and development periods, the international community passed it by, choosing instead to reinforce previously existing patterns of discrimination. As a consequence, women faced many barriers in their access to justice, services, and resources, with many governments refusing to recognise, let alone remedy, the laws and practices perpetuating women's inequality. While some countries took positive steps toward ensuring women's equality, patterns of discrimination against women surfaced in the laws, policies, and practices of governments and non-governmental bodies around the world.

The Taliban militia in Afghanistan, having gained territorial control of 90 per cent of the country, continued to enforce official gender-based discrimination unparalleled in its harshness. The discriminatory measures imposed by the Taliban not only completely marginalised Afghan women from the mainstream of political life, they placed women's very survival, and that of their families, at risk. The enforcement of the Taliban's strictures on women varied to some extent in different areas of the country, but this geographical variation in enforcement was largely a matter of degree rather than substance. The restrictions had a severely detrimental effect on women's health, security, and personal freedoms in all areas under Taliban control.

In most parts of Afganistan, the education of girls and the employment of women outside the health sector remained banned or severely restricted. In some areas, however, home- or mosque-based education for girls was reportedly permitted. In most areas, women could not appear in public without a *burqa*, a garment that cloaks the head, face, and body. Women's freedom of movement was severely curtailed as they were generally required to appear in public escorted by a male relative or *mahram*. Punishments for violations of these edicts were extremely harsh.

## Violence against Women in Armed Conflict

During times of armed conflict, women's rights were in particular jeopardy. During these periods, judicial structures that should both prevent violence against women and respond to it were in disarray, could not be relied on and, in some cases, were controlled by the very people who were instigating or participating in rapes. In every civil conflict in recent memory-including East Timor, Afghanistan, Angola, Indonesia, Sierra Leone, Kosovo, the Mexican state of Chiapas, Algeria, Bosnia, the Democratic Republic of Congo-women were targeted for sexual violence.

One of the most promising developments of 1999 was that important international actors such as the United Nations successfully identified gender-specific abuses committed against women at the start of conflicts, rather than not at all or only once those conflict were long over, as had been the pattern in the past. This early recognition, however, was still not matched by vigorous investigation and prosecution of perpetrators of rape, tasks that were often left to post-conflict national authorities.

The international community was able to do very little to prevent sexual violence in conflict. In fact, combatants defied international standards prohibiting rape and, in some cases, made sexual assault a deliberate weapon. As a consequence, in 1999 many women were treated as reward for soldiers, targeted for forced marriage and domestic labour, and attacked as substitutes for their male relatives or as symbols of communities' honour and reproductive capacity.

Women of Sierra Leone faced severe sexual abuse in country's eight-year civil war, mainly at the hands of Revolutionary United Front (RUF) rebel forces. In January 1999, RUF rebels launched an offensive against the capital, Freetown, temporarily capturing it from government troops and the soldiers of the Nigerian-led peacekeeping force. During this attack, RUF rebels detained women at base camps, raped them daily for weeks, and forced them to cook and clean for rebel leaders. The fragile July peace agreement crafted between the government of Sierra Leone and the RUF merely recognised the violence that women suffered and called for special attention to integrating women into post-conflict reconstruction and development, while, at the same time, granting a blanket amnesty to combatants.

During Serbian-Kosovo war, Serbian paramilitaries entered the homes of ethnic Albanians and raped women and girls in front of their families or outside in their gardens. An unknown number of women and girls died after these attacks. In other instances, Serbian paramilitaries, many of them volunteer irregular soldiers bussed in from Serbia, demanded money from fleeing Kosovar Albanians, threatening to rape, kill, or torture those who did not comply.

Serb paramilitaries subjected an unknown number of women to gang rapes in forests, in trucks, or along the road. They held women captive for periods ranging from twenty minutes to several days. In some cases, paramilitaries forced women to undress and subjected them to physical searches and interrogations. Many women found these searches terrifying, fearing that they were a precursor to rape.

Violence against women in conflict situations remained so persistent that governments consistently failed to hold perpetrators accountable post-conflict. Women raped in conflict had to contend not only with post-conflict impunity for what happened to them, but also with the dire health consequences of rape. In addition to psychological trauma, physical injuries, and sexually transmitted diseases, sexually abused women faced HIV infection, a potential death sentence, especially in countries in which health care and medicine were scant.

## Custodial Violence against Women

Custodial violence against women is widespread. Women are physically or verbally abused; they also suffer sexual and physical torture. According to Amnesty International, thousands of women held in custody are routinely raped in police detention centres worldwide. States should prosecute those accused of abusing women while in detention and to hold them accountable for their illegal actions.

## STATES' RESPONSE TO VIOLENCE AGAINST WOMEN

Despite some positive efforts by state and non-state actors, abuses against women were carried out frequently and with virtual impunity, as states largely failed to fulfil their obligations to prevent and provide redress for such crimes. States were particularly negligent in addressing violence in the family. This problem received widespread international attention in recent years, but concrete action was slow in coming. Japan, for example, only began to consider specific legislation and support services to combat domestic violence in mid-1999.

The United Nations International Children's Emergency Fund (UNICEF) reported in 1999 that violence against women was rising in post-communist countries as economic crises increased women's financial dependence upon men. In many of these states, domestic violence was not prohibited by law and marital rape was not recognised as a crime. Speaking on a more global level, in her 1999 report to the UN Commission on Human Rights, the special rapporteur on violence against women noted the growing prevalence of violence against women generally and domestic violence specifically.

Russian attempts to pass national legislation on women violence against women, the topic failed, and little was done to improve the state response to the abuse. The federal government did not make financial resources available for combating violence against women. Activists, expressing frustration with the lack of progress nationally, focused their attention on local level initiatives, establishing cooperative links with local law enforcement, city officials, and journalists.

The number of non-governmental crisis centres grew across the country, while the few existing government-sponsored centres and shelters closed due to budget cuts. Crisis centre leaders travelled throughout Russia, training judges, police, and activists on rape and domestic violence issues. The Russian Association of Crisis Centres for Women officially registered in 1999 and held a national meeting in September to coordinate its activities.

According to current estimates in Pakistan eight women were raped every twenty-four hours and 70 to 95 per cent of women had experienced domestic or familial violence. Extreme forms of familial violence included so-called honour killings and bride burnings, with both practices claiming the lives of hundreds of women every year. Women victims of violence who turned to the criminal justice system confronted a discriminatory legal regime, venal and abusive police, untrained doctors, incompetent prosecutors, and sckeptical judges. As a result, few women reported crimes of violence, and fewer still saw their attackers punished.

The Mexicoan government revised its rape law in several important ways. A provision was eliminated that allowed a man who raped a minor to avoid prosecution if he agreed to marry her. Now judges are required to hand down a decision regarding access to an abortion within five working days.

The government of Canada announced a new four-year Family Violence Initiative intended to mobilise community action, strengthen Canada's legal framework, establish services on Indian communities, develop resources to help victims and stop offenders, and provide housing for abused women and children.

A Ministry of State for Women was established in Turkey, whose main goals are, among others, to promote women's rights and strengthen their role in economic, social, political and cultural life. Legal measures are being adopted towards the elimination of violence against women. The establishment of special courts to deal with violence is envisaged. Psychological treatment for abused women is also planned, along with the establishment of women's shelters around the country. Specially trained female police officers could provide assistance to victims of violence.

Many governments have introduced police units specially trained for dealing with spousal assault. It is a well known fact that states have tended to adopt a passive attitude when confronted by cases of violations of women's rights by private actors. Most laws fail to protect victims or to punish perpetrators. Passing laws to criminalise violence against women is an important way to redefine the limits of acceptable behaviour. States should ensure that national legislation, once adopted, does not go unenforced.

State responsibility is clearly underlined in Article 4 of the Declaration on the Elimination of Violence against Women, which stipulates that "States should exercise due diligence to prevent, investigate and, in accordance with national legislation, punish acts of violence against women, whether those acts are perpetrated by the State or by private persons". Any approach designed to combat violence must be twofold, addressing the root causes of the problem and treating its manifestations. Society at large, including judges and police officers, must be educated to change the social attitudes and beliefs that encourage male violence.

Combating violence against women requires challenging the way that gender roles and power relations are articulated in society. In many countries women have a low status. They are considered as inferior and there is a strong belief that men are superior to them and even own them. Changing people's attitude and mentality towards women will take a long time—at least a generation, many believe, and perhaps longer. Nevertheless, raising awareness of the issue of violence against women, and educating boys and men to view women as valuable partners in life, in the development of a society and in the attainment of peace are just as important as taking legal steps to protect women's human rights. It is also important in order to prevent violence that non-violent means be used to resolve conflict between all members of society.

## ROLE OF INTERNATIONAL COMMUNITY

The international community is confronting the challenges of protecting and promoting women's human rights in conflict and post-conflict situations. Although some significant steps were taken toward greater protection of women's rights, the conflict in Kosovo reminded human rights defenders yet again how sexual violence against women paradoxically can be used to rally support for military intervention and yet risk being ignored when holding perpetrators of human rights violations accountable.

### United Nations

On twentieth anniversary of the Convention on the Elimination of All Forms of Discrimination against Women (CEDAW), Deputy Secretary-General Louise Frechette recognised how violence and discrimination against women pushes them to society's margins: Women are more commonly found in part-time work in the informal sector, among the unemployed and the underemployed. Women's work in subsistence farming and in family enterprises is ignored and there are no social security, health or old age benefits attached to such work.

Aware of its role in ending the human rights violations that reduce women's status, the United Nations and its various programmes and agencies continued their slow progress in integrating protection of women's rights into their work. For example, the UN Food and Agricultural Organisation (FAO) conducted an analysis of the impact of education of women on food production and determined that increasing women's primary schooling alone could increase agricultural output worldwide by 24 per cent.

After determining that information provided by agricultural extension agents to male heads of households is rarely conveyed to women in the same households, FAO implemented programmes to ensure that women, particularly those cultivating subsistence crops, received information and services. In addition, UNESCO organised, in partnership with governmental and non-governmental groups, a Pan African Women's Conference on a Culture of Peace in Zanzibar in May to design ways for women to influence the making of policy, particularly as the policies pertain to conflict prevention, conflict resolution, and peace building.

The final Zanzibar Declaration and Women's Agenda for a Culture of Peace was to be submitted to the United Nations, the Organisation for African Unity (OAU), and the World Bank for approval and financial support. At the same time, diminishing voluntary contributions from governments threatened to close the International Research and Training Institute for the Advancement of Women (INSTRAW), the only UN institute focusing exclusively on women.

The UN's ability to galvanise successfully government funding to save INSTRAW has to be a measure of its commitment to programmes supporting women's rights. The Commission on the Status of Women took a significant step toward protecting women from human rights violations by adopting, after four years of negotiations, an optional protocol to CEDAW. The protocol, which was to enter into force after ratification by ten states, would enable women to submit claims of rights violations to the Committee on the Elimination of Discrimination against women, and would create an inquiry procedure enabling the committee to initiate investigations into situations of grave or systematic violations of women's rights. On October 6, 1999, the UN General Assembly adopted without vote the optional protocol to CEDAW.

The International Criminal Tribunal for the former Yugoslavia (ICTY) appeared to have increased its credibility among women reporting conflict-related violations. Women meeting at a July conference in Vienna on rape in the Kosovo conflict expressed hope that perpetrators of sexual violence in Kosovo would be brought before the ICTY. However, all participants agreed that the women victims and witnesses needed to be represented by their own counsel to protect their interests.

The ICTY still had not created a witness protection and assistance unit which women trusted. Bosnian women scheduled to testify before the ICTY on rape charges told Human Rights Watch that they had no luck seeking help with immigration claims and relocation issues. With the threat of forced repatriation hanging over their heads, witnesses temporarily residing in Germany and other third countries feared what they perceived as the potentially deadly consequences of testifying without a guarantee that they would not be forcibly returned to Bosnia.

UNHCR was inundated with funds to provide for the refugees, and the media tracked it's every move. This contrasted sharply with the inattention of the international community and media to ongoing and larger refugee crises in Africa. Yet UNHCR demonstrated in Kosovo that, if adequately resourced, it could respond better to these crises and the specific protection needs of women refugees.

UNHCR largely ignored sexual and domestic violence in the emergency phase of the camps and later responded to the problems in an ad hoc manner. Only in the first half of 1999 did UNHCR adopt a more comprehensive and coordinated response to violence against women in the camps. In February 1999, Human Rights Watch met with UNHCR staff in Geneva to discuss UNHCR's response to sexual and domestic violence in the Tanzanian camps and to underscore the need to better implement UNHCR's policies on protecting refugee women in all refugee settings and to adopt policies addressing domestic violence.

New protection initiatives of UNHCR included providing firewood to vulnerable refugees, i.e., unaccompanied minors living alone, unaccompanied elderly men and women, elderly couples, handicapped and terminally ill persons, trauma victims, and some single female and male heads of household. UNHCR provided some victims of domestic violence with alternative shelter on a short-term basis, and strengthened ongoing community education on gender violence and counselling services to victims of sexual attacks.

## European Union

The European Union (EU) has declared a campaign against violence against women in Western Europe. As part of the campaign, the European Commission supported a comprehensive study on the prevalence of domestic violence in the region. The Commission also funded a meeting on rape as a war crime in Kosovo, which brought together activists and experts from the Balkans, other parts of Europe, and the United States. The Balkan Stability Pact Summit for South Eastern Europe, held in July in Sarajevo and attended by President Clinton and fifty other world leaders, was designed to develop a comprehensive strategy for political stability and economic reform in the Balkans.

The Organisation for Security and Cooperation in Europe (OSCE) made some moves to integrate women's human rights into its efforts to monitor human rights violations and develop policies to curtail such abuses. But women's groups in the region, and even in the Sarajevo office of the OSCE, protested that planners had left women off the agenda and excluded them from the meeting. An appeal signed by women's human rights activists throughout the region demanded an equal and active role for women in the development and implementation of the Pact. In December 1998, the Permanent Council allocated funds for gender issues and activities, such as women in politics trainings in Kazakhstan and Poland, and called on member states to provide voluntary contributions for staffing. The British and Swiss governments each seconded a staff member to serve as gender advisors to the OSCE, one in Warsaw and one in Vienna. A gender focal point person continued to work in the secretariat in Vienna. To some extent, human rights reporting and field activities increased their attention to women's human rights. In Tajikistan, a local OSCE staff member initiated a project working with traumatised women survivors of the civil war.

During the crisis in Kosovo, female OSCE human rights officers successfully documented cases of rape and other violations against women. Their achievement was all the more noteworthy given that none of the OSCE monitors received instruction in the challenges of interviewing female rape victims and only three per cent of the OSCE staff in Kosovo was female. The OSCE's public commitment to women's rights did result in several positive developments. The OSCE held a supplementary Human Dimension Meeting on gender issues, where non-governmental organisations were allowed to participate actively in creating recommendations for the institutions of the OSCE.

## United States

The US government's commitment to women's rights around the world was jeopardised by two competing foreign policy concerns: the desire to promote advantageous economic and strategic relations with other governments regardless of human rights considerations, and the desire to protect US practices at home and abroad from scrutiny and criticism on human rights grounds. The US government demonstrated leadership in the area of trafficking, an activity that traps hundreds of thousands of women in exploitative working conditions and debt bondage with little legal recourse.

In 1999, the United States played a critical role in crafting a new, markedly improved international protocol on trafficking of persons. The protocol, proposed in the process of negotiating a new Convention against Transnational Organised Crime, would create a new international standard on trafficking to afford trafficked people greater rights and protections. During the negotiations, the US advocated a broad, inclusive definition of trafficking. Despite this positive step, the US stopped short of further advancing trafficked people's rights by failing to provide sufficient support for protocol provisions that would offer greater protections to victims of trafficking.

Preoccupied with keeping US citizens outside the court's jurisdiction, the US played an obstructionist role at the February and August Preparatory Committee meetings for drafting the rules of evidence and procedure and elements of crime for the ICC; it seemed intent on either undermining the power of the court or negotiating a blanket agreement that would exempt any US national from being tried before it. Moreover, the US delegation remained a reactionary force in areas that directly affected women's rights.

The commitment of US government to protect women's rights in the refugee context was evidenced by its attention to Kosovar women refugees. In July 1999, the US government pledged $10 million for the Kosovar Women's Initiative (KWI), which was being implemented by UNHCR. This initiative, which will continue through September 2000, addressed the immediate survival needs of Kosovar women refugees affected by rape and other gender violence by, among other things, providing psychosocial support and counselling, programmes to re-establish women into their communities.

The US government avoided addressing the substantive findings of the report of the UN special rapporteur on violence against women that detailed human rights violations of women in detention in the US, including extensive sexual misconduct and systematic violations of women's right to privacy. The US delegation to the UN Commission on Human Rights insisted that women incarcerated in the US have protection from and recourse against human rights violations, even though passage of the Prison Litigation Reform Act of 1995 made it extremely difficult for women to bring legal claims against corrections departments, especially in cases of sexual assault and abuse.

The CEDAW which languished in the Senate Foreign Relations Committee. While the Clinton Administration stepped up its efforts to promote ratification of this treaty, which included attempts to cultivate Senate leadership on this issue and the unveiling of a White House ratification strategy, those efforts were minimal, and had not yet resulted in the treaty being offered for a vote. The Clinton administration was a steadfast critic of women's rights violations in areas where the sheer scale and severity of the physical violence could not be ignored. However, the US government was much less critical about blatant sex discrimination practised in places like Mexico, its second largest trading partner.

## REFERENCES

Aggarwal, B., 'Gender and Command over Poverty: A Critical Gap in Economic Analysis and Policy in South Asia', in *World Development*, vol. 22, no. 10.

Friedman, E., *Women's Human Rights: the Emergence of a Movement*.

*Human Rights Watch Global Report on Women's Human Rights*, New York, 1993 and 1995

Peters J. and A. Wolper., *Human Rights: International Feminist Perspectives*, edited by Roudedge, New York, 1995.

Stamatopoulou, E., *Women's Rights and the United Nations: Human Rights Discourse*.

*The Education for Girls and Women: Towards a Global Framework for Action*, UNESCO, Paris, 1995.

Tomasevski, K., *Women and Human Rights*, Zed Books, London, 1993.

Youssef, N.H., *Women's Access to Productive Resources: the Need for Legal Instruments to Protect Women's Development Rights*.

# 9

# Refugees and Human Rights

When their human rights are at grave risk, people become refugees. They sever the link with their own state, and seek the protection of another state, because their own government is persecuting them or cannot be relied on to protect them. When refugees seek the protection of another state, they rarely receive a warm welcome. Many are turned back at the border without a hearing; detained as illegal immigrants; subjected to further violence or squalid conditions in refugee camps; put through summary and unfair asylum procedures; or sent back to the country they fled.

## PROBLEM OF FORCED DISPLACEMENT

Security of many people is currently being threatened by a complex mixture of factors: by unbalanced development, economic decline and environmental degradation; by state collapse, state formation and the authoritarian exercise of state power; and by new forms of violence and warfare, which, although based in many instances on communal allegiances, also serve as a camouflage for personal or factional gain.

Given the difficulties involved in quantifying human security and insecurity, it is not easy to say whether such threats are more widespread and intense today than they were in the past. On one hand, there are many analysts who point to 'the new world disorder' and 'the coming anarchy'. Taking it as almost self-evident that life in the contemporary world is nastier and more brutish than it was in previous years, the representatives of such schools of thought tend to envisage a future which in certain parts of the world is characterised by mounting lawlessness, an irreversible process of social and political fragmentation, as well as growing conflict over scarce natural resources. On the other hand, there are scholars who believe that such pessimism is unwarranted and based upon a faulty reading of both historical and contemporary evidence.

Mass population movements are now assuming a larger scale and occurring within a shorter time-frame than in previous years. This trend has been witnessed most graphically in the flight of more than a million Iraqi Kurds after the war in the Persian Gulf, the internal and external displacement of two to four million people by the conflict in former Yugoslavia, the exodus of over a million Rwandese citizens after the 1994 genocide, as well as the movement of more than two million displaced people within and from Liberia. A number of trends appear to have contributed to the growing scale and speed of forced displacement in these and other parts of the world: the emergence of new forms of warfare, entailing the destruction of whole social, economic and political systems; the spread of light weapons and landmines, available at prices which enable whole populations—including their youngest members—to be armed; and, perhaps most significantly, the use of mass evictions and expulsions as a weapon of war and as a means of establishing culturally or ethnically homogeneous societies.

In an era when so many people have become the victims of ethnic cleansing and other forms of mass expulsion, others have found it impossible to escape from their own country and to find refuge elsewhere. In some cases, as in Bosnia or Sri Lanka, for example, their departure has been blocked by government or opposition forces who wish to maintain control over the civilian population. As the Haitian refugee problem also suggests, the problem of forced displacement has become increasingly enmeshed with the broader pattern of international migration. Rightly or wrongly, people wishing to move to the world's more affluent countries have increasingly sought entry to such states by submitting claims to refugee status. This trend is a result not only of the material insecurity of life in many parts of the world, but also the progressive closure of official immigration channels in the industrialised states and the penetration of the international media, communications and transportation networks into the remotest corners of the earth. Diaspora communities, many of which are themselves the product of forced population displacements, have played an important part in maintaining the volume and determining the direction of such migratory movements.

While the problem of forced displacement has certainly grown in scale and complexity during the past few years, it has also assumed a new degree of public and political importance. Not so long ago, the refugee question was primarily the preserve of relief agencies, development organisations and human rights bodies. Of course, this issue played an important part in both the ideology and the practice of the cold war; the western states were particularly adept at using exiled populations to discredit and in some cases to undermine those governments allied to the Soviet Union.

In recent years the problem of forced displacement—and humanitarian issues more generally—have been the subject of increasing discussion in political and military fora such as the UN Security Council and the North Atlantic Treaty Organisation (NATO). This development derives in part from the changing nature of the international security agenda, the central role of forced displacement in so many of the world's recent crises, and the fear that growing numbers of uprooted people might try to make their way to richer and more stable parts of the globe.

One forcibly displaced person or population may straddle several categories simultaneously or over time; someone may initially be displaced within their own county, then become a refugee in its neighbouring state, then be displaced again within their country of asylum, before finally repatriating to their homeland. Such categorisations are also of little relevance when different types of displaced persons—not to mention the local population—are living alongside each other in equally difficult circumstances. It is for this reason that UNHCR and other humanitarian organisations often provide relief and rehabilitation assistance on a community-wide basis and to all needy people in a given geographical area, irrespective of whether they are refugees, returnees, internally displaced people or local residents.

## HUMANITARIAN ACTION AND INTERVENTION

There has been a growing recognition of the need to respond to the problem of forced displacement on a regional basis, rather than establishing separate humanitarian programmes for individual countries. There was broad international consensus that UNHCR could only respect its humanitarian and non-political status by confining its activities to those countries of asylum and by responding to refugee movements once they had taken place. Any effort to address the problems of human insecurity and displacement within countries of origin, it was agreed, would have involved the organisation in activities which fell beyond the scope of its mandate. In recent years, a number of different factors have combined to bring about a fundamental reassessment of this traditional approach to the refugee problem. These include:

i) the mounting concern of host and donor countries about the financial and other costs incurred in providing refugees with indefinite protection and assistance, and their growing unwillingness to admit large numbers of displaced people;

ii) a growing awareness that refugee movements can constitute a serious threat to national, regional and even international security;

iii) the changing military and strategic value of refugee populations in the post-cold war period;

iv) an initial willingness amongst some of the world's more powerful states to intervene in countries affected by acute political and humanitarian crisis, particularly when those states are weak or have some strategic significance;

v) a recognition of the need to protect, assist and find solutions for groups of uprooted and vulnerable people other than refugees, especially those who are displaced within their own countries; and,

vi) a desire to consolidate peace and prevent the recurrence of violence in war-torn societies through measures designed to ensure the return and effective reintegration of displaced populations.

As a result of such developments, a new international consensus has emerged, recognising the need to address humanitarian problems within countries of origin and to avert those situations in which people are obliged to abandon their homes in order to survive. The traditional right to asylum, as enshrined in the Universal Declaration of Human Rights and other international instruments, should be joined by another: the right to stay in one's own country and community, in conditions of physical, material, legal and psychological security. While this right has not been formalised in international law, the UN Human Rights Commission has affirmed "the right of persons to remain at peace in their own homes, on their own lands and in their own countries."

Today, the world's more powerful states are becoming increasingly reluctant to take the decisive action that is sometimes required to avert political crises and bring an end to massive human rights abuses. As the International Institute for Strategic Studies has observed, such countries "are in no mood to sacrifice their well-being for supposed international advantage.... Even the brief post-cold war sense of humanitarian obligation has begun to give way to colder realpolitik calculations of what can be done." The exceptions to this statement tend to prove the rule. It is now widely acknowledged, for example, that the eventual decision of the NATO states to intervene more actively in former Yugoslavia was prompted as much by the need to sustain the North Atlantic alliance as any humanitarian consideration. Similarly, there is little doubt that in the more recent case of Albania, the eagerness of certain states to lend military support to the delivery of humanitarian relief has derived primarily from a desire to stem an unwanted exodus of asylum seekers.

At a Security Council debate on the protection of emergency assistance held in May 1997, the permanent members of that body effectively buried the concept of 'humanitarian intervention' which had achieved such prominence in the early 1990s. As the US government stressed, "the UN cannot send peacekeepers into each and every emergency."

Nevertheless, and as the case of former Yugoslavia demonstrates again, it has proved impossible for the industrialised states simply to turn their back on complex emergencies taking place in other parts of the world. Prompted in many instances by public opinion and the international media, states have often responded to situations of armed conflict and forced displacement with humanitarian action, often on a massive scale.

During the past decade, the resources devoted to humanitarian assistance have soared. Among official aid agencies, spending on emergencies has increased five-fold over the last decade. The rise in the share of emergency assistance in the total bilateral aid spending of the industrialised countries is even more dramatic, increasing from 1.5 per cent in 1991 to 8.4 per cent in 1994.

Although the two trends may not be directly linked, it is significant that this increased spending on emergency aid has been matched by a steady decline in the level of official development assistance. Only in the last two years has the amount spent on emergency relief started to decline. The expansion of the humanitarian sector has gone hand-in-hand with a decline in the role of state structures in the provision of basic public services in low-income states.

Today, some 1,500 non-governmental organisations (NGOs) are registered with the United Nations, many of whom act as competing subcontractors for UN agencies and donor states. Between 1990 and 1994, for example, the proportion of European Union relief funding channelled through NGOs increased from 45 to 67 per cent. In countries such as Liberia, Rwanda, Sierra Leone and Somalia, such agencies have tried to plug the gap created by the disintegration of state structures, ensuring the provision of a whole range of services that would normally be considered the responsibility of government: food, shelter, health care, water supply, education, transport, commercial contracts and jobs.

It is, therefore, not wholly accurate to suggest that the world's wealthier states are reluctant to intervene in complex emergencies. In many senses, that function has been devolved to humanitarian organisations. The growth of the humanitarian sector has clearly been facilitated by the growing ability of humanitarian organisations to work in situations of ongoing violence. Due to the importance attached to the principles of sovereignty and non-interference during the cold war years, the governments of war-torn countries often denied relief agencies access to areas controlled by rebel groups. Relief assistance therefore tended to be channelled through state structures, or simply dealt with the symptoms of war by means of refugee assistance programmes.

The principal exceptions to this pattern were to be found in the cross-border relief operations established by international NGOs and indigenous agencies, such as those from eastern Sudan to Eritrea and from Pakistan to Afghanistan. This situation has changed quite dramatically in recent years, facilitated to a large extent by a succession of Security Council resolutions, enabling the UN and other agencies to mount emergency operations inside conflict-affected countries and to gain direct access to uprooted and besieged populations. Sometimes undertaken on the basis of negotiated agreements with governments and rebel groups, and sometimes backed by the deployment of UN-mandated forces, either in a logistical or more assertive capacity, these initiatives have established a new paradigm of humanitarian action and intervention.

In recent years humanitarian organisations have been able to expand their operations geographically and extend their activities functionally. In the process, they have saved an unknown number of lives, reunited many families, educated large numbers of children and assisted massive numbers of people to return to their homes. In situations where the relationship between state and citizen has broken down, humanitarian action can help to compensate for the absence of national protection and provide affected populations with a degree of security which they would otherwise lack. While few commentators would query such achievements, it has become increasingly clear that humanitarian action has some important constraints and limitations, and that it can also have a number of unintended and negative consequences.

## REFUGEE PROTECTION PRINCIPLES

The first institution of refugee protection was born in Europe, and it is in Europe today that the adequacy of that system is being tested. As authors of the international law relating to refugees, governments in Europe and other affluent regions have a historical and a moral responsibility to uphold the right of asylum. Although no right to receive asylum yet exists in international, regional or municipal law, a willingness to provide asylum is the litmus test for the commitment by affluent states to human rights.

Affluent states cannot expect other, more vulnerable nations to execute demanding reforms or improve human rights conditions and at the same time claim that it is beyond their own substantial means to sustain a commitment to asylum. In practice, this entails much more than simply giving rhetorical support to the principles of international refugee and human rights law.

First, it means eschewing restrictive interpretations of the 1951 UN Refugee Convention, such as the proposition that only states can act as agents of persecution.

Upholding access to asylum procedures is a second pre-condition for upholding the principle of asylum. A great deal of effort has been expended by the industrialised states in the attempt to prevent asylum seekers from even setting foot on their territory. Technically, it is true, some of the measures employed to reach this objective are not specifically banned by the international refugee instruments. But as restrictive practices of this kind make no distinction between legitimate and unfounded claimants, they are clearly contrary to the spirit of the 1951 Refugee Convention.

The third area where reforms are required concerns the notions of safe countries of origin and safe third countries, as well as the related question of responsibility for examining asylum requests. The safe country of origin notion is an inherently dangerous one, as there is an evident potential for persecution to occur in any state, however democratic its constitution. The notion of safe countries of origin is also susceptible to political manipulation.

While considering the safe of Third World countries, there is an evident value in arrangements which limit the ability of asylum seekers to apply for refugee status in one country after another. Governments have argued—and some legal experts agree—that asylum seekers should in principle submit their claim to refugee status in the first country they reach which has fair and effective determination procedures. But this should not take precedence over every other consideration. Some asylum seekers have substantive connections with a particular country, whether through past residence, the presence of family members or through linguistic or cultural ties. Such connections, which in general are quite easy to verify, may make integration much easier for asylum applicants who are eventually granted refugee status. They may also help to reduce the social welfare costs incurred by the receiving state. If asylum seekers are to be turned away from certain states on the grounds that they failed to apply for asylum in their previous country of transit, then it is imperative to ensure that high standards of protection are available in the place to which they are returned.

## The Asylum Procedures

While considering the situation of people who have entered the refugee determination procedure, states should place much greater emphasis on the quality of the first instance interview and decision which they grant to asylum seekers. If these are of a high standard, undertaken fairly and thoroughly by properly qualified personnel, then there is likely to be less need for states and asylum seekers to become involved in lengthy appeals and legal proceedings. Decisions on asylum applications should also be made on the basis of an accurate understanding of conditions in countries of origin.

The states should develop their own human rights information centres, such as those which exist in Canada and the USA, which have established publicly verifiable databases of information, drawn from a broad range of official and other sources. Making the information used in decision-making available to all of the parties involved would enhance the quality, speed and perceived fairness of the process. During the past decade, states have regularly copied each other in the formulation and implementation of new restrictive measures. In fact, they have established a multitude of inter-governmental fora with precisely this purpose in mind. Regrettably, much less attention has been paid to identifying examples of good state practice which might usefully be replicated in other countries.

In this respect, some particularly useful lessons can be learned from examples such as the Danish asylum model. Since the mid-1980s, Denmark has introduced a succession of useful reforms to its refugee determination procedures. Responsibility for initial asylum interviews was reallocated from the border police to a civilian body, the Aliens Directorate. The impartiality of the procedure was strengthened by authorising a non-governmental organisation, the Danish Refugee Council (DRC), to interview asylum seekers who were deemed by the Directorate to have manifestly unfounded claims. The DRC was authorised to veto the Directorate's decision, thus enabling the applicant concerned to enter the asylum procedure. Accuracy of interpretation and a better record of gathering case information were also improved through the employment of different interpreters by the DRC and the Directorate.

As a result of these reforms, both the government and refugee advocates agree, the impartiality and efficiency of Denmark's asylum procedures have been enhanced. The DRC's participation has helped to shield asylum decisions from foreign policy concerns, and has facilitated the identification of people who are at special risk. At the same time, the direct involvement of an independent body has legitimised the asylum procedure and has made it easier for the authorities to remove those people whose applications are manifestly unfounded.

Systematic efforts should be made to ensure that the best practices of states with well-established asylum systems are emulated in countries which are now dealing with refugee issues for the first time. It is for this reason that a growing proportion of UNHCR's activities in low and middle-income countries are devoted to the establishment and reinforcement of national determination procedures by means of training programmes, the dissemination of information and other capacity-building measures. While thoroughness should never be sacrificed to speed, all of the parties to any asylum decision have an interest in it being taken with the minimum of delay.

Indeed, the so-called asylum crisis could probably have been avoided if the industrialised states had taken much earlier steps to establish effective determination procedures.

## Treatment Standards of Refugees

The 1951 UN Refugee Convention focuses almost exclusively on the rights and obligations of recognised refugees. It is for this amongst other reasons that asylum seekers in the industrialised states receive widely differing standards of treatment with regard to social welfare benefits, access to public services, the right to work, housing entitlements and conditions of detention. To address this neglected problem, UNHCR, the states concerned and other interested parties should develop a set of agreed standards, applicable to people who are waiting for their status to be determined. Such standards should evidently discourage governments from introducing some of the more oppressive restrictive measures witnessed in recent years, particularly the withdrawal of social welfare benefits and the detention of asylum seekers.

The establishment of relatively open but monitored reception centres might be considered as an alternative to the imprisonment of asylum applicants who are thought likely to abscond. The heavy demands that asylum seekers can make on public resources and services should not be discounted, particularly in those lower-income countries which are beginning to receive substantial numbers of asylum seekers for the first time. Particular efforts could be made to determine whether non-governmental organisations, voluntary agencies, religious institutions and refugee community groups could make a contribution in this area, freeing state resources for those asylum seekers whose needs cannot be met in any other way.

## Temporary Protection

Temporary protection is linked with the persistence of the causes of persecution. It is provided for a limited period of time.

Many developing countries admit refugees to their territory on a temporary basis, making it clear that the people concerned will be expected to go home when it is safe for them to do so. This has, for example, always been the position of the Pakistani authorities with regard to the exiled Afghans on its territory, for many years the largest refugee population in the world. People who have been granted refugee status in the industrialised states have normally been allowed to stay and settle permanently in their country of asylum, even if there has been a fundamental and durable improvement to the human rights situation in their homeland. There was a tentative move away from this approach in the 1980s, when the industrialised states began to grant various forms of 'humanitarian status' to asylum seekers who were in need of international protection, giving them a temporary right to remain in the country. This arrangement, it was felt, might facilitate the eventual repatriation of the people concerned.

However, most of the people who were granted humanitarian status have been allowed to stay in their country of asylum on a long-term basis, often because of their inability or unwillingness to go home and the reluctance of the industrialised states to initiate deportation proceedings against people who had started to integrate in their society. The policies pursued by the industrialised states took a decisive turn as a result of events in former Yugoslavia.

In 1992, the number of asylum applications submitted in western Europe reached an all-time high, placing heavy pressure on the asylum procedures of the countries concerned. At precisely the same time, substantial numbers of people from former Yugoslavia began to arrive in the region, escaping from the escalating war in the Balkans. It was against this background that in July 1992, the UN High Commissioner for Refugees urged states to grant temporary protection to asylum seekers from former Yugoslavia, pending the time when the war had come to an end and they could go back to their own country. In the period which followed the High Commissioner's request around 15 states, primarily in western Europe, agreed to implement the temporary protection proposal.

Altogether, more than half a million people have benefited from this arrangement, the largest number of them in Germany, perhaps, the most important benefit of the temporary protection approach has been that it provided immediate security to a large number of people whose lives and liberty were at risk, and spared them the anxiety associated with a long and complex refugee status determination procedure.

Given the traumatic circumstances that forced people to flee from former Yugoslavia, the advantage of this arrangement cannot be overestimated. At the same time, the temporary protection proposal has relieved states of the need to examine many thousands of individual asylum applications—a time-consuming and expensive process—and has enabled them to adopt a more generous asylum policy than might otherwise have been the case. Publicly and politically, the admission of former Yugoslav citizens became more acceptable because of the understanding that they would repatriate once conditions had improved at home.

In this sense, as the UN High Commissioner for Refugees has observed, "Temporary protection is an instrument which balances the protection needs of people with the interests of states receiving them." The temporary protection principle has also had some broader benefits in terms of defending the principles of international protection in a situation of mass influx.

The industrialised states have in recent years tended to apply restrictive definitions of the refugee concept. People from countries affected by war and generalised violence those states have argued, should be granted protection only if they can demonstrate that they have been singled out for persecution. With the introduction of temporary protection, however, those same states have acknowledged a broader humanitarian obligation to provide a place of safety to people who have fled from a war-torn state. Temporary protection has helped to reassert the principle of international responsibility sharing.

By admitting a substantial number of refugees from former Yugoslavia, the countries of western Europe provided a concrete demonstration of their commitment to the principle of international protection and thereby provided a positive example to actual and potential host countries in other parts of the world.

Temporary protection is not in itself a solution to refugee problems and that this approach should not be applied in an isolated manner. If it is to have a real value, temporary protection must form part of a comprehensive international strategy, designed to deal with both the causes and the consequences of a refugee-producing conflict. Although temporary protection is intended to be provisional and essentially short-term, people who benefit from this arrangement should evidently be granted a formal legal status, clearly defined residence rights, as well as access to adequate housing, welfare benefits, health care, psychosocial support and family renunciation arrangements. The children of asylum seekers who have been granted temporary protection must receive a proper education, including mother-tongue language classes, during their time in exile.

The rights and benefits accorded to people with temporary protection must be progressively improved if it becomes necessary for them to stay longer in their country of asylum than was initially expected. Housing, welfare and work entitlements that are suitable for a few weeks or months, for example, may not be appropriate for a stay of several years. Such improvements do not necessarily contradict the principle that people with temporary protection should eventually go back to their own country.

Temporary protection should not be extended indefinitely. As UNHCR has suggested in a paper submitted to its Executive Committee, "If return remains impossible after a prolonged stay of no more than five years, states should review the situation of temporarily protected persons, with a view to reducing their psychological uncertainty and to identifying long-term solutions for them." Such solutions might include integration in the country of asylum, resettlement in a third country, or voluntary relocation to a secure area in the country of origin.

Great care is needed in facilitating or encouraging the return of populations with temporary protection, not least because a proportion of the people concerned might have qualified for refugee status if they had been able to apply for it on an individual basis. Both legally and ethically, therefore, such people must benefit from the principle of non-refoulement. It is for this reason that UNHCR has argued against the involuntary return of Bosnians originating from areas of the country where they would be a member of the ethnic minority. Temporary protection should be brought to an end if there is a fundamental change in the circumstances that caused people to flee.

Individuals who require continued protection in their country of asylum must evidently be allowed to remain for as long as necessary. While the temporary protection approach does not exclude the involuntary repatriation of people who no longer need to seek safety in another country, considerable caution must be exercised in this area. As UNHCR has affirmed in relation to the deportation of Bosnians with temporary protection, it is impermissible for people to be returned to places where their lives or liberty would be at risk, where violence and human rights violations are still occurring and where the necessities of life are unavailable.

In situations where forms of ethnic cleansing have taken place, moreover, it may eventually be necessary for people to go back to a new location within their country of origin, rather than their previous place of residence. UNHCR's caution in relation to the involuntary return of people with temporary protection also derives from the organisation's awareness that such repatriation movements are likely to act as a destabilising factor in war-torn societies. This issue has arisen not only in Bosnia, but also in relation to the US government's efforts to repatriate Central American asylum seekers whose temporary right of residence has expired.

## AMNESTY INTERNATIONAL AND PROTECTION OF REFUGEES

Every day governments are violating the principle of non-refoulement, the fundamental basis of refugee protection. UNHCR, the agency set up to guarantee international protection for refugees, appears unable to ensure that states fulfil even their minimum obligations towards those forced to flee their country. The 1997 Amnesty International report, *Refugees: Human Rights have no Borders*, outlines why people flee, why they need protection and the system that should, but does not always, provide that protection. It demonstrates that refugee crises cannot be resolved unless the underlying human rights issues are addressed.

Amnesty International therefore calls on all governments to take concrete measures to prevent human rights violations and to live up to their obligations under international law to protect the fundamental human rights of their citizens. It also urges all armed opposition groups to abide by the principles of international humanitarian law. One essential element in restoring respect for human rights in countries where abuses have been widespread is ending impunity. Amnesty International calls on all governments to end impunity by investigating reports of human rights violations and bringing those responsible to justice. This would be a major step towards breaking the cycle of violence and giving refugees the confidence to return home.

Many armed conflicts that cause refugees to flee are fuelled by outside powers that supply arms, personnel and expertise to protagonists known to disregard human rights. It therefore calls on all governments to end transfers of equipment and training for military, security or police forces that are used to commit or facilitate human rights abuses. The international system to protect refugees is in crisis. Many people who deserve protection are falling through the net: denied access to asylum procedures; wrongly told they do not qualify as refugees; sent back to countries where they will not be safe.

However, instead of enhancing refugee protection, governments are trying to restrict even further the definition of who qualifies for protection and the degree of protection they should receive. The stark reality is that governments, both individually and collectively, are unwilling to commit themselves to a greater degree of protection. This has led Amnesty International to conclude that this is not a time to call for bold new measures by the international community, such as the development of new international standards. Rather, it is a time to remind the world's governments of their existing obligations towards refugees and to urge them to ensure that these minimum standards are respected.

Amnesty International calls on the international community to ensure that the full framework provided by international human rights law is applied to the protection of refugees. The organisation believes that basic human rights principles provide an inviolable standard of protection for all people, regardless of asylum decisions made by individual states. The organisation opposes the return of anyone to a situation where they may be at risk of execution, disappearance, torture or imprisonment as a prisoner of conscience. The main thrust of Amnesty International's work is to combat the human rights abuses that force so many people to flee their homes in terror. In its 1997 campaign on the human rights of refugees, Amnesty International is focusing on the way governments treat refugees.

Amnesty International urges governments in countries of asylum to:

i) Build awareness and public support for the rights of refugees.

ii) Ratify and implement international treaties.

iii) Stop forcibly returning refugees to countries where they are at risk of serious human rights violations.

iv) End practices that prevent or deter asylum-seekers pursuing claims.

v) Provide refugees with a fair and satisfactory asylum procedure.

vi) Accept responsibility for examining asylum claims.

vii) Recognise and meet the special needs of particular groups of asylum-seekers.

viii) Protect the rights of refugees in situations of mass exodus.

ix) Base repatriation programs on human rights standards.

x) Strengthen international solidarity and responsibility sharing.

xi) Make the international system more accountable.

xii) Ensure that internally displaced people are protected.

*Build awareness and public support for the rights of refugees*: In countries of asylum governments often obscure the relationship between human rights violations and the protection needs of refugees. As the number of those seeking protection increases, governments seem less willing to live up to their international obligations. Many governments which have offered people asylum in the past are now restricting access to their countries, often justifying such actions on the grounds that they are responding to economic difficulties or anti-immigrant attitudes and growing xenophobia within their societies. Host countries should conduct public information campaigns drawing attention to the human rights concerns underlying the plight of refugees and the obligations of states to protect them.

*Ratify and implement international treaties*: Ratification of international treaties relating to the protection of human rights and the rights of refugees demonstrates states' commitment to the values endorsed by the international community and allows them to be held accountable for their actions. All states should accede to and implement the 1951 Convention relating to the Status of Refugees and its 1967 Protocol, as well as relevant additional regional refugee treaties. They should also accede to and implement international and regional human rights treaties, including in particular the International Covenant on Civil and Political Rights (ICCPR); the International Covenant on Economic, Social and Cultural Rights (ICESCR); and the Convention Against Torture and Other Cruel, Inhuman Degrading Treatment or Punishment.

The states who have declared reservations to the UN Refugee Convention, or maintain a geographical limitation incompatible with the intention of the 1967 Protocol, should withdraw them and extend the scope of protection to all refugees. All states should apply the full range of refugee and human rights treaties in determining who is entitled to protection as a refugee.

*Stop forcibly returning refugees to countries where they are at risk of serious human rights violations*: The established principle of non-refoulement is the fundamental basis of international refugee law. This prohibits states from sending anyone against their will to a country where they would be at risk of serious human rights violations. It is a norm of customary international law, binding on all states irrespective of whether they are party to the UN Refugee Convention, and states cannot derogate from it.

All states must scrupulously observe the principle of non-refoulement, and not forcibly return refugees, in any manner whatsoever to frontiers of territories where they may face serious human rights violations. They should adhere to the full range of other international human rights standards so that no one is sent back to a situation where they may face grave human rights violations, such as torture, disappearance or execution. They should ensure that all asylum-seekers are referred to an independent and specialised body responsible for deciding asylum claims.

Border officials should never decide claims; they should be instructed to refer each asylum-seeker to the responsible body. States should ensure that the principle of non-refoulement applies irrespective of whether an asylum-seeker has been formally granted refugee status. They should not interpret the term coming directly in Article 31 of the UN Refugee Convention in a manner that excludes refugees who merely travel through another country before applying for asylum and should not penalise asylum-seekers for illegal entry.

*End practices that prevent or deter asylum-seekers pursuing claims*: In its 14.1st article, the Universal Declaration of Human Rights states that everyone has the right to seek and to enjoy asylum from persecution. While governments are entitled to control immigration and entry to their territory, they should ensure that asylum-seekers have access to a fair and satisfactory asylum procedure. They should ensure that there are no restrictions on entry or border control measures that in practice obstruct access. They should not detain asylum-seekers in violation of international law. They should not deny asylum-seekers the means of adequate subsistence while their asylum claims are being considered, which can in practice force refugees to withdraw their claims because they cannot survive.

Governments should ensure restrictive measures, such as visa controls, carrier sanctions and interdictive border controls, do not in effect prevent asylum-seekers obtaining access to their jurisdiction or asylum procedures. All asylum-seekers, in whatever manner they arrive at the border or within the jurisdiction of a state, must be referred to the body responsible for deciding asylum claims. Detention of asylum-seekers should normally be avoided. No asylum-seeker should be detained unless it has been established that detention is necessary, is lawful and complies with one of the grounds recognised as legitimate by international standards. In all cases, detention should not last longer than is strictly necessary.

All asylum-seekers should be given adequate opportunity to have their detention reviewed by a judicial or similar authority. States should never detain asylum-seekers in order to deter people from seeking asylum in their country, to impede their asylum claim or to induce them to abandon their claim. Governments should not deny asylum-seekers access to adequate means of subsistence while their asylum application and any appeal is being considered.

*Provide refugees with a fair and satisfactory asylum procedure*: A fair and satisfactory asylum procedure is the only effective way to ensure that people who would be at risk of serious human rights violations if returned to a particular country are identified and offered protection. In each state, the body responsible for deciding asylum claims must be independent and specialised, with sole and exclusive responsibility for dealing with such claims. The decision-makers must have expertise in international human rights and refugee law. Their status and tenure should encourage the strongest possible guarantees of their competence, impartiality and independence. Decision-makers should be provided with objective and independent information about the human rights situation in asylum-seekers' countries of origin or any countries to which they might be sent. Asylum applicants should have the opportunity to be heard in person by the decision-maker when their claim is examined in the first instance. There should be an individual and thorough examination of all the circumstances of each case.

An asylum-seeker should have the right to legal counsel, be notified of that right, have access to qualified interpreters, and have the right to contact UNHCR and relevant non-governmental organisations. Asylum-seekers should be given, in a language they fully understand, the necessary guidance about the procedures to be followed and full information about their procedural rights. If their claim is initially rejected, they should be given the reasons for the decision in writing, in a language they fully understand, so that they can pursue satisfactorily any appeals. Every asylum-seeker must have the right to appeal. Appeals should normally be of a judicial nature and heard by a different body than that which heard the case in the first instance. An appeal should include a full examination of the case given the gravity of the interests at stake.

Asylum-seekers must be allowed to stay in the host country during the asylum determination procedure, including any appeals. All officials and procedures dealing with asylum-seekers should take into consideration the special situation of refugees. It is not always possible for an asylum-seeker to prove every part of her or his case. If an asylum-seeker's account is credible, she or he should be given the benefit of the doubt, unless there are good reasons to the contrary.

*Responsibility for examining asylum claims*: Many states are avoiding their responsibility for examining asylum claims or transferring it to other countries. They use 'safe third country' practices, measures such as 'white lists' which exclude asylum-seekers based on the presumption that the country they fled is safe, readmission agreements between states which lead to the automatic return of people from one country to another, temporary protection schemes or other measures where the substance of the claim is not adequately assessed. The state in which an asylum-seeker lodges an asylum claim should normally assume responsibility for substantively examining that claim. All 'safe third country' practices and similar bilateral and multilateral arrangements that allow asylum-seekers to be sent to a country where they would be at risk of direct or indirect refoulement or serious human rights violations should be ended immediately.

Governments should not transfer their responsibility for examining an asylum claim to a third state unless they have received explicit consent that the refugee will be admitted and explicit guarantees that the applicant's claim will be examined in a fair and satisfactory asylum procedure and that the asylum-seeker will not be subject to refoulement. Procedures for dealing with claims presumed to be manifestly unfounded or submitted by asylum-seekers from countries presumed to be safe should offer the opportunity for a thorough and substantive examination of the claim using fair and satisfactory methods. While temporary protection schemes, or the granting of *de facto* or some form of humanitarian status, may sometimes provide interim protection, they should not be used to deny asylum-seekers access to a determination of the substance of their claim under the UN Refugee Convention. All those who are granted some form of interim protection must be given an opportunity to have their individual asylum claim assessed in a fair and satisfactory procedure, to determine if they are still in need of protection, before a decision is made to remove them from the country of asylum.

*Recognise and meet the special needs of particular groups of asylum-seekers*: Some kind of asylum-seekers have special protection concerns due to their particular vulnerability or circumstances. For example, the protection needs of women, children and those persecuted because of their sexual orientation are often misunderstood or wrongly interpreted. All states should, as a minimum, adopt and implement the recommendations of the UNHCR Guidelines on the Protection of Refugee Women and the numerous EXCOM Conclusions concerning refugee women. These recognise and address the particular concerns of women while in flight, in camps and during asylum determination procedures. Governments should recognise that women may be forced to flee as a result of persecution in the form of sexual violence or other gender-related abuses, as acknowledged by the world's governments in the Beijing Declaration and Platform for Action adopted in 1995.

Governments should ensure that asylum decision-makers understand that sexual violence and other gender-related abuses can constitute persecution under the UN Refugee Convention definition of a refugee. Governments should offer protection to women who fear persecution because they will not conform to, or have transgressed, gender-discriminating religious or customary laws or practices of their society. Governments should recognise that asylum claims on these grounds fall within the ambit of the UN Refugee Convention and international human rights instruments. Governments should take measures, including following guidance issued by UNHCR, to address the special protection needs of unaccompanied minors and of children in their own right.

*Protect the rights of refugees in situations of mass exodus*: Human rights violations cause mass exodus. In some circumstances, when hundreds of thousands of people flee their country, governments may not be in a position to examine every individual case, but will grant asylum to the whole group. In effect, there is a *prima facie* presumption of refugee status. Before any person who has been part of a mass exodus is returned to the country they fled, they should be given an opportunity to identify themselves as having individual grounds for continuing to fear persecution if returned. States should explicitly, endorse the fundamental obligations established in EXCOM Conclusion 22:

i) In situations of mass exodus asylum-seekers should be admitted to the state where they first seek refuge. If that state is unable to admit them on a long-term basis it should always admit them on at least a temporary basis pending arrangements for a durable solution. In all cases the fundamental principle of non-refoulement, including non-rejection at the frontier, must be observed scrupulously.

ii) Asylum-seekers in mass exodus situations should not be penalised or treated unfavourably solely on the grounds that their presence in the country is considered unlawful. They should not be subjected to restrictions on their movements except those which are necessary in the interest of public health and public order.

iii) States where large groups of refugees seek asylum should respect the refugees' fundamental civil rights and should ensure that they have the basic necessities of life. The refugees should not be subjected to cruel, inhuman or degrading treatment and should not suffer discrimination.

iv) States should provide the means for asylum-seekers to stay in a place of safety. This should not be close to dangerous border areas.

v) All governments should provide effective assistance, including financial support and resettlement opportunities, to states that host large numbers of refugees, for as long as it is required.

Governments should agree standards for the use of temporary protection schemes in situations of mass exodus. Such temporary protection schemes should not be used by states to undermine existing standards under the UN Refugee Convention. I should ensure that all those given temporary protection have the right to have their individual case for asylum examined before they are removed from the host state.

*Base repatriation programs on human rights standards*: According to the internationally agreed standard on repatriation, the voluntary and individual character of repatriation and the need for it to be carried out under conditions of absolute safety should always be respected. Recent experience shows that many repatriations are not genuinely voluntary; rather there is premature, forced and coerced return to less than safe conditions. Equally fundamental to any decision that a refugee can repatriate is an assessment of their safety upon return, measured according to human rights standards. Any decision on repatriation should be based on an independent, impartial and objective assessment of the human rights situation in the country of return, with a view to the durability of that safety. The principle of non-refoulement must never be violated by repatriation schemes.

Repatriation programmes should include human rights guarantees at all stages of the return. Repatriation should not be imposed until there is a fundamental and lasting change in the human rights situation in the country of return. The human rights situation in the country of return should be subject to independent and impartial assessment based on publicly available information before, during and after any repatriation.

International human rights treaty bodies, thematic mechanisms and country rapporteurs should have an active role in this assessment. The international community, including governments, international organisations and non-governmental organisations, should immediately agree on how to provide an independent human rights assessment and monitoring system for repatriation programs. They should determine what type of organisations and agencies should be involved on an ongoing basis. Efforts should be made to ensure the involvement of a representative cross- section of the refugee community in assessing when return is possible.

Governments of the countries from which refugees have fled should cooperate with UNHCR, other international organisations, and non-governmental human rights and humanitarian organisations in the pursuit of durable solutions to refugee problems. They should allow access to their countries so that the human rights situation can be properly assessed throughout any repatriation programme. Individuals should have the right not to repatriate without an adequate opportunity for an individual assessment of their asylum claim. When refugees are repatriating spontaneously rather than as part of an organised program, governments, UNHCR and other agencies should continue to exercise responsibility for ensuring that refugees are not put under undue pressure to return, and that measures are taken to ensure the safety of returning refugees.

*Strengthen international solidarity and responsibility sharing*: All states should share equitably the responsibility for hosting refugees and funding their support. States should not bear a disproportionate share of the responsibility simply because of their geographic location. States hosting refugees should receive the full support of the international community.

International organisations responsible for providing refugee protection and assistance should be able to operate without political interference by governments and with secure funding. UNHCR funding arrangements should urgently be reviewed to create an adequate mechanism for funding ongoing programmes and, in particular, to improve the support for those states which bear the overwhelming responsibility for hosting refugees. UNHCR should be enabled to implement in full its protection mandate in a consistent manner and should be shielded from the political agendas of donor countries. Responsibility sharing should not be used to prevent refugees from seeking asylum in the country of their choice or to limit protection to the region of origin.

*Make the international system more accountable*: At present little information is provided by governments about the protection they offer refugees and how they apply international refugee law. This makes it more difficult to hold governments to account if they fail to live up to their obligations towards refugees. States should comply with their reporting obligations under the UN Refugee Convention. UNHCR should submit these reports to the UN General Assembly annually. To monitor the compliance of States Parties to the UN Refugee Convention and its 1967 Protocol, an independent, impartial mechanism should be established.

*Ensure that internally displaced people are protected*: While the internally displaced often flee for the same reasons as asylum-seekers who have fled to other countries, only people outside their country of origin can receive international protection as refugees. The discrepancy between the protection accorded to refugees outside their country and the lack of protection for those who are internally displaced should receive greater international attention and concern. The issue of the protection and assistance needs of the internally displaced is especially urgent in view of the increased number of such people in many parts of the world and their particular vulnerability to gross human rights abuses. Measures taken by the international community for the protection of internally displaced people should not limit their right to seek and to enjoy asylum in other countries. All states should support the work of the Representative for Internally Displaced Persons of the UN Secretary-General by allowing access to their countries and by providing adequate resources.

The role of the Representative should be strengthened to enable the Representative to identify perpetrators of human rights abuses against internally displaced people so as to ensure that they are held to account. The international community should take concrete measures to ensure that internally displaced people are protected. The Representative should develop guidelines for the protection of internally displaced people, based on the full range of existing human rights and humanitarian law, addressing any current gaps in the protection of internally displaced people.

## REFERENCES

Aga Khan, Sadruddin, "Legal Problems Relating to Refugees and Displaced Persons", *Recueil Des Courts*, Collected Courses of the Hague Academy of International Law, 1976, 1, p. 293.

Batchelor, C., 'Stateless persons: some gaps in international protection', *International Journal of Refugee Law*, vol. 49, no. 1, 1995.

Chimni, B.S., "Rights of Refugees, Including the Right to Return: The Language of Protection and the Reality of Rejection: End of Cold War and Crisis in Refugee Law", paper presented in the World Congress on Human Rights, New Delhi, December 10-15, 1990.

Cohen, R., 'Protecting the internally displaced', in *World Refugee Survey* 1996, United States Committee for Refugees, Washington DC, 1996.

Hyndman, P. 'Refugees Under International Law with a Reference to the Concept of Asylum', 60 *Australian L. J.* 1986, 148.

Patil, V.T. and Trivedi, P.R., *Refugees and Human Rights*, Authorspress, New Delhi, 2000.

Rizvi, Z., 'Causes of the Refugee Problem and the International Response', in A. Nash (ed.) *Human Rights and the Protection of Refugees under International Law*, 1988, p.111.

Singh, Nagendra, *The Role and Record of the UN High Commissioner for Refugees*, Macmillan India Ltd., New Delhi, 1984, p.74.

Smith, R. 'Refugees, immigrants and the claims of the nation-state', *Times Literary Supplement 1422* December 25-31, 1987.

Vernant, J. *The Refugee in the Post-War World*, 1953, p.5.

Weiner, M. and Munz, R. "Migrants, refugees and foreign policy: prevention and intervention strategies", *Third World Quarterly*, vol. 18, no. 1, 1997.

Weiss, T. and Collins, C. *Humanitarian Challenges and Intervention: World Politics and Dilemmas of Help*, Westview Press, Boulder, 1996.

# 10

# Minorities and Human Rights

Over the centuries, minorities questions have led to interventions, aggressions, and wars, both local and general. Today they lead to friction between states, intervention by one state in another or to appeals to United Nations for international intervention. States in which minorities live are sometimes concerned about the possibility of a sessionist movements by minorities, threatening in territorial integrity of the state, or about the danger of the interference by other states with which the minorities are connected by ties of race, national origin, language, or religion.

International community has sought to assure minorities equal rights and freedom from invidious discrimination. There has also been international concern to assure that minorities will flourish so as to preserve that diversity of the human race, which, since the beginning of mankind, has provided a motive power for the development of civilisation and culture by weaving many strands into a single multicoloured tapestry. In a democratic state too, there is some danger that the majority which determines the laws and institutions and the behaviour of national authorities may not take into account the special character and needs of minorities.

Minorities are of several kinds. They may members of the indigenous inhabitants of a territory conquered by another race; members of a nation completely absorbed by another state; some inhabitants of a territory transferred from one country to another; a group that has maintained its identity though scattered among many countries by events of history; compact groups of permanently established immigrants who are trying to preserve the traditions of the country from which they came; or diverse components of a multi-national, multi-racial, multi-religious, or culturally pluralistic state.

Due to the diversity of circumstances that have led to the emergence of minority groups in various states, it has not been easy to obtain agreement on a definition of minorities or on the rights to which they should be entitled. In particular, doubts have been expressed about the possibility of establishing world-wide standards which could be applied to all minorities, since they differ in character and circumstances from region to region, from country to country, and even in the same country.

Provisions for the protection of religious and other minorities have been included in various treaties since the seventeenth century, in several of the multi-lateral treaties which followed the First World War, and though one of the main activities of the League of Nations was to protect various minorities in Central and Eastern Europe and in the Middle East, the need for such protection would be eliminated, and the political difficulties incident to the protection of the minorities would be avoided by general recognition of the basic human rights of all. This was accomplished by providing the UN Charter for the promotion of human rights and fundamental freedoms for all without distinction as to race, sex, language, or religion.

The Commission on Human Rights, established in 1946, was authorised to submit to the economic and social council proposals, recommendations, and reports regarding the protection of minorities. In 1947 the Commission established a Sub-Commission on Prevention of Discrimination and Protection of Minorities and authorised it to give recommendations to the Commission undertake studies and to suggest remedies concerning the protection of racial, national, and linguistic minorities. During the discussion in the Sub-Commission of the implementation of the General Assembly's

1948 Resolution, it was agreed that the most effective means of securing the protection of minorities would be the inclusion of an article on the subject in the proposed International Covenant on Civil and Political Rights. The first draft of the minorities' article of the Covenant read as follows:

> Ethnic, religious and linguistic minorities shall not be denied the right to enjoy their own culture, to profess and practice their own religion, or to use their own language. It was objected, however, that minorities as such had no juridical personality and that one should speak instead of persons belonging to minorities; the idea might be expressed by recognising their rights in community with other members of their group.

The major obstacle to granting any special protection to minorities was the fear that they might then invoke the principle of self-determination, leading ultimately to secession. The problem was compounded by the use in the self-determination articles of the Covenants of the expression 'peoples'.

Those countries opposed the inclusion in the Covenants of a provision on self-determination insisted that such a provision would encourage a minority to claim autonomy or independence; there was no criterion to determine whether or not such a minority should be regarded as a people; and proclaiming such an undefined right might easily be construed as an appeal to secession. Other states insisted that self-determination was primarily a problem of non-self-governing territories and could not be applied to sovereign countries; that self-determination applied only to national majorities living in their own territory but unable freely to determine their political status; that a minority in a community was entitled to the fullest possible safeguards, but was not entitled to obstruct the will of the majority; and that minority rule would be dictatorship not democracy.

Article 27 is strictly limited to three specific rights and clearly avoids dealing with such broader political issues. It was understood throughout the drafting process that this restrictive formulation of the rights of persons belonging to minority groups was necessary to avoid tendencies dangerous for the unity of states and to discourage activities that might impair national unity or security.

In 1954, the UN Sub-Commission on the Prevention of Discrimination and Protection of Minorities suggested a thorough study of the present position of minorities throughout the world. For that it proposed the following definition for the term minority. "The term minority shall include only those non-dominant groups in a population which possess and wish to preserve ethnic, religious or linguistic traditions or chara-cteristics markedly different from those of the rest of the population." It also proposed that the following factors should be considered while carrying out the study.

i) Among the nationals of many states, there are distinctive population groups possessing ethnic, religious or linguistic traditions or characteristics, different from those of the rest of the population, and among these are groups that need to be protected by special measures, national and international, so that they can preserve and develop their traditions or characteristics.

ii) Among minority groups who not requiring protection are those seeking complete identity of treatment with the rest of the population, in which case their problems are covered by those articles of the Charter of the UN, the Universal Declaration of Human Rights and the draft international covenants on human rights that are directed towards the prevention of discrimination.

iii) It is most undesirable to hinder by any actions spontaneous development of minority groups towards integration with the rest of the population of the country in which they live, which takes place when impacts such as those of a new environment, or that of modern civilisation, produce a state of rapid racial, social, cultural, or linguistic evolution.

iv) Minorities should settle down happily as citizens of the country in which they live, and therefore in any measures that may be taken for the protection of their special traditions and characteristics, including the study, nothing should be done that is likely to stimulate their consciousness of difference from the rest of the population.

v) Minorities must include a sufficient number of persons to preserve by themselves their traditions and characteristics.

vi) Account should be taken of the circumstances under which each minority group has come into existence, for example, whether it owes its existence to a peace treaty or to voluntary immigration.

Later, in a study prepared for UN Commission on Human Rights, Francisco Capotorti defined minority as a group numerically inferior to the rest of the population of a state, in a non-dominant position, whose members being nationals of the state possess ethnic, religious or linguistic characteristics differing from those of the rest of the population and show, if only implicitly, a sense of solidarity, directed towards preserving their culture, traditions, religion or language.

However, several objective criteria were included in this definition. In the first place, the existence, as a question of fact, of a distinct group within a state's population possessing stable ethnic, religious or linguistic characteristics that differ sharply from those of the rest of the population. Second, the concept of a 'minority' implies a group that is numerically inferior to the majority group. In the third place, it is only a non-dominant minority that needs to be protected. Fourth, only citizens of the state are entitled to protection as minorities; foreigners must rely on other rules of international law for their protection.

While drafting Article 27, there was strong emphasis on making clear that recent immigrant to South and North America should not be treated as minorities. This was the reason for including the opening phrase, 'in those states in which ethnic, religious or linguistic minorities exist.' It was thus agreed that the article should cover only groups 'long-established on the territory of a state.' Some countries emphasised the relevance of the willingness of the minority to maintain its special characteristics. The Yugoslav government wishes to underscore its conviction that the so-called subjective factor is in many respects dependent on the political atmosphere, and the cultural and social circumstances prevailing in the individual social communities in which the members of minorities live and work.

Among societies with a prevailing negative attitude of the 'majority' towards the 'minority', the members of the minorities are fearful that any declaration of one's national, ethnic, cultural and other characteristics might be interpreted as a so-called 'civil disloyalty' on his part as citizen of the country concerned. Therefore, it would be inappropriate to ascribe too much importance to the need of a 'declaration of desire' by the members of any minority in order to preserve their own national, ethnic, cultural and other features and to manifest their awareness of their affiliation to a particular minority, especially in the case of a minority which has for decades been subjected to the pressures of systematic assimilation and denationalisation. To the requisite size of the minority, there was general agreement that 'minority' is a group that is numerically less than 50 per cent of a state's population. Some emphasised that the group should be a sizeable one, as otherwise it might be too difficult to provide it with the ordinary facilities required by minorities; and it might not have enough capacity and talent to preserve its traditions and institutions.

The most important right of members of a minority group is the right to equality. It is provided in Article 2(1) of the Covenant, which imposes the obligation on state parties to respect and to ensure to all individuals within their territories. The rights recognised in the Covenant without distinction of any kind, such as race, colour, sex, language, religion, political or other opinion, national or social origin, property, birth or other status. Thus ethnic, religious, or linguistic differences cannot form the basis for discrimination; and there is a positive duty to prevent discrimination against anyone on these grounds.

In addition to protection against discrimination, members of minority groups need special rights to enable them to preserve and develop their ethnic, religious, or linguistic characteristics. Most treaties for the protection of minorities concluded after the First World War, and those concluded after the Second World War, also contained special provisions to that end. These provisions were explained as follows by the Permanent Court of International Justice:

> The idea underlying the treaties for the protection of minorities is to secure for certain elements incorporated in a state, the population of which differs from them in race, language or religion, the possibility of living peaceably alongside that population and cooperating amicably with it, while at the same time preserving the characteristics which distinguish them from the majority, and satisfying the ensuing special needs.
>
> In order to attain this object, two things were regarded as particularly necessary, and have formed the subject of provisions in these treaties. The first is to ensure that nationals belonging to racial, religious or linguistic minorities shall be placed in every respect on a footing of perfect equality with the other nationals of the state. The second is to ensure for the minority elements suitable means for the preservation of their racial peculiarities, their traditions and their national characteristics.
>
> These two requirements are indeed closely interlocked, for there would be no true equality between a majority and a minority if the latter were deprived of its own institutions, and were consequently compelled to renounce that which constitutes the very essence of its being as a minority.

The Court pointed out that, for a minority, having its own charitable, religious and social institutions, schools and other educational establishments is indispensable to enable the minority to enjoy the same treatment as the majority, not only in law but also in fact.

The special rights to be protected has occupied the Commission on Human Rights and its Sub-Commission on the Prevention of Discrimination and the Protection of Minorities, from the very beginning. It was agreed that members of minority groups should be entitled to enjoy their own culture, practise their religion, and use their own language. Several proposals would have expressly provided the right of minorities to use their own language in judicial proceedings, at least where the minority members did not speak or understand the language ordinarily used in courts. Some proposals specified the right of minorities to establish their own schools, and a right to receive teaching in the language of their own choice in those schools.

Even though the Article 27 is limited to the right 'to enjoy' their own culture and the right 'to use' their own language, it is accepted that it includes the right to have schools and cultural institutions of their own. The article assumes that the individual rights protected by this article are not to be sacrificed to such concerns, however sincere and *bona fide*.

The right to profess and practice one's own religion is protected by Article 18. Article 18(4) also expressly obligates states to respect the liberty of parents to ensure the religious and moral education of their children in conformity with their own convictions. Article 18 is not subject to derogation even in time of public emergency. The basic freedom of thought, conscience and religion, moreover, is not subject to any limitations whatsoever. The freedom to manifest one's religion or belief, however, may be subject to such limitations as are prescribed by law and are necessary to protect public safety, order, health, or morals or the fundamental rights and freedoms of others.

The rights protected by Article 27 have been the subjects of proposals for special implementation by additional multi-lateral instruments. Several proposals for a declaration or convention to protect the rights of members of minority groups were made in the UN in the early years, without success and the subject was revived when Capotorti suggested that a declaration be prepared which could provide guidance for governments by throwing light on the various implications of Article 27 and by specifying the measures needed for the observance of the rights recognised by the article.

The Sub-Commission on Prevention of Discrimination and Protection of Minorities recommended to the Commission on Human Rights that such a declaration be drafted and Yugoslavia presented to the Commission a draft declaration. The draft read as follows:

Article 1

National, ethnic, linguistic or religious minorities have the right to existence, to respect for and promotion of their own national, cultural, linguistic and other characteristics and to enjoyment of full equality in relation to the rest of the population, regardless of their number.

Article 2

1. Members of minorities shall enjoy all the human rights and fundamental freedoms without any discrimination as to national, ethnic or racial origin, language or religion.

2. Any propaganda or activity aimed at discriminating against minorities or threatening their right to equal expression and development of their own characteristics is incompatible with the fundamental principles of the Charter of the United Nations and the Universal Declaration of Human Rights.

Article 3

For the purpose of realising conditions of full equality and complete development of minorities as collectivities and of their individual members, it is essential to take measures which will enable them freely to express their characteristics, to develop their culture, education, language, traditions and customs and to participate on an equitable basis in the cultural, social, economic and political life of the country in which they live.

Article 4

1. In ensuring and promoting the rights of minorities, strict respect for the sovereignty, territorial integrity and political independence and non-interference in the internal affairs of those countries in which minorities live should be observed.

2. Respect for the aforementioned principles shall not prevent the fulfilment of the international commitments of states members of the United Nations in relation to minorities. Member states should fulfil in good faith the commitments they have assumed under the Charter of the United Nations and international instruments and under other treaties or agreements to which they are parties.

Article 5

1. The development of contacts and cooperation among states and the exchange of information and experience on the achievement of minorities in cultural, educational and other fields create favourable conditions for the promotion of the rights of minorities and for their general progress.

2. States members of the United Nations are invited to take the needs of minorities into account in developing their cooperation with other states, especially in the fields of culture, education and related areas of particular importance for minorities.

Austria suggested the addition of the following provision:

a) No one belonging to a national, ethnic, religious or linguistic minority shall be expelled by means either of an individual or of a collective measure from the territory of the state of which he is a national.

b) Genocide against national, ethnic, religious or linguistic minorities should be considered as a crime against humanity.

c) The changing of the demographic composition of a territory in which national, ethnic, religious and linguistic minorities live is incompatible with the spirit of international human rights instruments.

On 18 December, 1992, United Nations came out with a third Declaration on the rights of minorities, issuing a mandate to the nations. This Declaration stated states shall protect the existence of the national or ethnic, cultural, religious and linguistic identity of minorities within their respective territories and shall encourage conditions for promotion of that identity. For carrying out this mandate, the 1992 Declaration asked all the nations to take measures to ensure that person belonging to minorities may exercise fully and effectively all their human rights and fundamental freedoms without any discrimination and in full equality before the law. The United Nations made it absolutely clear that rights of minorities constitute an internationally accepted, legally recognised, logically sound, jurisprudently tenable and morally justified social norm.

## ETHNIC, SOCIAL AND RELIGIOUS CONFLICTS

The prevention of discrimination seeks to secure that everyone, as individuals, are treated on an equal basis. In the human rights system the state is the nexus or the focal point, where the rights are organised and balanced. Firstly, the state itself is obliged not to discriminate. It shall not give preference to anyone, or exclude anyone, on the basis of race, religion, language, ethnic, etc. Secondly, the state is obliged also to protect the individual from social discrimination. Thirdly, the state is obliged to take affirmative action in order to compensate for past discrimination which have placed members of discriminated groups at a disadvantage.

The question of minority rights was very active during the preparation of the UDHR. Even the secretariat went to the extent of endeavouring to include in the UDHR a provision for the protection of the rights of a minority to use its own language and to maintain schools and other cultural institutions. However, this attempt was defeated by the argument that the principle of absolute equality enshrined in the UN Charter and in many national constitutions militate the idea of minorities. Further, it was argued that the UDHR should not deal with rights, which did not have universal applicability.

The most effective means of securing the protection of minorities would be the inclusion of an article in the proposed International Covenant on Civil and Political Rights—the numeric size of the minority in regard to the dominant groups of the country, the question whether members of the minority were living geographically concentrated or whether they were dispersed among the other member of society, the national characteristics of the state, the origin of the state formation in the state, and the question, whether they were totally or only partially incorporated within the state's territorial jurisdiction.

It should be remembered that Article 27 of the ICCPR has been interpreted in various ways as to find out whether it in fact ensures the minorities rights for the individuals constituting the minority. In this regard mention can be made to the individualist approach as different to that of the collective approach. However, it is submitted that the right guaranteed by Article 27 is a weak right, only establishing the responsibility of states, not to prevent individuals who belonged to a minority to do what is stated in Article 27.

It is also argued that the practice of states and the Human Rights Committee under the Covenant dictates that state parties are under a positive duty to assist ethnic minorities in the preservation and development of their culture, language and religion. It was stated in the committee that Article 27 was drafted in a negative way as this gives an assumption that minorities have rights, but Article 27 merely called on states to ensure that persons belongings to such minorities should not be denied specific rights it mentioned.

Reference can be made to the specific arrangements of the UN Commission on Human Rights, which adopted two procedures to ensure the protection of minority rights in very general forms. First of those is the ECOSOC resolution 1235 (1967) which has secured powers to receive information about violation of human rights from all available sources. Secondly, by resolution 1503 (1970) of the ECOSOC the Sub-Commission appointed a working group to meet at least once a year, to receive communications and replies of the state parties. The Sub-Commission, however, deals with cases showing consistent pattern of gross and reliably attested violations of human rights including racial discrimination, segregation, apartheid, etc. A similar arrangements is provided for Human Rights Committee under Article 28-44 of the ICCPR. As for the UN system is concerned, in relation to the protection of minorities, attention could be warranted to the following international instruments:

i) UN Declaration on the Elimination of all Forms of Racial Discrimination (1963);
ii) International Conventions on the Suppression and Punishment of the Crime of Apartheid (1973);
iii) Convention on the Prevention and Punishment of the Crime of Genocide (1973).

In regional set-ups, the most important investment dealing with minority rights is the European Convention on Human Rights (1950). Article 14 of this Convention expressly refers as national minorities whose enjoyment of fundamental rights is secured within the jurisdiction of a High Contacting Party. The Convention has seriously stipulated an international protection of minorities living within Europe. In addition to this arrangement, the Council of Europe has adopted a considerable number of reports, resolutions and recommendations concerning specific types of minorities. The European system further provides instruments dealing with fixed problems like discrimination, participation in public life, improvement in Europe of mutual understanding between ethnic communities, minority flows concerning Latin America, missing persons, deportation etc.

The Preamble of African Charter on Human and Peoples Rights speaks in unequivocal terms against racial discrimination. It aims at eliminating every kind of discrimination, especially those based on race, origin, the colour of skin, sex, language, religion or political views. Article 2 of the Charter prohibits discrimination on the basis of national or social origin and seeks to ensure the rights and freedoms recognised and guaranteed by the Charter for every human being. According to Article 13 (2) all citizens are entitled to the equal right to access to public service of the country. This right is further strengthened by Art 13(3) as that guarantees equality in the access tc public property and services. Protection of these rights have been entrusted in the hands of the African Commission on Human and Peoples' Rights established under Article 30 of the Charter.

Another characteristic feature of the Charter is the duty-oriented obligations imposed on people. Article 29(4) of the Charter places duty on individuals to preserve and strengthen social and national solidarity particularly when the latter is under threat. The drafters of the Charter conceive that the emphasis on minority groups rights should not be a threat to national unity but go hand in hand with the national integrity. However, it is submitted, that this view cannot be extended to all cases where the people's right to self-determination is involved. Article 17(2) provides that the promotion and protection of morals and traditional values recognised by the Community shall be the duty of the State.

The Charter of the Organisation of American States has provided, a system of individual liberty and social justice based on respect for the essential rights of man. Article 5 of the Charter recognises the fundamental rights of the individual without distinction as to race, nationality, creed or sex. Economic and religious rights are guaranteed by Article 29(a), Article 74(c) of the Charter places the responsibility of promoting basic educational programmes on one of the organs of OAS.

In 1978, the American Convention on Human Rights (1969) came into force. Its preamble reaffirms the intention of the signatories to consolidate a system of personal liberty and social justice. As widely enough to cover the minority rights, this Convention proclaims in its preamble that the above rights are not derived from one's being a national of a certain state but as based upon attributes of the human personality and therefore demanding for international protection. Article 1 declares that these rights should be protected and respected by states without any discrimination for reasons of race, colour, sex, language, religion, political or other opinion, national or social origin, economic status, birth or any other social condition.

A notable defect in this Convention is the absence of the right to self-determination which has been accepted as peoples includes minorities, the absence of this right diminish the standard setting quality of this instrument in the international forum. Further, there is no clear statement or provision regarding the right of minorities.

It is consistently pleaded by the Third World Human Rights activists that there must be an adoption of human rights instrument at least at sub-regional levels. Organisations like ASEAN, SAARC, ESCAP, etc., could provide general support for establishing a Regional Organisation to adopt a convention setting out the rights guaranteed by international instruments. However, due to the diversities of cultural and linguistic backgrounds and to the pluralism in the legal systems make this task very difficult to the Asian countries to successfully draft a Convention.

In the process of harmonising these differences, attempts are being made in certain quarters towards the adoption of some sort of a bill of rights document applicable to Asian countries with their traditional and sensitive area of rights concept. Since these countries are confronted with major problems that have human rights dimensions and most of these cases are directly involved with minority rights, it is highly desirable to have regional cooperation to face these calamities. Major violations of human rights are reported from this region due to the application of draconian laws such as Prevention of Terrorism Act and Prevention of Terrorist and Disruptive Act indiscriminately to the issues of minority rights cases. The provisions of the national constitutions have proved to be failure to prevent abuse and misuse of executive and legislative powers in victimising minorities.

## REFERENCES

Bandaraga, A., *Colonialism in Sri Lanka: Political Economy of the Kandyan Highlands, 1833-1886,* Berlin: Monton, 1983.

Banerjee, Sumanta, (ed.), *Shrinking Space: Minority Rights in South Asia,* Kathmandu: South Asia Forum for Human Rights.

Capotori, Francesco, 'Study on the rights of Persons Belonging to Ethnic, Religious and Linguistic Minorities', *UN Document* E/ CN 4/ Sub. 2/384/Rev. 1, p. 9.

Lawson, Edward, *Encyclopedia of Human Rights,* 2nd ed., Washington: Taylor Francis, 1996.

Peocock, Olive, *Minority Politics in Sri Lanka: A Study of the Burghers,* Jaipur: Arihant Publishers, 1988.

Vije, Mayan, *Where Serfdom Thrives: The Plantation Tamils of Sri Lanka,* Madras: Tamil Information Centre, 1987.

Subrmanaian, Nirupama, 'Rage in the hills', *Frontline,* November 24, 2000, pp. 59-60.

Sahadevan, P., *India and Overseas Indians: The Case of Sri Lanka,* Delhi: Kalinga Publications, 1995.

# 11

# Business and Human Rights

The links between business and human rights are becoming increasingly clear and higher on the international agenda in these days. The Global Compact initiative has provided a much needed common framework for tackling these and other issues by aiming to develop what UN Secretary-General Kofi Annan's Millennium Report refers to as 'global policy networks'—bringing together international institutions, civil society, private sector organisations and national governments in pursuit of common goals. Deciding to work together through such a network is no small commitment. The business leaders, labour representatives and non-governmental partners who are adding their voices to the Secretary-General's call for a Global Compact should be commended for taking this important step in developing a new form of partnership.

The High Commissioner for Human Rights presented a document titled *Business and Human Rights* at the 2000 meeting of the World Economic Forum in Davos. It was a Progress Report which took stock of the corporate initiatives giving effect to the Global Compact principles. The present report is intended to provide a brief update on some of the recent developments relating to business and human rights both within and outside the UN system. They are:

i) Steps taken by the UN Security Council with regard to trade in diamonds.

ii) The inclusion of corporate social responsibility issues in the five-year review of the Copenhagen World Summit for Social Development.

iii) activities of UN human rights rapporteurs involving the corporate sector in addressing particular human rights issues;

iv) the work of other international organisations such as the World Bank and the OECD;

v) recent initiatives by companies and trade unions and;

vi) the impact of ongoing litigation at the national level alleging corporate liability *in tort* with regard to serious violations of human rights in other countries.

For there can be little doubt that helping companies develop strong human rights policies and sound implementation strategies will be key tests both in overcoming increasing public concerns about globalisation and in ensuring that it becomes an effective tool for improving the lives of people.

## UN DEVELOPMENTS

Within the business community, the need for engagement in human rights is backed up by a recent survey by the Ashridge Centre for Business and Society which found that human rights issues have caused 36 per cent of the biggest 500 companies to abandon a proposed investment project and 19 per cent to disinvest from a country. The survey also found, however, that only 44 per cent of the companies' codes of conduct made explicit reference to human rights.

Much work still remains in better defining businesses' human rights obligations. The United Nations system has taken steps in this direction in recent months. The UN Security Council recently took an important step in identifying the links between business activities and human rights violations by expressing its concern at the role played by the illicit trade in diamonds in fuelling the conflict in Sierra Leone. In its Resolution 1306 the Security Council called on the international diamond industry to cooperate with a ban on all rough diamonds from Sierra Leone. The Council also requested the Secretary-General to appoint a panel of experts to monitor implementation of the ban and the Government of Sierra Leone to ensure the effective operation of a certificate of origin regime for trade in the country's diamonds. The resolution calls on States, international organisations, members of the diamond industry and other relevant entities in a position to assist the Government of Sierra Leone in further developing a well-structured and well-regulated diamond industry that provides for the identification of the provenance of rough diamonds.

The recent meeting of the World Diamond Congress in Antwerp resolved to track each stage of diamond transactions and to keep conflict diamonds out of the rough diamond market. A proposed International Diamond Council made up of producers, manufacturers, traders and governments and international organisations would be established to oversee the new system of verification.

According to Global Witness, the group which has been a leader in raising public awareness on this issue, the proposed measures could have an important impact in preventing rebel groups from funding their war efforts through diamond sales. The industry's decision to address this issue is evidence of the growing awareness of the private sector's responsibility to ensure that its activities do not indirectly lead to violations of human rights.

The issue of corporate social responsibility was on the agenda of the recent General Assembly special session to review progress since the 1995 Copenhagen World Summit for Social Development. In the final outcome document adopted by the General Assembly on 1 July 2000, governments agreed on further initiatives aimed at eradicating poverty, promoting full employment and universal access to social services, and ensuring that everyone has equal opportunities to participate in society. The document makes specific references to the role and responsibilities of the private sector and calls for a multi-sectoral approach. References in the outcome document to the private sector include:

i) encouraging corporate social responsibility by fostering awareness about the relationship between social development and growth, by providing a legal, economic and social policy framework to promote corporate social responsibility and by enhancing partnerships with business, trade unions and civil society at the national level in support of the goals of the Summit.

ii) promoting a dialogue among government, labour and employer groups to achieve broad-based social progress.

iii) realising an open, equitable, secure, nondiscriminatory, predictable, transparent and multilateral rule-based international trading system, maximising opportunities and guaranteeing social justice, recognising the interrelationship between social development and economic growth.

The UN Development Programme's Human Development Report 2000 for the first time takes as its theme human rights. The report, titled *Human Development and Human Rights*, calls for greater accountability of non state-actors. It points out that global corporations can have enormous impact on human rights—in their employment practices, in their environmental impact, in their support for corrupt regimes or in their advocacy for policy changes. The priorities set out in the report include strengthening non-state actors' commitments through better implementation of corporate codes of conduct.

The report acknowledges the adoption of codes of conduct and social responsibility policies but goes on to state: 'many fail to meet human rights standards, or lack implementation measures and independent audits'. It suggests that the use of human rights indicators be extended to include the rôle of corporations. The report also calls for a multi-actor approach to accountability, taking into account the influence and power of the media, corporations and international bodies like the WTO and the Bretton Woods Institutions as well as addressing schools, families, communities and individuals.

The UN High Commissioner has found a growing eagerness on the part of the business community to engage in dialogue on human rights issues as well. The High Commissioner has noted that global corporations are under pressure to demonstrate social concerns and values beyond straight shareholder return. Human rights are at the centre of this picture. In the last few years, perceived corporate complicity in human rights abuses has damaged corporate reputation and, in some cases, share price.

The High Commissioner has increasingly been invited to meet with business leaders to discuss areas of common concern. In May 2000 she met with leaders of the Brazilian business community and members of the Ethos Institute. In addition to discussing business initiatives to promote respect for human rights throughout Brazil, the meeting focused on how the business community could support the Global Compact and be involved in major UN events.

In May 2000, the Office of the High Commissioner (OHCHR) took part in a meeting organised by the International Organisation of Employers (IOE) and the International Labour Organisation (ILO) which brought together business leaders from developing countries to discuss the Global Compact. The meeting provided an important exchange of experience on the obstacles such as poverty, corruption, weak judicial systems and trade disadvantages faced by many businesses in developing countries when trying to improve human rights, labour and environmental practices. There was strong support among the business representatives for being proactive with their governments and in their separate spheres of influence in advocating respect for human rights, good governance and the rule of law.

Each year hundreds of thousands of individuals, the majority of them being women and children from less developed and transitional countries of Asia and Eastern/Central Europe, are tricked, sold, coerced or otherwise procured into situations of exploitation from which they cannot escape. These women and children have become the commodities of a transnational industry that generates billions of dollars and is conducted with a frightening level of impunity and official complicity. OHCHR is committed to working with governments, regional intergovernmental organisations, UN agencies and programmes, civil society organisations and the business community to address this emerging global challenge.

Experts appointed by the UN Commission on Human Rights to report on specific human rights, or to focus on the human rights situation in a particular country, have also increasingly sought to enhance cooperation and contact with the business sector in the course of their work. During the June 2000 annual meeting of these Special Rapporteurs and Independent Experts, there was a discussion on involving the private sector when addressing different human rights issues.

Examples of such an approach can be seen in the work of the Special Rapporteurs on Sudan and on Afghanistan, both of whom have held dialogues with oil companies in these countries, the Special Rapporteur on toxic waste who has met with a pharmaceutical company, and the Independent Expert on Structural Adjustment policies who during a visit to Zambia met with the country's Chamber of Commerce to discuss how HIV/AIDS could be addressed through debt relief. A further example can be found in the work of the Special Rapporteur on the sale of children, child prostitution and child pornography who has decided to focus this year on the role of the international business community in addressing human rights violations concerning children.

During her country visits the Special Rapporteur has held discussions with business leaders in different parts of the world. In June 2000, the Special Rapporteur wrote to members of the International Chamber of Commerce around the world introducing her own initiative and requesting information about company initiatives benefiting children which could be proposed and replicated in other parts of the world.

## POLICY DEVELOPMENTS

The UN Sub-Commission for the Promotion and Protection of Human Rights, an expert body elected by the governments who are members of the UN Commission on Human Rights, has established a Working Group to examine the effects of the working methods and activities of transnational corporations on human rights. The Working Group will discuss at its meeting in August of this year a report containing draft principles relating to human rights conduct of companies.

The draft is intended to be a comprehensive guide by addressing a wide range of human rights issues including non-discrimination and freedom from harassment and abuse, slavery, forced labour and child labour, healthy and safe working environment, fair and equal remuneration, hours of work, freedom of association and the right to collective bargaining as well as war crimes, crimes against humanity, respect for national sovereignty and the right of self-determination. It constitutes an adaptation and combination of relevant language from codes of conduct and similar documents by the UN, the OECD, the ILO, corporations, unions, NGOs and so on.

The *Human Development Report 2000* emphasises the fact that international law places primary responsibility for human rights on states, but a series of new developments deserve mention in the current context as well. They all point to the fact that promises by non-state actors in the field of human rights are being taken seriously; and they demonstrate that new ways are being found to hold all actors accountable for human rights violations.

The potential for new forms of cooperation and accountability between corporations and trade unions was given an important boost in April 2000, when an agreement on worker rights was reached between Telefonica, the global telecommunications company, and Union Network International, the newly formed international union organisation representing 7.5 million workers in service related industries worldwide. The agreement commits Telefonica to guaranteeing core ILO labour standards such as forbidding the use of forced or child labour as well as gender and racial discrimination in all its Global operations.

In 1993, the World Bank created a three member body—The Wolrd Bank Inspection Panel—to respond to private individuals who believe their interests could be harmed by a World Bank financed project. An example of the Panel's work can be seen in the recent investigation of a Bank financed project in China. In September 1999, the Bank's Executive Board of Directors formally requested the Bank's Inspection Panel to undertake an investigation into the Qinghai component of the China Western Poverty Reduction Project to see whether Bank Management had observed its policies and procedures with regard to involuntary resettlement, indigenous peoples, and environmental assessment.

Earlier, the Panel had received a Request for Inspection from the International Campaign for Tibet claiming that the proposed migration of about 60,000 poor people from six counties in eastern Qinghai Province to Dulan County would adversely affect the lives and livelihoods of 4,000 Tibetan and Mongolian ethnic peoples. In April 2000 the independent Inspection Panel delivered its Report to the Bank Management. The Management and Board are currently considering the Report. This process is an interesting example of the possibilities of independent monitoring of internal directives and codes of conduct. There are growing expectations that avowed human rights policies should be held up for scrutiny where harm is threatened.

The Organisation for Economic Cooperation and Development (OCED) adopted revised Guidelines for Multinational Enterprises on 27 June 2000 at its annual Ministerial meeting in Paris. The recommendations by the 29 OECD governments plus four non-member countries: Argentina, Brazil, Chile and Slovakia, are supported by follow-up procedures in the participating countries. Again, guidelines are increasingly being monitored through flexible complaints mechanisms which are not necessarily to be compared to litigation or other traditional forms of legal complaint. The guidelines are addressed to multinational enterprises operating in or from the 33 adhering countries and are to apply to business operations worldwide.

The guidelines are intended to supplement applicable law and to complement and reinforce codes of conduct and other private efforts to implement responsible business conduct. The revised guidelines have added a human rights obligation in the context of general policies. The guidelines cover the fields of employment, industrial relations, protection of the environment, and the question of bribery among other topics. The institutional follow-up does not represent a judicial or even quasi-judicial finding but rather a series of procedures for requesting consultations, good offices, conciliation or mediation as well as clarifications of the guidelines. Non-governmental organisations have criticised the implementation measures as resting almost entirely on the will of governments through their National Contact Points (NCPs). Nevertheless, all sides, governments, business, trades unions and interested non-governmental organisations have stated that they will work to make the guidelines better known, to promote effective use of the guidelines and ensure their application in a consistent and fair manner.

Human rights litigation against businesses for violations of international law taking effect abroad has raised awareness of the international obligations of companies. There is also a realisation that a corporate defendant could be liable for large sums of money which would be enforceable in the national legal order where the corporation has considerable assets. A recent ruling by the House of Lords held that claimants could bring claims against an English-based multinational in the English courts concerning a claim by workers from mines in South Africa suffering from asbestos related diseases. This judgement is expected to open the door to complaints against companies for illegal conduct committed in countries where at this stage there is no appropriate access to justice for similar large claims or class actions.

Of course many issues remain to be resolved regarding the extent of the duty of care owed by the parent company and the actual liability of the company, but the idea that claims can be litigated away from the country where the harm occurred is certain to open up new legal challenges for businesses operating on the world stage. Even though a company cannot be a defendant in a case in the International Court of Justice or the International Criminal Courts established by the UN Security Council, disrespect of international human rights law can give rise to litigation at the national level.

Of course we are now a long way from the everyday world of business but the public is on guard to condemn and shun businesses that violate 'the law of nations'. Such allegations have to be addressed and are shaping perceptions of the whole business and human rights debate. Furthermore, anyone who commits acts of genocide, war crimes, crimes against humanity, piracy, or engages in the slave trade will be violating international law and there could be individual criminal liability and punishment.

Although corporate criminal responsibility is a notion which finds a place only in some legal systems, few would disagree that such acts need to be both prevented and punished. It is the abhorrence of impunity and the instinctive quest for justice which has translated international obligations in the context of forced labour and ill-treatment into new offers of compensation for abuses suffered during the Second World War.

Human rights talk has to be matched by concrete commitments. The sums being negotiated in the context of the slave labour settlements with respect to Germany and German industry testify to the beginning of a new approach to accountability for human rights abuses. Even if the horrors of the Second World War seem rather disconnected from current business practice, the message is becoming clearer.

There are international legal limits to what is acceptable and a new triangular constellation of governments, victims and businesses can be observed attempting redress and justice. However, it is the new use of international law and national courts which has changed how many see the obligations of business in the human rights field.

From upheavals in the diamond industry to the adoption of new inter-governmental guidelines for companies, the message seems clear: international duties are being defined and implemented. The Security Council sanctions represent one extreme form of legal reaction but law is increasingly playing a role whether through new forms of litigation at the national level or through new forms of good offices, conciliation or mediation procedures.

The biggest challenge for the credibility of the companies involved in the Global Compact is the implementation and monitoring of their human rights commitments and in particular their support for the nine principles at the heart of the Compact. There are now increasing expectations on companies. Perhaps a goal which could be achieved by the next Davos meeting would be to establish a task force or group of businesses working with trade unions and both local and international non-governmental organisations exploring ways to have credible independent monitoring of human rights commitments in the business sector.

The Global Compact will remain credible as long as it acts in a self-critical way and invites outside appreciation of its efforts. If the businesses involved become a cosy club, closed to outside evaluation of their codes and practices, none of the sincere commitments will mean much in practice. Governments are taking an increasing interest in ensuring that business behaves in ways which are good for sustainable development, for human rights and for international cooperation. Even though states retain the primary responsibility for ensuring the protection of human rights under the human rights treaties, there is a new awareness that such responsibility entails ensuring that companies operating from or in their jurisdiction must not undermine existing human rights obligations or the international rule of law.

## REFERENCES

Alan, Gewirth, *The Community of Rights*, Chicago and London: University of Chicago Press, 1996.

Thomas, Henk, ed., *Globalisation and Third World Trade Unions*, Indian reprint, Delhi: Madhyam Books, 1995.

Saksena, K.P., 'South in Bloc-dominated Economy', *International Studies*, Vol. 27, No. 4, December, 1990.

Edward, Bloustein, J., 1984, 'Dignity and Privacy' in *Philosophical Dimensions of Privacy*, ed., Ferdinand D. Schoeman, 156-202. Cambridge: Cambridge University Press.

Jeremy, Rifkin, *The End of Work: The Decline of the Global Labor Force and the Dawn of the Post-Market Era*, New York: G.P. Putnam's Sons, 1995.

# 12

# Globalisation and Human Rights

Realisation and protection of human rights depends on the extent to which the government of the country concerned is democratic and responsive to the needs and aspirations of the people. They depend on popular participation in all spheres of the state's activity. Human rights belong to the people and it is the vigilance and capacity to resist the authority when abused by the people themselves which would ensure observance and protection of human rights.

In the contemporary world, global factors operate to the advantage of the industrially advanced nations at the cost of developing countries. External factors operating at the global level are managed by a group of industrialised powers. Their control is so deeply entrenched, both historically and institutionally, as to be beyond the influence of governments and people of developing countries constituting the South or the Third World.

The 21st century is engulfed by the phenomenon of globalisation. The world rapidly being turned into an integrated whole via international trade, internationalisation of production and financial market and the internationalisation of consumer-culture, promoted by an increasingly networked global telecommunication systems. How the forces of globalisation, moving as they are, at an escalated pace, going to affect the day-to-day lives, i.e., human rights, of the people having different needs and aspirations? As a prefatory to the discussion on these and related questions, let us look at the factors that led to the current pace of change and intensity of challenges which the globalisation presents.

## GLOBALISATION AND HUMAN DEVELOPMENT

The basis of various facets of globalisation that we are witnessing today could be traced to the colonialist-imperialist era which had its beginning in the 17th century when Europeans successfully attempted to reach various parts of the globe. The colonial system matured, by the end of the 19th century, as capitalism or monopoly capitalism.

### Transactional corporations (TNCs)

The growth of large scale industries and concentrations of economic power in the hands of a relatively small number of major companies and banks provided the background for the emergence of large business corporate what are widely referred to as multinational corporations (MNCs), and what in the UN terminology are aptly called transnational corporations (TNCs). TNCs have huge funds and technical know-how which the Third World countries are very much in need for their economic development.

The reach and magnitude of their impact on world economic development can be gauged by recalling that the total assets of some or the largest TNCs exceed the GDP of many medium-sized countries. TNCs can play and are playing a significant role in the economic development of the developing countries. But their motivating force is profit; they exploit cheap labour and resources of the country where they operate. Thus, in many cases the role of TNCs runs counter to, and in conflict with, the mandate of the state to protect and safeguard the human rights of its people. This conflict arises out of divergence between the profit objectives of the TNCs and the socioeconomic goals pursued by national governments.

TNCs can act both as engines of development and the destroyers of it. The TNCs could help bring in foreign direct investments (FDI), instituting training facilities to the local employees, setting up expansion of export trade, introducing modern management techniques for increasing productivity and providing for adequate safeguards for the community against hazards from the nature of manufacturing operations.

The International Labour Organisation (ILO) report indicates that even while labour is organised through trade unions yet they are no match to TNCs gigantic bargaining power. TNCs have an integrated worldwide economic system which allows them to easily exploit the local labour by not giving equal pay for equal work, allowing labour to live in unhealthy and filthy conditions, taking advantage of their total helplessness particularly when they are unorganised.

TNCs are free to move with their capital machinery and equipments from one country to the other in search of cheaper labour and resources/raw material. The situation has been further aggravated by the refusal of TNCs to provide any guarantee of environment and the possibility and the threat of temporary or permanent transfer of their operations to other countries.

Instead of laying down a code of conduct for TNCs, the industrialised countries, are preparing drafts for Multilateral Agreement on Investment (MAI) The United Nations attempted to do its part of monitoring their activities and preventing their misuse of power. For several years United Nations also tried to work out a code of conduct for TNCs but after more than two decades of negotiations and drafting of the code, the attempt was abandoned in the late 1980s.

## Debt Crisis

Debt crisis broke into public awareness in the late 1970s, although it was brewing up since the early 1950s, as a result of the policies of US and its allies to promote export of their capital goods and Cold War strategies. The developing countries after gaining independence, soon discovered that the prices of primary commodities and semi-manufactures, they exported were going down and capital goods and equipments that they imported for their economic development from industrialised countries were going up. They also learnt that their currency had no value beyond their national frontiers; whatever they needed to import, have to be paid in hard currency, invariably in US dollars which they could earn only through their export. Any country that, over the long term runs a trade-deficit, would run out of both dollars and the ability to borrow them. Thus, the options for the Third World countries were either to slow down their plans for economic development or stop running into trade deficit or borrowing.

Between 1956 and 1972 all major Third World countries like Argentina. Brazil, Chile, Ghana, India, Indonesia, Pakistan, Peru and Turkey were knocking at the doors of the 'Paris Club' seeking rescheduling of payments for debt services and debt owed to government creditors. By 1970s, the debt burden of the developing countries had reached a crisis proportion.

The oil price hike by the Organisation of Petroleum Exporting Countries (OPEC) further aggravated the crisis. By that time, the Third World as a whole was approaching the break-even point at which debt service exceeded new capital inflows. At this moment commercial banks with headquarters in North America and Europe chose to abandon their long-held skepticism on the safety of international lending and began to throw hundreds of million of dollars at the Third World countries, which were already in heavy debt.

The OPEC price-hike in early 1970s generated huge petrodollars which were invested back in industrialised countries of the Europe and North America in real estate or placed in deposits with commercial banks. Thus, commercial banks were loaded with money and were faced with the problem of finding profitable outlets for their money. They found ready customers in the Third World countries, particularly the non-oil producing countries who had suffered much because of oil price hike. They needed money which was readily offered to them by the commercial banks. Once they failed to pay the interest and instalments, they were obliged to borrow higher amount to avoid default, to pay the arrears and debt servicing; thus got caught in debt-trap. A study conducted by the World Bank in 1993 showed that from 1980 to 1992 developing countries have paid more than $400 billion as interest and part payment of debt. Thus, there has been a reverse flow of capital from the South to the North.

## Global Money

Global money is another phenomenonal characteristic of globalisation. It is owned, controlled and managed by non-governmental institutions or non-territorial centres of power and speculators who indulge in the sale and purchase of domestic currencies, resulting in sharp decline or rise of exchange rates of a national currency specifically of the developing countries.

Speculators and financial investment institutions are dominating global currency market. Not so many years ago there were only seven stock markets around the world in which one could invest. Investors can now buy and sell securities wherever and whenever they wish, within 24 hours. The motivating force is profit and these investors easily panic or get too excited or act as such; they withdraw their investments by selling the stocks.

Global money is being created by currency-trading as virtual money rather than real money. It fits none of the traditional definitions of money, whether standard of measure, storage of value or medium of exchange. It is totally anonymous but its power is real. The volume of this money is so gigantic, the author goes on to say, that its movements in-and-out of a country have greater impact than the flows of financing, trade or investment. This money has total mobility because it serves no economic function. And because it serves no economic function and finances nothing, this money also does not follow the economic logic or rationality.

## Market Economy

The US and UK aggressively promoted market economy. The two powers, in conjunction with their European allies, first attempted to weaken the economic and social sector of the UN system arguing that UN economic and social programmes promote 'statism'. Their efforts paid dividend as a result of ending of the cold war and the fast changing international scenario. In 1990, they did succeed in getting adopted a set of resolutions which endorsed private entrepreneurship and market economy, This was for the first time when the world organisation made recommendation in support of a particular economic system. These resolutions were supported by all countries, including Soviet Union and East Europeans, with one exception, that of Cuba which voted against. Thus, market economy became the major thrust of not only industrialised nations.

Under private entrepreneurship all economic activities would lead to better and more production of goods and services, both in terms of quality and quantity. Incentives of profit and competition among private entrepreneurs or business corporates would be beneficial for the economy of the country and add to the overall prosperity of the people. TNCs with massive capital and technical knowhow and based in the industrialised countries of the North, should be allowed, without any restriction, to operate in the Third World countries.

Free movement of goods and capital is being proposed to the Third World countries as a panacea of their economic and social problem. TNCs, international agencies like the International Monitory Fund (IMF) and World Bank and their media spokes people have been saying that free markets promote economic growth and progress and globalisation.

The process of globalisation is the product of concatenation of parallel, but interlinked set of developments the expanding role of TNCs, the debt crisis, the emergence of global money, ending of the Cold War, disintegration of the Soviet Union, accompanied by an aggressive push to market economy. To cap it all came, beginning the last decade of this century, revolutionary innovations in informations and communication technology.

In 1947, when the UN Commission on Human Rights was preparing a draft of the Universal Declaration of Human Rights, Harold J. Laski forcefully argued that unless institutions so well entrenched both at national and global level, were removed, the declaration would only raise false hopes and its contents on human rights do not have prospect of being fulfilled.

Globalisation demands the removal of all trade barriers allow free flows of goods and capital, which would usher in economic growth and development, so the rhetoric goes. However, the industrialised countries of Europe and North America themselves are resorting to protectionist measures and formation of regional trade blocs. Thus, while consumers goods produced in industrialised countries could have unrestricted entry in developing countries, goods produced, for instance, in India cannot have the same unrestricted access in North America or Europe.

Trade between the West and countries in the non-Western world may destroy subsistence agriculture, coopting Third World farmers into production for the international market-place, while their societies are made dependent on imported foods. Local artisanal production can be wrecked by international competition, causing more unemployment than the new employment produced by international investment.

Free trade is of mutual benefit when the countries trading goods are roughly at the same level of industrial development and have sophisticated economic structures and legal system as in the case of trade between the United States and Europe and

Japan. But when barriers between advanced and backward economies are destroyed, a new form of human exploitation can follow, resembling that of colonialism in the 19th and early 20th centuries, complete with new forms of indentured labour.

Free market economy sets the goal of more production at less cost and more profits; glossed over in this approach is the human face and day-to-day problems faced by the common people. Such an approach not only ignores human rights aspect but further widens the gap between the rich and the poor and aggravates, what Peter Drucker calls, social crisis.

The *Human Development Report 1997* provides arresting evidence of how globalisation and the systematic violation of human rights go hand in hand. Its statistics provide gloomy confirmation of the fact that many countries are worse off today than they were one, 10 or 30 years ago and that the global distribution of income is the worst it has been for at least three decades.

The report indicates that in 1997 30 developing countries have registered a decline in their 'human development index', a construct based on life expectancy, literacy and income, more than in any other year since the United Nations Development Programme (UNDP) began publishing its annual reports in 1990. And the share of the world's poorest 20 per cent in global income is only 1.1 per cent, down from 2.3 per cent in 1960. On an average, the world's richest 20 per cent earned 78 times more than the poorest 20 per cent. Globalisation attempt to merge socioeconomic conditions of industrially advanced countries with developing countries when the US and the European Union are currently earning about $85 a day, are not on a level-playing field, could face gales ahead.

The OECD Report 1997, published that the number of unemployed workers in the industrialised nations has tripled to 35 million since 1970s. Popular protests against economic policies and further stringent measures in many European countries have been made. In most of the industrialised countries, business corporates have increasingly acquired domineering influence over the top echelon of the government and its policies. Thus, a fear expressed by President Eisenhower in his farewell address regarding the role of military-industrial complex has not only come true, but a new nexus has been added what economist Jagdish Bhagwati refers to as treasury wall street complex.

The real choice of governments is not how to fight globalisation but how to manage it. In a way, globalisation posits a challenge to the concept of nation-state. Market economy and global money could be utilised for more production at minimum cost and economic growth could alleviate poverty. Globalisation could be utilised, especially the global media, and information technology, to remove illiteracy, superstitions, etc., and to generate wider awareness of human rights issues. It could be utilised by drawing attention of the governments and the people to violation of human rights happening anywhere in the world.

International institutions such as IMF, World Bank government creditors and commercial banks should either accept moratorium on debt or should write them off. Indeed, debtor countries have already paid more money by way of debt servicing, interests and annual part payment of the principal to the creditors, such a move alone would help bring developing countries to a level-playing field in competitive global economy. Globalisation could lead to mutual benefit provided the powers-that-be are ready to have an equitable management of global economy, an international code of conduct for TNCs and an equitably managed global institution to regulate global money—the rapid flows of investment that moves in and out of developing countries.

## GLOBALISATION IN THE INDIAN CONTEXT

For nearly 40 years, India did not very much open up to Foreign Direct Investment (FDI) and exercised its discretion of such offers on case by case basis. To pursue its objectives, India attempted to regulate the industry and market through licensing-controls and other bureaucratic practices, in the belief that market forces alone cannot achieve growth with equity, it was seeking.

Market forces, if they are fully competitive can at best achieve efficiency in production but not of distributive justice. India for long relied on Indian private entrepreneurs and Public Sector Units (PSUs) to do their part, but they failed, with few exceptions, even in the achievement of efficiency. At the same time, economic growth rates have been very slow because of the framework adopted was inward looking and counterproductive and India continued to have a declining share of world trade. From 2.5 per cent in 1947, it has come to less than half of one (0.59) per cent.

Moreover, public sector enterprises became very dominant and unprofitable and had a multiple effect because they were at the commanding heights. Another problem was the rampant, inexplicable expansion of licensing. The failure to achieve equity, elimination of poverty was partly a result of the failure to achieve economic growth and more so because of rampant corruption. Indeed, what was worse was that a system of regulated economy gave birth to bureaucratisation, red-tapism and corruption.

By 1991-92, because of forces of globalisation and other external factors, India's foreign exchange reserves had reached an alarmingly low levels 1.2 billion in June 1991. It was also no longer in a position to meet its debt ratios, which had reached a figure of $92 billion. Even then the short-lived coalition government in 1990-91 was hesitant to open up its economy and to carry out necessary reforms. But after the elections and advent of a new government, India decided to take the necessary steps and to approach the IMF and World Bank for massive loans to meet its financial challenges. The IMF/World Bank conditionalities for development aid or loans to promote market-economy are well-known. They assured India of their assistance provided India was ready to open its economy to market forces. Subsequently, IMF assistance and structural adjustment loans from the World Bank helped India to face the financial challenges.

In June 1991, India initiated the new economic policy by devaluation the macro policy changes to liberalise its economy, sought Foreign Direct Investment (FDI) to cut down subsidies, and opted for free-trade and market based policies. What may appear as if India acted under compulsion was in a sense, its a continuation of the policy pursued, though haltingly since the mid-1980s. Thus, India began its experiment with the forces of globalisation, beginning 1991. We are experiencing a changed situation in certain respects. One significant development has been better annual economic growth ranging between five per cent and seven per cent.

Indian markets are flooded with consumer goods. Foreign made colour TVs, cellular phones and various models of cars-German, French, Japanese, South Korean, Italian cosmetics, textile, ready-made clothes, shoes, etc., have flooded the market. Food joints such as Kentucky Fried Chicken, Pizza Hut have their restaurants and food shops all over India. The two cold drinks—Pepsi and Coke, have captured soft-drink market. The Indian companies have vanished.

The arrival of TNCs have increased the rentals and market value of real-estate many-folds depending on the site and the precise areas/locality in the metropolitan areas. On the other hand, Delhi itself continues to experience acute shortage of power and water supply. States like Bihar, U.P., Madhya Pradesh, Rajasthan continue to be in a worse state in terms of power and water supply. Of course, prices of electronic goods such as colour TVs, computers, refrigerators of various makes, which are now easily available, have came down, while the prices of essential commodities of day-to-day needs such as vegetables, food grains, edible oils, etc., have gone up.

Where the objective of policy is economic development with equity, liberalisation of markets must be attended with positive action for poverty alleviation, primary education, improved nutrition and regional balance. It is true that without deregulation of license and permits and opening up of the markets, costs of inefficiency can easily surpass the benefit of any other positive action. But without such other positive actions and deliberate policies of the government, deregulation alone cannot serve national objectives of economic growth with equity.

For an effective implementation, the government has to take certain necessary steps.

It has to create a transparent legal and regulatory framework for business to enter and exit a field; invest, expand, borrow and collaborate with others at home and abroad and then operate freely in buying, selling and producing goods and services. Within that framework, one should be able to function without anybody's permission. If a businessman violates the rules following the due process of law, then alone should he be liable to penalty. Otherwise he does not have to go from pillar to post from one office to another, for getting a permission here and business there as has been the practice in the past.

The need to be emphasised is that governments holding to those adversely affected by deregulation, may have to expand much beyond supplementing the worker's compensation. In every industrialised country, including the United States, there is a social security system which takes care of the unemployed persons, who have been thrown out from employment because the companies for one reason or another want to curtail the labour force.

Invitations to FDI create a situation where backward regions get more backward and the rich get richer through earning incomes and commanding the mode of goods they would like to consume. We should keep in mind that it is the responsibility of the government to protect human rights of the people. As such, the government will have to provide for new schemes and infrastructure support in the backward regions and further expand its anti-poverty programmes. Globalisation present certain opportunities for economic growth, but India has to move with utmost caution. It is necessary to keep the windows open; it is equally necessary that we refuse to be blown off our feet.

What India cannot ignore is its responsibilities of promoting and protecting human rights, particularly of the vulnerable segments of the society. Under market economy, India is expected to withdraw from economic production, market and distribution. But if the government opts for this kind of economy, consumerism would be the dominant ideology and principle of equity would take a back-seat. While the rich and upper-middle class will reap the benefits, the lower classes, i.e., lower-middle class, peasants, farmers and workers, who represent larger segment of our society could suffer increasing deprivation.

International Covenant of Economic, Social and Cultural Rights, Articles 6 to 15 emphasise on the right to work, the right to just and favourable conditions of work, the right to form and join trade unions, the right to social security and above all the right to adequate standard of living including food and shelter. Similarly, the Constitution of India has spelled out these rights and the directive principles of state policy has directed the state to secure a social order for the promotion and welfare of the people. The governments, both at federal and state level, cannot absolve themselves of these responsibilities. They cannot absolve themselves of the responsibility of providing primary education as well as to promote higher education. The government should not surrender its economic resources to private entrepreneurs, especially the TNCs.

## REFERENCES

Albrow, M. and King, E (eds.), *Globalization, Knowledge and Society*, 1990.

Charles, J. Hanley, 'Losers in a global race to the bottomline', *Times of India*, April 10, 1996.

Diwan, Ramesh, 'The New Colonial Threat', *Times of India*, July 24, 1997.

Harold, J. Laski, 'Towards a Universal Declaration of Human Rights', in UNESCO *Human Rights Comments and Interpretations* (London: Wingate, 1949), reproduced in *Human Rights Teaching* (UNESCO), Vol. IV, 1985.

Millikan Max and Walt W. Rostow, *A Proposal: Keys to Effective Foreign Policy*, New York., Harper, 1957.

Parekh, B., 'The Modem Concept of Right and its Marxist Critique', *The Right to be Human* . 1987.

Robert L. Rothstein, *The Weak in the World of the Strong: The Developing Countries in the International System*, New York: Praeger, 1977.

Saksena, K.P., 'South in Bloc-dominated Economy', *International Studies*, Vol. 27, No. 4, December, 1990.

Thomas, Henk, ed., *Globalisation and Third World Trade Unions*, Indian reprint, Delhi: Madhyam Books, 1995.

# 13

# Human Rights: Third Millennium Challenges

Rights are moral as well as legal, and it is their morality that underlies and justifies their legality. We must overcome the false opposition between human rights and community. Rights have as their objects the necessary goods and interests of individuals to which they are entitled and which require duties on the part of others. Human rights require community for their implementation, while community requires human rights as the basis of its morally justified economic, political and social operations and enactments. This chapter highlights some IT challenges to human rights in order to illustrate the moral justification of and limits to privacy regulation, and the need to reconcile rights and community in the digital age.

Smart cards may not be intrinsically detrimental to human rights if they merely provide customer service benefits, operational efficiency and security. But they can be used as a technology of surveillance and control and could lead to discrimination. The efficiency they offer ought not to override human freedom and well-being and ethical norms such as beneficence, informed consent, and so on.

Fingerprints, finger scans, retinal scans and hand geometry are unique biological characteristics of persons. If biometric encryption is not used as a unique identifier, but rather for the purpose of authentication of eligibility, then the technology can enhance privacy as long as necessary safeguards are in place. Metro Toronto City Council's implementation of a "Client Identification and Benefits System" was justified on the grounds that finger scanning is less cumbersome than existing identification methods, and stops welfare recipients from double-dipping and vendor fraud by service providers. Critics claim that finger scanning criminalises welfare recipients, perpetuates the myth that economic problems are caused by the poor, and violates rights to privacy.

Electronic Monitoring (EM) is a non-violent offender supervision programme that uses technology to verify that an offender remains within his or her home during specified periods as a condition of early release from jail. A tamper-resistant ankle bracelet contains a miniature radio transmitter that sends a radio signal to a receiver connected to the wearer's home telephone line. The receiver then transmits data via the telephone line to a central monitoring computer. Societal protection is a key value. EM is also viewed as safe, cost effective, and an alternative to imprisonment that provides family support and community integration to the offender.

Use of closed circuit television cameras for the sake of crime prevention and public safety has an intuitive appeal. The commodification of surveillance data contravenes an implicit contract that the data will be used only for agreed-upon law enforcement and public safety values. Representatives of the security industry admit that they have often failed to apply ethical standards, and that the industry is largely motivated by profits.

Massive Millimeter Wave Detectors can now scan beneath clothing to detect guns and drugs from a range of 12 feet or more, and look through walls to detect activity. Computerised Facial Recognition Systems can be digitised and matched with facial images stored in databases. In Massachusetts this technology has already been used to develop a database with digitised photographs of 4.2 million drivers.

The global surveillance system of ECHELON allows spy agencies to monitor most of the world's e-mail, fax, telex, and telephone communications. The system is used for non-military targets such as governments, organisations, businesses, and individuals worldwide, and indiscriminately intercepts vast quantities of communications using five global surveillance stations. The stations target international telecommunications satellites, non-intelsat communications, and land-based systems involving cables under the oceans and microwave networks over land.

Computers or dictionaries in the ECHELON system perform real time searches through piles of intercepted messages for pre-programmed keywords that are, in turn, linked back through a four-digit code to the five agency headquarters. ECHELON is used for the collection of terrorist, economic, and especially political and military intelligence which assists allies to pursue their interests. British intelligence insiders who felt they could not remain silent about gross malpractice and negligence note how charitable organisations like Amnesty International and Christian Aid had their telephone calls targeted.

Genetic testing can provide information about a person's relatives and possible behaviours, and indicate what will or may happen to health in the future. Canadians have a right to reasonable expectation of genetic privacy even if there is a perceived good for society or for the person flowing from the testing. This includes the right not to have others know one's possible genetic destiny, and a right not to know about oneself.

Genetic testing may benefit the promotion of law enforcement goals, but problems arise when genetic information is passed to law enforcement agencies without legal approval. The commercial use of genetic information raises questions about employment and insurance discri-mination.

Case studies suggest discrimination linked to genetic testing. Distributive justice requires that insurance companies find a balance between information that is essential for insurance underwriting and basic equity where persons are not discriminated against on the basis of susceptibility.

Encryption technologies protect personal privacy, support e-commerce, and promote public safety and national security. But encryption is a two-edged, technological sword. Law enforcement and national security agencies are concerned that widespread use of strong encryption, without some ability for lawful access, will stymie security capabilities and the potential of e-commerce.

Some governments have sought to prevent widespread use of cryptography unless ubiquitous key recovery mechanisms can guarantee lawful and real time access by appeal to the 1996 Wassenaar Arrangement, the first global multilateral arrangement on export controls for conventional weapons and sensitive dual-use goods and technologies.

The Arrangement seeks to prevent military developments that threaten regional and international security and stability by restricting the proliferation of offensive strategic weapons. It interprets encryption as a munition, subject to restriction in the same way as weapons and yet, cryptographic products are vital for the continued growth of digital economies, for the development of secure electronic commerce and the protection of the privacy of citizens.

Many countries and businesses encourage a market-driven use, manufacture, sale and distribution of strong encryption products. The government of Canada Public Key Infrastructure (PKI) attempts to enable secure electronic transactions and exchange of sensitive information, provide confidentiality, access control, integrity, authentication, and non-repudiation services for e-commerce transactions.

Some top cryptographers argue that key recovery infrastructure provides a new and vulnerable gateway to unauthorised recovery of data. End-users lose complete control over the means to decrypt data. If criminals or hackers gain access to the caches of keys, they can intercept business correspondence, forge digital signatures and engage in fraudulent e-commerce transactions. Legislation that would prohibit the manufacture, import and use of non-key recovery products, prohibit real-time communications that are not in plain-text or encrypted with key recovery software, and limit the export of strong cryptography raises privacy concerns. The courts have interpreted Sections 7 and 8 of the Charter as guarding against unreasonable privacy invasions. Section 7 states that everyone has the right to life, liberty and security of the person and the right not to be deprived thereof except in accordance with the principles of fundamental justice. Section 8 states that everyone has the right to be secure against unreasonable search or seizure.

Article 17(1) of the International Covenant on Civil and Political Rights (ICCPR) provides that no one shall be subjected to arbitrary or unlawful interference with his privacy, family, home or correspondence, nor to unlawful attacks on his honour and reputation. Prohibitions against unreasonable search and seizure cover surveillance techniques such as wiretaps and interception of internet communication.

Section 2(b) of the Charter guarantees the right of free expression while article 19 of the ICCPR provides, in pertinent part, that Everyone shall have the right to freedom of expression; this right shall include freedom to seek, receive and impart information and ideas of all kinds, regardless of frontiers, either orally, in writing or in print, in the form of art, or through any other media of his choice, While there have been no attempts to criminalise on-line communications in Canada, it is still illegal to spread hate propaganda, child pornography and obscene material on the internet.

Section 1 of the Charter guarantees rights and freedoms only to such reasonable limits prescribed by law as can be demonstrably justified in a free and democratic society. Under the ICCPR, the communication of encryption programmes may be restricted only as necessary in a democratic society for interests such as national security or public safety. How the legal specification of the Section 1 proportionality test might apply to Canadian cryptography policies and practices remains to be seen.

Principles of human rights and criminal justice are premised on the idea that it is better that the guilty sometimes go free if that is necessary to protect the rights of the innocent. When the incremental utility of key recovery is weighed against the threat to speech and privacy of individuals worldwide, it is not at all clear that the balance is in favour of law enforcement.

Information Warfare (IW) refers to actions taken to achieve a goal by influencing and controlling adversary information, computer processes and information systems, while protecting one's own information, computer processes and information systems. IW is a world where logic bombs, computer viruses, Trojan horses, precision-guided munitions, stealth designs, radio-electronic combat systems, new electronics for intelligence-gathering and deception, microwave weapons, space-based weapons, and robotic warfare are being discussed, developed and deployed.

One way of simplifying IW is to reduce its basic components to cyberwar and netwar. Cyberwar is synonymous with command-and-control warfare. Netwar involves societal-level conflict waged through communications on the internet or intranets. A full-fledged cyber attack would disrupt the power grid, the flow of money, air traffic and transportation, and other information dependent items.

Cyber attacks are less risky than sabotage, assassination, hijacking or hostage-taking, and unlike conventional warfare there is a low cost for developing nations or terrorist groups. The right set of skills and less than $10,000 of computer equipment can turn anyone into an information warrior. Fifteen years ago the worldwide population with skills for conducting cyber attacks was in the thousands. In 1996 it was about 17 million, and by the year 2001 it was predicted to be about 19 million. Netwar may be a more immediate challenge to civil and political rights. Netwar applies to struggles most often associated with low-intensity conflict by terrorists, drug cartels, or black market proliferators of weapons of mass destruction, but also includes government antagonism to political activism by means of counter-intelligence programmes. Organised hackers daily steal proprietary designs, corporate merger and acquisition secrets, and new products coming out of research labs.

The San-Francisco-based Computer Security Institute estimates the total loss from netwar crime at more than $236 million dollars, and in 1997 losses from credit-card fraud totalled $88 million for Canadian banks. The fear is that more and more terrorist and criminal gangs will use hacking techniques to neutralise military, police and security services.

Law enforcement efforts to try to stop money laundering, credit-card fraud and computerised transfers of black (tax evasion) and dirty (illegal) money between Canada and other nations has been viewed as stymied by privacy laws and the need for search warrants, full disclosure of investigative methods and the like.

Transnational criminal organisations (TCO's) such as the Columbian drug cartels, Chinese triads, and Japanese *yakuza* undermine civil society, destabilise domestic politics and undercut the rule of law. Democratic governments are forced to work within a framework of rules. TCO's work outside the rules. RCMP Commissioner Philip Murray maintains that bikers, the Mafia, and Asian-based organisations are all on a roll today. It is because of organised crime that Canadians have higher taxes. Businesses are at a competitive disadvantage because others use laundered money to set up their competition.

## PRIVACY PROTECTION

Privacy protection in the public and private sphere is vitally necessary, yet insufficient, for coping with the ethical challenges of the information age. Privacy and the right to privacy are notoriously slippery concepts, especially if one consciously seeks to avoid question-begging definitions. Philosophers have viewed privacy as a claim-right of the person to determine what personal information about one's self may be communicated to others, or a condition of control over access to information about oneself, the intimacies of identity, or one's body. American jurists have interpreted privacy as an individual's right to be let alone or the respect due to one's inviolate personality.

Privacy is a set of torts dealing with intrusion upon one's solitude or private affairs, public disclosure of embarrassing private fact, publicity which places one in a false light in the public eye, and intangible property or appropriation of one's name or likeness for personal advantage. Or perhaps privacy is really a dignitary tort whose legal remedy merely represents a social vindication of the human spirit thus threatened rather than a recompense for the loss suffered.

People generally define the right to privacy as a right to be left alone, free from intrusion or interruption and the right to exercise control over their personal information. We view the ethical challenge of informational privacy as one of balancing the rights and responsibilities of data subjects and data users. Yet informational privacy fails to capture the import of privacy as related to individual freedom and well-being and to communal life. Social scientific studies, for example, corroborate the socially normative value of privacy across cultures, despite its cultural symbolisation.

In Canada, as a recent House of Commons Report notes, "if we approach privacy issues from a human rights perspective, the principles and solutions we arrive at will be rights-affirming, people-based, humanitarian ones, if we adopt a market-based or economic approach, the solutions will reflect a different philosophy, one that puts profit margins and efficiency before people, and may not first and foremost serve the common good". The term 'common good' here is ambiguous. The 'common good' might morally override the rights of individuals, e.g., when individual privacy must be balanced against the need to permit the collection, use and disclosure of personal information as part of a public health response to AIDS.

'Common good' may have a collective meaning in reference to the community as a whole as distinct from its individual members. This view of the 'common good' of community has been used as a utilitarian justification for infringing the rights or basic goods of a few if it would lead to maximisation of overall good. South African apartheid, forms of religious, nationalist, and ethnic intolerance provide examples of this collective conception of a common good. The term 'common good' may also be interpreted distributively where it refers to some good or goods equally common to, equally shared by or distributed among, all the members of a community.

Privacy rights protect the freedom and well-being that all persons share in common as persons who pursue purposive goals and ends of action. The privacy policy debate reveals the tension between individual privacy protection and interpretations of the collective value of information gathering for Canada's economic prosperity in a global information society.

The tension is part of the broader debate about globalisation, the political economy of information, competing visions of the internet, and IT regulatory standards and governance. The question of whether or not IT is a jobs-killer, explanations of the productivity paradox, and problems of unemployment are all debated. A proper understanding of the relation between rights and community need not make privacy rights and the market mutually exclusive. A community of rights can work to fulfil the economic and social rights of the most deprived members of society, including victims of roadkill on the information highway.

## RIGHTS AND COMMUNITY

Adversarial conception of individual rights and community, present in the foregoing survey of IT challenges and policy debates, is as old as the critique of rights by Bentham and Marx and as recent as the debates between communitarians and liberals. The usual contrast suggests that rights entail giving primacy to atomistic entities that have no inherent affective social relations. Rights presuppose competition and conflict as guarantees that self-seeking individuals will not be trampled in their conflictual relations with others. As such, rights submerge the values of community, obscure moral responsibility, and alienate persons.

Community, on the other hand, connotes common interests and cooperation, mutual sympathy, and fellow-feeling that ranges from one's family through one's ethnic and other groups to the nation-state. If persons would only develop moral and intellectual virtues and maintain ties of community that make for social harmony, then there would be no need for rights with their emotivist claims and ideological aims.

This adversarial view of rights and community is profoundly wrong. The community of rights involves not only duties of non-interference with respect to privacy as entailed by negative rights, but also positive duties and rights to productive agency, employment, economic and political democracy. The community of rights is a society whose government actively seeks to help fulfil the needs of its members, especially those who are most vulnerable, for the freedom and well-being that are the necessary goods of human agency, when persons cannot attain this fulfilment by their own efforts. The community must also have laws that threaten punishment to persons who, out of narrow self-interest, violate the requirements it sets up in accordance with the principle of human rights.

Gewirth's human rights theory starts with the universal purposiveness of human action as behaviour done voluntarily in order to achieve a freely chosen goal or end. It is by virtue of having an indispensable need for freedom and well-being as the necessary goods of action that every rational agent or prospective purposive agent is logically committed to hold that he or she has rights to these goods, and that others also have these rights with the correlative duties they entail. His theory eventuates in the Principle of Generic Consistency (PGC) Act in accord with the generic rights of your recipients as well as yourself.

The PGC combines formal considerations of consistency with the material consideration of the generic features of action. The PGC also serves to ground positive and negative rights to freedom and basic, non-substractive, and additive well-being. Basic well-being consists in having the essential preconditions of action and includes basic rights to life, physical integrity, and mental equilibrium. Non-substractive well-being consists in having the abilities and conditions necessary to maintain one's general level of purpose-fulfilment and capacities for action.

Non-substractive rights are violated when one is adversely affected in abilities to plan for the future, to have knowledge of facts relevant to projected actions, or to utilise resources to fulfil wants. Violations entail being lied to, cheated, stolen from, or defamed, and suffering broken promises or being subjected to dangerous, degrading, or excessively debilitating conditions of physical labour or housing when such resources are available for improvement.

Additive well-being consists in having the conditions and abilities necessary for actually augmenting or increasing one's purposes and capacity for action, e.g., right to education, self-esteem, and opportunities for acquiring an income and wealth. These goods of well-being fall into a hierarchy of progressively less needed conditions of action where the right to basic well-being takes precedence over other levels of well-being. So too, the kinds of freedom must be differentiated into occurrent or particular freedom and dispositional or long-range freedom, as well as different objects of freedom.

From the PGC we may derive a basis for the resolution of the conflict of rights. The criterion of degrees of needfulness for action states that when two rights conflict with one another, that right takes precedence whose object is more needed for action. Thus rights not to be stolen from or lied to are overridden by the rights not to starve or be murdered if the latter rights can be fulfilled only by infringing the former.

The PGC entails direct and indirect applications. In the direct applications, the PGC's requirements are imposed on the interpersonal actions of individual persons. On this basis, rights and duties are deduced in a determinate way ranging from duties not to kill innocent persons, duties to rescue, through duties not to lie or break promises, to duties to develop one's prudential virtues by education and other means, and duties to refrain from violence, coercion, and deception.

In the indirect applications, the PGC's requirements are imposed on various social rules that govern multi-person activities and institutions. The requirements of these rules are, in turn, imposed on the actions of individuals who participate in the activities and institutions in accordance with their governing rules.

Voluntary associations and the democratic state, through its use of consensual procedures, are the locus for applications of the right to freedom. The minimal state, which embodies the criminal law, and the supportive or welfare state, which provides basic goods such as food and shelter to those who cannot obtain them by their own efforts, are applications of the right to well-being.

Privacy is best understood as a non-substractive good whose object serves freedom and well-being as necessary conditions of action. When evaluated in the light of the criterion of degrees of needfulness for action, interferences with privacy entailed by tele-marketing and phone solicitation are not as serious as non-consensual medical and genetic privacy breaches that could drastically restrict highly valued actions. Smart cards may give the card-holder fraud-proof identification without necessarily invading privacy if consensual safeguards of the democratic state are in place and thereby serve basic, non-substractive, and additive well-being.

Video surveillance rules and health institutions must serve, through the indirect applications of the PGC, to protect and foster meaningful consent and the equal freedom and well-being of the persons subject to them. The PGC rules out secondary uses of information and requires restoring or aiding the mutuality of non-harm.

Electronic monitoring, as part of the rules of the minimal state, is instrumentally justified by the PGC in its attempt to uphold the freedom and well-being of all members of society, including the parole's own freedom. Since strong encryption is already available, and the hard-core cartels and syndicates will surely use it, this throws into question the usefulness of a global key recovery system and export bans for law enforcement. The surveillance capabilities that key recovery provides, even if it were economically and organisationally feasible, makes it a potential threat to millions of innocent, law-abiding citizens around the world.

A network may require its users to acknowledge that all traffic is public, though employees or individuals can make their own decisions about privacy. But mutuality is breached when intelligence agencies sniff ordinary e-mail and run anonymous remailers ostensibly designed to protect privacy. Information warfare raises a unique set of ethical concerns. The primary justification of the political authority possessed by states and governments is that they secure or protect certain important rights of individual persons.

There are many areas where the state justifiably limits persons' possession of objects the state is designed to protect. One such justification of state authority is that it protects the right to property while, at the same time, justifiably imposing taxes which remove from persons some of their property in order to further its necessary functions.

In the case of warfare, the state has even endangered life in-so-far as this is necessary to preserve it and help it carry on in its functioning. The advent of nuclear weapons challenged this view of *raison d'etat* for going to war. It remains to be seen what this same raison will mean for information warfare. The state may impose reasonable restrictions on privacy, even though this removes some individual freedom, in order to protect the basic well-being and dignity of persons that would be entailed by attacks against critical national infrastructures. But expanding strategic arsenals into the information realm will not safeguard the earth or human civilisation in the long term.

## REFERENCES

John, Arquilla and Ronfeldt, David, 'Cyberwar Is Coming!', *In Athena's Camp: Preparing for Conflict in the Information Age*, pp. 23-60. Santa Monica, Ca: Rand, 1997.

Benn, Stanley I., 'Privacy, Freedom, and Respect for Persons', in Schoeman, ed., *Philosophical Dimensions of Privacy*, Cambridge: Cambridge University Press, 1984.

Berkowitz, Bruce D., 'Warfare in the Information Age', *Issues in Science and Technology*, Fall 1995, 59-66.

Flaherty, David H., 'On the Utility of Constitutional Rights to Privacy and Data Protection' *Case Western Reserve Law Review*, vol. 41, No.33 (1991):831-855.

Foot, Richard, 'Computer Criminals Wave of the Future', *The Ottawa Citizen*, May 13, 1998.

Gilc, 'Global Internet Liberty Campaign', *Cryptography and Liberty: An International Survey of Encryption Policy*, February 1998.

Lafleur, Brenda and Peter Lok, *Jobs in the Knowledge-based Economy: Information Technology and the Impact on Employment*. Ottawa: Conference Board of Canada, 1997.

Mendes, Errol P., 'Human Rights and the New Information Technologies: The Law and Justice of Proportionality and Consensual Alliances', *Human Rights Research and Education Bulletin*, Number 34, December, 1997. Ottawa: Human Rights Research and Education Centre, 1997.

Steeves, Valerie, 'Humanizing Cyberspace: Privacy, Freedom of Speech, and the Information Highway', *Human Rights Research and Education Bulletin*, No. 28 June 1995.

*Appendix*

# Human Rights in Africa: Challenges of the New Millennium

Achieving genuine respect for human rights may constitute the greatest challenge facing Africans in the new millennium. After 51 years of the United Nations having adopted the 1948 Universal Declaration of Human Rights and almost nineteen years after the Organisation of African Unity (OAU) having adopted its own African Charter on Human and Peoples' Rights, the human rights situation on the African continent is decidedly bleak. In June 1999 UNESCO Director-General the Federico Mayor expressed his deep concern over the ever increasing number of African countries afflicted by war and associated human rights abuses. Fighting has raged in Sierra Leone, Guinea Bissau, Angola, Congo, the Democratic Republic of Congo, Somalia, Rwanda and Burundi, Ethiopia and Eritrea.

Twenty-four African countries had serious and widespread human rights violations in 1998 and armed conflicts, social and political unrest continued unabated, leading to appalling human rights abuse throughout the continent. The United Nations High Commissioner for Refugees estimated that in 1998 there were about 3.5 million refugees in Africa, 80 per cent of them women and children under the age of five. In its 1999 survey, Human Rights Watch (HRW) reported that Africa's refugee population had increased to 6.3 million. Of the ten top refugee producers in the world, five were African: Burundi, Eritrea, Sierra Leone, Somalia, and Sudan.

## REASONS FOR HUMAN RIGHT VIOLATIONS

A recent OAU report attributed Africa's poor human rights record mainly to racism, post-colonialism, poverty, ignorance, disease, religious intolerance, internal conflicts, debt, bad management, corruption, the monopoly of power, the lack of judicial and press autonomy, and border conflicts. More than 75 per cent of the continent's 700 million people live below the poverty line, and 10 of the world's 13 poorest countries are in Africa. Africa's troubling situation, however, is not unique.

In many of the world's poorer countries, the following elements comprise the system leading to human rights violations:

i) Undeveloped economies, with limited resource bases and insufficient employment/income opportunities for large segments of the population resulting in widespread poverty.

ii) High population growth rates further straining the natural environment and local resources, while intensifying competition for resources.

iii) Ethnic diversity and/or regional factionalism promoting local/particularistic identifications, while hindering the development of a national identification.

iv) Ethnic and/or class politics involving competition among leaders of different language, cultural, or regional populations for state positions of political and economic power with the spoils of victory going to supporters.

v) Lack of regime legitimacy as those large segments of the population not culturally and/or politically affiliated with the ruling elite and not sharing in the spoils refuse to recognise the regime as legitimate.

vi) Resort to military/police force to maintain power by suppressing political opponents and disgruntled civilians.

vii) Violation of economic, civil, and political rights by the regime on the pretext of national security.

## COLONIALISM IN AFRICA

European imperialists imposed the state structure on collections of ethnopolitical communities that historically lacked intercommunal coherence. The imperialists forced communities that lived independently of each other to live together in the newly-created colonial state. Most of these new citizens lacked any nationalistic bond to the colonial state. Today, only a few African states bear any territorial resemblance tc the political communities that existed prior to European colonialism. The resulting disconnection between Africans and the modern African state has created a crisis of cultural, social, and political identity.

The new African states have failed to inspire loyalty in the citizenry; to produce a political class with integrity and a national interest; to inculcate in the military, the police, and the security forces their proper roles in society; to build a nation from different linguistic and cultural groups; and to fashion economically viable policies. This historic, psychological process has adversely affected many African political leaders, who, lacking a genuine national committment and sense of obligation, exploit state budgets and power to strengthen their ethnic power bases, enhance personal privileges and thus retain power.

African leaders have relied on ethnic support in order to achieve and maintain positions of power. In return, these leaders have often favoured their supporters with privileged access to the limited available resources. Such politics, by favouring the few over the many, has not and cannot generate the generality of legitimacy necessary for regime stability and internal security.

Ethnonationalism or politicised ethnicity represents a major legitimator and de-legitimator of regimes. A government's legitimacy rests, in significant degree, on its ability to convince the governed that it shares, represents, or respects their ethnicity. In many countries with multi-ethnic populations, the classic nation-state has proved to be a dangerous fiction. Attempts by state governments to force diverse cultural populations into a dominant ethnic mold have led to human rights abuses. The bias of the UN and existing states against autonomy or secessionist movements by cultural minorities seeking self-determination and political independence from dominant ethnic power-holders could very well prove detrimental to both the stability of states and the human rights process.

Historically, diverse ethnic populations with a tradition of mutual animosity have not found common citizenship in a single state a sufficient basis for social harmony. In cases of intrastate, inter-ethnic strife involving cultural populations who are numerically dominant in different regions of the country, at least two political paradigms or structural alternatives to the pluralistic state are possible. One structural solution involves replacing the state with autonomous, ethnic cantons that can opt for confederation on the Swiss model. Another possibility is the creation of small independent ethnic states whose leaders may opt for some form of interstate integration on the European Union model. Both the Swiss cantons and the states comprising the European Union opted for forms of legal integration to achieve anticipated political and economic benefits.

In cases of intrastate, inter-ethnic conflict involving populations intermingled within the same territory, a culturally pluralistic, single-state solution may be necessary. In order to significantly reduce and, hopefully, eliminate the causes of minority oppression and state instability, the following minimal measures must be taken:

i) states must establish an independent judiciary.

ii) states must incorporate the various UN human rights conventions into its domestic law.

iii) state constitutions must place a duty on the state to guarantee all citizens legal equality and non-discrimination, while also granting injured citizens standing in court to initiate claims when these guarantees have been broken.

— state constitutions must guarantee minority cultural rights, including the rights to speak, teach, and write their own language; practice their own religion; and practice other aspects of their cultures to the extent that such practice does not infringe on the rights of others.
— government and military officials as well as the powerful elite must be responsive to judicial decisions.
— minority populations must be permitted some effective means of participating in the political process.
— minority populations must be permitted some effective means of participating in the economic process.

The minority populations must accept the inevitable fact that the majority or plurality population and culture will be predominant at the national/state level. For example, in states where numerous minorities and languages exist, the selection of a single, official national language will be necessary for the practical purposes of facilitating national and international communication.

## AFRICAN HUMAN RIGHTS CHARTER

The African Charter on Human and Peoples' Rights created under the auspices of the OAU, entered into force on 21 October 1986. With the ratification of this Charter, Africa joined Europe and the Americas as one of the three world regions with its own human rights convention. The great majority of African states had previously ratified the United Nations Covenant on Civil and Political Rights and the Covenant on Economic, Social and Cultural Rights. Okoth-Ogendo argues that this is because many African leaders felt the need to develop a scheme of human rights norms and principles founded on the historical traditions and values of African civilisations rather than simply reproduce and try to administer the norms and principles derived from the historical experiences of Europe and the Americas.

Charter Articles 3-17 list a fairly typical array of individual rights, including rights to equal protection of the law, to life and security, to due process, to education, to own property, to work under equitable and satisfactory conditions, to enjoy the best attainable state of physical and mental health, and to assemble with others. These articles also promise individuals freedom of expression, movement, conscience, religion, and political participation. The Charter grants all peoples the rights to equality, to self-determination, to freely determine their political status and economic development. In addition, all peoples shall have the right to national and international security and the right to a general satisfactory environment favourable to their development.

The Charter lists obligations that states incur, including the obligation to eliminate every form of discrimination against women and also ensure the protection of the rights of the woman and the child as stipulated in international declarations and conventions; the obligation to eliminate all forms of foreign and domestic economic exploitation of natural resources; the obligation to promote and ensure the Charter; the obligation to guarantee the independence of the courts; and, what is especially African, the obligation to assist the family which is the custodian of morals and traditional values recognised by the community.

Charter Articles 27-29 list the duties that an individual incurs towards his family and society, the state and other legally recognised communities and the international community. More specifically, these include duties to exercise rights and freedoms with due regard to the rights of others, collective security, morality and common interest; to respect fellow-beings without discrimination; to respect the family and parents at all times, and to maintain in case of need, to serve the national community, both physically and intellectually; not to compromise the security of the state; to preserve and strengthen national solidarity, independence and territorial solidarity; to pay taxes; to preserve and strengthen positive African values; and to promote African unity.

## AFRICAN HUMAN RIGHTS COMMISSION

The African Human Rights Commission was created by OAU in 1987, in accordance with Charter Article 30, to promote human rights and to monitor compliance by African states with their obligations under the Charter. The Commission is comprised of 11 persons chosen from amongst African personalities of the highest reputation, known for their high morality, integrity, impartiality, and competence in matters of human and peoples' rights; particular consideration being given to persons having legal experience.

The Assembly of Heads of States and Governments of the OAU elects members of the commission from a list of persons nominated by states parties to the Charter. Commissioners serve for a renewable term of six years. The commissioners elect a chairman and vice-chairman from among themselves every two years. Members of the Commission are elected to serve in their individual capacities and should, therefore, act independently.

State parties to the Charter are obligated to cooperate with the Commission and to submit to it a report every two years in which the state explains the measures it has taken and needs to take to ensure its citizens the rights and freedoms guaranteed by the Charter. As of 1998, however, 30 of the 51 states parties to the Charter had failed to submit a single report, and all other states, except Zimbabwe, were in arrears.

African states generally have not given the commission significant cooperation. In addition to failing to fulfil their reporting obligations, many refuse to respond to the Commission's requests for information. In one case, the Commission sent 20 unanswered inquiries to Zaire requesting a response to allegations contained in complaints of gross violations of human rights. There also have been cases in which state parties have refused to admit the Commission on missions into their territories to investigate complaints of gross human rights violations.The Commission has had to rely on grants from West European countries for basic operating expenses. The Charter allows for an interstate complaint procedure whereby one state can charge another state with human rights violations before the Commission. Yet, despite the existence of widespread and grave violations in many countries, not a single state has ever filed an interstate complaint. The Commission has received petitions only from a limited number of individuals and NGOs.

The absence of adequate institutions to monitor, promote and protect human rights has tarnished Africa's image, so that many view it as being a continent without the rule of law. Africa's Human Rights charter has failed because politicians and strong men have refused to support it. Despite or because of the shortcoming in human rights achievements under the Charter and Commission, African leaders have decided to begin the process of creating a human rights court.

In 1998, members of the OAU meeting in Burkina Faso initiated the process for the creation of an African Court on Human and Peoples' Rights. To come into effect, the protocol for the proposed court requires the ratification of 15 OAU member states. As of late 1999, only Burkina Faso and Senegal had ratified it. According to the protocol, the court shall consist of 11 judges elected by the Assembly of Heads of state and Government of the OAU from a list of nominees proposed by OAU member states. The assembly shall ensure that there is adequate regional and gender representation among the selected judges. The envisioned court will complement the protective mandate of the African Commission on Human and Peoples' Rights.

As for its sources of law, the court shall apply the provisions of the African Charter on Human and Peoples' Rights and any other relevant human rights instruments ratified by the states concerned. This is a very significant provision, because the great majority of African states have ratified many of the major United Nations human rights conventions, including the Convention on the Elimination of Discrimination against Women and the Convention on the

Rights of the Child. African states, the Commission, the OAU and African inter-governmental organisations will be able to submit cases to Court. Individuals and NGOs, however, may not file a petition with the court against any state that has not explicitly made a declaration under Article 36(6) of the protocol recognising the competence of the Court to consider such petitions.

Unfortunately, this protocol provision permits states to shield themselves from complaints by their own citizens and NGOs who allege human rights violations. Since governments will be reluctant to make such declarations, and because no state has ever filed a human rights complaint against another state before the Commission, it is unlikely that the court will see much business. The protocol authorises the court to issue appropriate orders to remedy a human rights violation, including the payment of fair compensation or reparation to the injured party (Art. 27). States recognising the court promise to comply with its judgments (Art. 30), and the OAU Council of Ministers will be charged with monitoring the execution of court judgments on behalf of the OAU Assembly (Art. 31). Presumably, the Council of Ministers will pressure a non-complying country into honouring a court judgment.

## CHALLENGES AND PARADIGMS

In April of 1999 the OAU held its first ever Ministerial Conference on Human Rights. At that conference, held at Grand Bay, Mauritius, OAU Secretary-General, Salim, called for the integration of human rights in school curricula and the strengthening of institutions responsible for promotion and respect for human rights. Africa needs to inculcate in its people a culture of peace, tolerance and respect of human rights, to energetically fight poverty, illiteracy and intolerance, to strive to overcome the scourge of conflicts and ensure that human rights violations are not only condemned but also effectively opposed and eliminated. The ministers concluded the conference with a Declaration and Plan of Action that reaffirmed their commitments to human rights, the rule of law, and democracy. They recognised that human rights are founded on respect for the sanctity of life, human dignity, tolerance of differences, prosperity and stability.

The declaration urges all African states to work assiduously towards the elimination of discrimination against women and the abolition of cultural practices which dehumanise or demean women and children. The declaration also calls on African states to eradicate genocide on the continent and to ratify the African Charter on the Rights and Welfare of the Child, the Protocol on the Establishment of an African Court on Human and Peoples' Rights, the Four Geneva Conventions, the UN Statute of the International Criminal Court, and a number of other major UN human rights conventions.

Today Africa is suffering from severe economic, demographic, health, and political problems and cannot easily achieve the human rights status its people want. Speakers at the first African Development Forum emphasised the need for a new paradigm for African development based on a vibrant domestic private sector, a stable state, effective policy analysis, and good governance. Such a paradigm will also need a marked change in Africa's relations with international financial institutions and donor states.

## REFERENCES

Amnesty International, 'Rwanda: human rights overlooked in mass repatriation', report no. AFR47/02/97, London, 1997.

Ketel, H., *Tanzania: environmental assessment report of the Rwandese refugee camps and the affected local communities in Kagera region*, Geneva, May 1996.

Okechukwu lbeanu, "Apartheid, Destabilisation and Displacement: The Dynamics of Refugee Crisis in Southern Africa" *Journal of Refugee Studies*, Vol.3, No. 1, 1990, pp.47-63.

Woodward, P. 'Political Factors Contributing to the Generation on Refugees in the Horn of Africa' (1987), 9(2) *Intl. Relations* 111, at 112.

# Bibliography

*A Human Rights Approach to UNICEF Programming for Children and Women*, Part I, C3.

Aga Khan, Sadruddin, "Legal Problems Relating to Refugees and Displaced Persons", *Recueil Des Courts*, Collected Courses of the Hague Academy of International Law, 1976, 1, p. 293.

Aggarwal, B., 'Gender and Command over Poverty: A Critical Gap in Economic Analysis and Policy in South Asia', in *World Development*, vol. 22, no. 10.

Alan, Gewirth, *The Community of Rights*, Chicago and London: University of Chicago Press, 1996.

Albrow, M. and King, E (eds.), *Globalization, Knowledge and Society*, 1990.

Amnesty International, 'Rwanda: human rights overlooked in mass repatriation', report no. AFR47/02/97, London, 1997.

An-Na'im, Abdullahi, Ahmed, *Toward an Islamic Reformation: Civil Liberties, Human Rights and International Law*, Syracuse University Press, 1990.

Avishai, Margalit, *et. al.*, "The Uniqueness of the Holocaust', *Philosophy and Public Affairs*, 1996.

Bandaraga, A., *Colonialism in Sri Lanka: Political Economy of the Kandyan Highlands, 1833-1886,* Berlin: Monton, 1983.

Banerjee, Sumanta, (ed.), *Shrinking Space: Minority Rights in South Asia,* Kathmandu: South Asia Forum for Human Rights.

Batchelor, C., 'Stateless persons: some gaps in international protection', *International Journal of Refugee Law*, vol. 49, no. 1, 1995.

Benn, Stanley I., 'Privacy, Freedom, and Respect for Persons', in Schoeman, ed., *Philosophical Dimensions of Privacy*, Cambridge: Cambridge University Press, 1984.

Bentham, Jeremy, "Anarchical Fallacies; being an examination of the Declaration of Rights issues during the French Revolution", Jeremy Waldron (ed.), *Nonsense Upon Stilts: Bentham, Burke and Marx on the Rights of Man*, New York: Methuen, 1987.

Berkowitz, Bruce D., 'Warfare in the Information Age', *Issues in Science and Technology*, Fall 1995, 59-66.

Berman, Marshall, 'Modernism and Human Rights Near New Millennium', *Dissent*, 1995.

Binion, Gayle, "Human Rights: A Feminist Perspective", *Human Rights Quarterly*, 1995.

Capotori, Francesco, 'Study on the rights of Persons Belonging to Ethnic, Religious and Linguistic Minorities', *UN Document* E/ CN 4/ Sub. 2/384/Rev. 1, p. 9.

Charles, J. Hanley, 'Losers in a global race to the bottomline', *Times of India*, April 10, 1996.

Chimni, B.S., "Rights of Refugees, Including the Right to Return: The Language of Protection and the Reality of Rejection: End of Cold War and Crisis in Refugee Law", paper presented in the World Congress on Human Rights, New Delhi, December 10-15, 1990.

Cohen, R., 'Protecting the internally displaced', in *World Refugee Survey* 1996, United States Committee for Refugees, Washington DC, 1996.

Cranston, *What are Human Rights*?, The Bodely Head, 1973.

Diwan, Ramesh, 'The New Colonial Threat', *Times of India*, July 24, 1997.

Donnelly, Jack, *Universal Human Rights in Theory and Practice*, Ithaca: Cornell University Press, 1989.

Edward, Bloustein, J., 1984, 'Dignity and Privacy' in *Philosophical Dimensions of Privacy*, ed., Ferdinand D. Schoeman, 156-202. Cambridge: Cambridge University Press.

Flaherty, David H., 'On the Utility of Constitutional Rights to Privacy and Data Protection' *Case Western Reserve Law Review*, vol. 41, No.33 (1991):831-855.

Foot, Richard, 'Computer Criminals Wave of the Future', *The Ottawa Citizen*, May 13, 1998.

Friedman, E., *Women's Human Rights: the Emergence of a Movement*.

Gewirth, Allan, "Why There Are Human Rights", *Social Theory and Practice*, 1985.

Gilc, 'Global Internet Liberty Campaign', *Cryptography and Liberty: An International Survey of Encryption Policy*, February 1998.

Gomango, S. P., *Child Labour: A Precarious Future*, Authorspress, New Delhi, 2001.

'Governance for Sustainable Human Development', *Policy document*, 1997.

Harold, J. Laski, 'Towards a Universal Declaration of Human Rights', in UNESCO *Human Rights Comments and Interpretations* (London: Wingate, 1949), reproduced in *Human Rights Teaching* (UNESCO), Vol. IV, 1985.

*Human Rights Watch Global Report on Women's Human Rights*, New York, 1993 and 1995.

Husak, Douglas, "The Motivation for Human Rights", *Social Theory and Practice*, 1985.

Hyndman, P., 'Refugees Under International Law with a Reference to the Concept of Asylum', 60 *Australian L. J.* 1986, 148.

Ichimare S. and B.P. Kirtisinghe, 'Human Rights and the Buddhist Concept of Law and Norm' in A. Adikari (ed.), *Sambbasha, the Mahadodhi Centenary Commemorative Volume*, Ministry of Education & Higher Education, Battaramulla, Sri Lanka, Vol. 1. No. 2, 1991.

Jeremy, Rifkin, *The End of Work: The Decline of the Global Labor Force and the Dawn of the Post-Market Era*, New York: G.P. Putnam's Sons, 1995.

John, Arquilla and Ronfeldt, David, 'Cyberwar Is Coming!', *In Athena's Camp: Preparing for Conflict in the Information Age*, pp. 23-60. Santa Monica, Ca: Rand, 1997.

Kalaiah, A.B., *Human Rights in International Law*, 1986.

Ketel, H., *Tanzania: environmental assessment report of the Rwandese refugee camps and the affected local communities in Kagera region*, Geneva, May 1996.

Lafleur, Brenda and Peter Lok, *Jobs in the Knowledge-based Economy: Information Technology and the Impact on Employment*. Ottawa: Conference Board of Canada, 1997.

Lawson, Edward, *Encyclopedia of Human Rights,* 2nd ed., Washington: Taylor Francis, 1996.

Lee-Wright, P., 1990, *Child Slaves*, London, Eathscan.

Leonardo Despouy, *Conflict Prevention and Poverty Alleviation*, 1996.

Mayer, Ann, E., *Islam and Human Rights: Tradition and Politics*, 2nd ed., Boulder, CO: Westview Press, 1995.

Mendes, Errol P., 'Human Rights and the New Information Technologies: The Law and Justice of Proportionality and Consensual Alliances', *Human Rights Research and Education Bulletin*, Number 34, December, 1997. Ottawa: Human Rights Research and Education Centre, 1997.

Millikan Max and Walt W. Rostow, *A Proposal: Keys to Effective Foreign Policy,* New York., Harper, 1957.

Moltmann, Jurgen, The original study paper: a theoretical basis of human rights and of the liberation of human beings, in Allen and Miller (eds.), *A Christian Declaration on Human Rights*, 1977.

Nicholas, J.H., *Democracy and the Churches*, Westminster Press, Philandelphia.

O'Manique, John, "Universal and Inalienable Human Rights: A Search for Foundations", *Human Rights Quarterly*, 1990.

Okechukwu lbeanu, "Apartheid, Destabilisation and Displace-ment: The Dynamics of Refugee Crisis in Southern Africa" *Journal of Refugee Studies*, Vol.3, No. 1, 1990, pp.47-63.

Paine, Thomas, *The Rights of Man*, New York: Penguin Books, 1985.

Parekh, B., 'The Modem Concept of Right and its Marxist Critique', *The Right to be Human*, 1987.

Patil V.T. and Trivedi, P.R., *Migration, Refugees and Security in the 21st Century*, Authorspress, New Delhi, 2000

_______________ P.R., *Human Rights and Refugees*, Authorspress, New Delhi, 2000.

_______________ , *Refugees and Human Rights*, Authorspress, New Delhi, 2000.

Peocock, Olive, *Minority Politics in Sri Lanka: A Study of the Burghers,* Jaipur: Arihant Publishers, 1988.

Peters J. and A. Wolper., *Human Rights: International Feminist Perspectives*, edited by Roudedge, New York, 1995.

Piggozzi, Mary Joy, *Implications of the Convention on the Rights of the Child for Education Activities Supported by UNICEF*, UNICEF, New York, March 1997.

Rai, Rahul, *Human Rights: UN Initiatives*, Authorspress, New Delhi, 2000.

*Report on Conference on Governance, Leadership and Poverty Eradication*, Ougodougou, Burkina Faso, 1996.

*Report on International Conference for Sustainable Growth and Equity*, New York, 28-30, July 1997.

*Report on the Regional Conference on Governance and Social Development*, Beirut, Lebanon, 1997.

*Report on the Third International Conference of the New and Restored Democracies on Democracy and Development*, Bucharest, Romania, 2-4, September 1997.

*Report on the Third International Human Rights Conference*, Riga, Latvia, 1997.

Rizvi, Z., 'Causes of the Refugee Problem and the International Response', in A. Nash (ed.) *Human Rights and the Protection of Refugees under International Law*, 1988, p.111.

Robert L. Rothstein, *The Weak in the World of the Strong: The Developing Countries in the International System*, New York: Praeger, 1977.

Robertson, A.H., *Human Rights in the World*, 1972.

Sahadevan, P., *India and Overseas Indians: The Case of Sri Lanka*, Delhi: Kalinga Publications, 1995.

Saksena, K.P., 'South in Bloc-dominated Economy', *International Studies*, Vol. 27, No. 4, December, 1990.

Singh, Nagendra, *The Role and Record of the UN High Commissioner for Refugees*, Macmillan India Ltd., New Delhi, 1984, p.74.

Smith, R. 'Refugees, immigrants and the claims of the nation-state', *Times Literary Supplement 1422* December 25-31, 1987.

Stamatopoulou, E., *Women's Rights and the United Nations: Human Rights Discourse*.

Steeves, Valerie, 'Humanizing Cyberspace. Privacy, Freedom of Speech, and the Information Highway', *Human Rights Research and Education Bulletin*, No. 28 June 1995.

Subrmanaian, Nirupama, 'Rage in the hills', *Frontline*, November 24, 2000, pp. 59-60.

*Survey of UNDP Activities in the Field of Human Rights*, 1997.

Thakur, L.K., *Comparative and International Human Rights*, Authorspress, New Delhi, 2000.

*The Education for Girls and Women: Towards a Global Framework for Action*, UNESCO, Paris, 1995.

Thomas, Henk, ed., *Globalisation and Third World Trade Unions*, Indian reprint, Delhi: Madhyam Books, 1995.

Tomasevski, K., *Women and Human Rights*, Zed Books, London, 1993.

Torres, Rosa Maria, "Repetition: A Major obstacle to Education for All", *Education News*, No.12, UNICEF, April, 1995.

United Nations Commission on Human Rights, *Report of the Working Group on Contemporary Forms of Slavery* (Geneva): Annual Reports, see especially 1985-87.

Vernant, J., *The Refugee in the Post-War World*, 1953, p.5.

Vije, Mayan, *Where Serfdom Thrives: The Plantation Tamils of Sri Lanka,* Madras: Tamil Information Centre, 1987.

Weiner, M. and Munz, R., "Migrants, refugees and foreign policy: prevention and intervention strategies", *Third World Quarterly*, vol. 18, no. 1, 1997.

Weiss, T. and Collins, C., *Humanitarian Challenges and Intervention: World Politics and Dilemmas of Help*, Westview Press, Boulder, 1996.

Woodward, P. 'Political Factors Contributing to the Generation on Refugees in the Horn of Africa' (1987), 9(2) *Intl. Relations* 111, at 112.

Writte, John, Jr., and Johan van der Vyver, eds., *Religious Human Rights in Global Perspectives: Religious Perspectives*, Dordrecht: Martinus Nijhoff, 1966.

Youssef, N.H., *Women's Access to Productive Resources: the Need for Legal Instruments to Protect Women's Development Rights.*

# Index